Unbridled Spirit

The Untold Story of the 2018 Extraordinary Palio
in Siena, Italy

Thomas W. Paradis

Copyright © 2020 by Thomas W. Paradis

All rights reserved. No part of this publication may be reproduced, distributed or transmitted in any form or by any means, without prior written permission of the publisher, except in the case of brief quotations embodied in critical reviews and certain other noncommercial uses permitted by copyright law.

Thomas W. Paradis has no responsibility for the persistence or accuracy of URLs for external or third-party Internet Websites referred to in this publication and does not guarantee that any content on such Websites is, or will remain, accurate or appropriate.

Library of Congress Control Number: 2020902334

Published by Thomas W. Paradis
Indianapolis, IN. USA

Includes bibliographic references and notes.
Book Layout © 2017 BookDesignTemplates.com
Typeset in Alegreya
Edited by Elizabeth Koozmin
Cover designed by Anna Burrous

All photos (cover and interior) by Thomas W. Paradis
Map of Siena's Contrade provided by David Lown: www.picturesfromitaly.com.

Unbridled Spirit -- 1st ed.
ISBN: 978-1-7334838-0-3 (paperback)
ISBN: 978-1-7334838-1-0 (ebook)

Contents

Introduction 1

PART I: PREPARATIONS 5

1. October Skies 7
    Legacy of the Republic 9
    Basics of the Palio 13
    An Unlikely Straordinario 16
    The Partiti 18
    Uncharted Territory for the Senesi 19

2. The Chosen Ones 23
    Extraction of the Contrade 23
    Most and Least Likely to Win 25

3. Transatlantic Journey 31
    An Impulsive Decision 32
    Tempting Fate 32
    Course Correction 33
    An Unexpected Companion 37

4. Presentation of the Drappellone 43
    Evolution of Drappellone Design 44
    The Bersaglieri 46
    A Palazzo Entrance Strategy 49
    Montesano's Drappellone 53
    The Masgalano 55
    Beware the Internet 56

PART II: PERSPECTIVES 61

5. Dario's World 63
Return to the Caterpillar 64
Cow's Stomach and Wild Boar 68
Origins of the Straordinario 70
Reflections on World War I 73
An Increasingly Rare Occasion 77

6. Mutilated Victory 83
Aperitivo on the Campo 83
Learning about World War I 84
Italy Enters the War 87
A Farewell to Arms 89
Along the Italian Front 91
The Paris Peace Conference 94
Aftermath of the War 96
Victory Speech 99

7. Generations Apart 103
A Myriad of Concerns 103
Choosing the Horses 106
Voting for the Straordinario 109
A Generational Paradox 111
Dissecting the Vote 115
Lunch in the Goose 118

8. Assignment of the Horses 125
Ceramic Shop Reunion 128
The Palio as a Strategic Game 130
Leveling the Field 136
The Drawing Proceeds 140

9. Four Days and Three Laps 145
Third Places 146
Palio Philosophy 149

Speculations about the Straordinario 152
Jockeys of Past, Present, and Future 155

10. A Stalloreggi Lunch 159
My Shifting Universe 159
Eating in Traffic 162
Tuscan Antipasti 164
Thoughts on the Palio 166

PART III: PARTICIPATION 173

11. The Third Trial 175
Stall Tactics 176
An Impromptu Palazzo Tour 178
The City Council Chambers 179
Preparations for the Trial 182
The Lineup Ritual 186
A Symbolic Finish 190

12. Blessing at San Domenico 193
Procession of the Drappellone 193
Communing with Saint Catherine 196
A Memorial at San Domenico 197
The Procession Arrives 199
One More Quest 204

13. Homecoming at Due Porte 207
Cena della Prova Generale 207
Second Thoughts 209
The Bàrberi 211
Making an Entrance 214
Guess Who's Coming to Dinner 216
Main Course 223
Radiational Cooling 225
A Promising Invitation 226

PART IV: PALIO STRAORDINARIO 229

14. The Protectors 231
Uneven Population Growth 231
Contemplating Contrada Membership 234
A Protector of the Panther 238
Lingering Concerns about the Race 239
Contrada Budgeting 242

15. Curve of San Martino 247
Acquiring Palio Tickets 248
Into the Bleachers 249
Earth-Sun Geometry 252
Pre-Palio Festivities 254

16. Shaken 265
Lining Up for the Race 265
Three Laps of Chaos 269
Aftermath in the Campo 275
Exit Strategy 279
Dario's Revelation 281

17. A Walk in the Park 283
Mixed News from the Palio 284
A Social Memorial to the War 287
Personal Takeaways 290
Two Parallel Paths for Siena 293
What Future for the Straordinario? 297

Acknowledgments 303

Glossary 305

Notes 311

Bibliography 315

Author's Note

To protect the trust and identities of individuals mentioned throughout the book, I have replaced their real names with pseudonyms. The exceptions to this are my wife, the jockeys, and any authors or local experts whose books and research are referenced.

Introduction

Following the publication of my previous book, *Living the Palio*, the last thing on my mind was a second, follow-up volume about the community's centuries-old horse race. Then again, the Senesi (English: Sienese) never imagined during summer 2018 that they would soon be engaged with an additional "Extraordinary" Palio (Palio Straordinario) later that year. This startling turn of events not only took me by surprise, but it shocked the sensibilities of the Senesi as well. Siena's summer Palio "season" of 2018, which included the usual two races, had already ended before anyone caught wind of a possible third race later that year. As the turf in Piazza del Campo was being swept up and hauled away following the August race, most were simply anticipating yet another "winter"—the long span following the summer Palii (plural of Palio)—that would predictably descend upon them.

Then in late August, a mysterious proposal landed on a desk at the Palazzo Pubblico (Siena's city hall). The idea had surfaced somehow to hold a Palio Straordinario to commemorate the one hundredth anniversary of the conclusion of World War I—or what was once referred to as la Grande Guerra (the Great War).

The rest, as they say, is history. The events and perspectives I share here transpired within the span of two short months in 2018. Upon learning that the community would muster its energy and resources to throw together its first Palio Straordinario in eighteen years, I became convinced that an incredible story was about to unfold. And someone would definitely need to tell it. Such special, third Palii were becoming less common in today's more complicated and costly modern era. Who knew whether this would be the last such event for quite some time, if not ever?

Beyond question, my effort to comprehend this special event has been among my most rewarding escapades. Diving back into the world of the Palio further encouraged me to learn more about the historical contexts of World War I, especially with respect to Italy's lesser known involvement and implications. My goal here is therefore to immerse readers within a very rare

Palio Straordinario while also featuring various Palio-related rituals and events not covered in my earlier book. That said, *Unbridled Spirit* is written to stand on its own. The first two chapters include a "crash course" about Siena and the Palio, setting the stage for the Straordinario and related events.

It follows that a litany of intriguing questions comes to mind about this particular Palio. For instance, in what ways would an "extra" Palio in autumn be organized and run differently than its normal summer counterparts? Certainly, the shorter length of daylight and unpredictable autumn weather would hold as-yet-unforeseeable implications. Further, to what extent did the Senesi accept or even applaud the idea to undertake a Palio at such a late time of the year? Do virtually all Senesi collectively rise in celebration at any potential opportunity to hold another Palio? And what of the event's unprecedented haste and lack of forewarning? Would the Senesi generally find value in commemorating the end of World War I with less than two months to prepare?

To seek answers to these and related questions, I obtained necessary permissions from my own university to undertake some legitimate human research. As a professor of geography and community planning, I came to Siena with a distinct plan on how to best answer my own questions in a relatively short period of time. In brief, I deployed a combination of three distinct social science methodologies. The first involved a set of questions that I relied upon to interview selected knowledgeable individuals. People of various backgrounds and affiliations with Siena and its contrade could shed direct light on local perspectives, beliefs, and how things function. In cases where it was not appropriate or possible to directly record a conversation or take thorough notes, I typed the narrative from memory immediately following the exchange, albeit with some occasional paraphrasing of dialogue.

In addition to these conversations, I further employed something called "participant observation," which is to experience events directly for myself while making my own interpretations. Third and just as important, I undertook some archival research before, during, and after my short expedition. This activity involved a thorough screening of online local news articles and related materials. With my hastily crafted plan ready to roll out, it was time to uncover what this special, third Palio had in store for everyone.

UNBRIDLED SPIRIT

The account that follows provides a roughly sequential story of my own experiences interlaced with personal conversations and supplemental perspectives from local media. In some cases, entire chapters are devoted to one particular conversation. Indeed, my admittedly small sample of local residents had a lot to say, and I am forever grateful that they entrusted me with their viewpoints. Now, on to the Palio Straordinario!

PART I:
PREPARATIONS

❈ CHAPTER 1 ❈

October Skies

O N THIS UNIQUELY SPECIAL EVENING OF SEPTEMBER 30, 2018, SIENA'S CITY hall—the venerable Palazzo Pubblico—could rival Disneyland as the happiest place on earth. Such hubs of local government cannot often claim such a thing. But here, at this very moment in Senese history, it would be difficult to find a wider variety of uplifting, joyful human emotions than what is on exhibit outside this fourteenth-century Gothic palace right now.

In the empty space remaining between the expectant crowd and the Palazzo Pubblico, two women emerge separately from the throng and run toward each other like powerful magnets attracting one another. Like long-lost sisters embracing for the first time since childhood, they collide and embrace in a strangling hug of sheer bliss. One of them is temporarily picked up off the ground, and both are screaming. Meanwhile, a few meters to their left, one young man is jumping up and down uncontrollably, bouncing around the open space as if on a trampoline. Others around him are doing the same while pointing to the sky or raising their fists with arms flailing. To the right of the women on this impromptu public stage is a group of five slower moving yet jubilant, middle-aged men (one in a sports coat) who appear from nowhere for a team hug. They don't seem to know how to satisfactorily express their collective, pent-up energy; their individual bodies shake uncontrollably while embracing one another. To see this out of context, one could reasonably presume they are celebrating a favored team scoring the winning goal in a World Cup match.

Soon thereafter, another group of young men and women suddenly appear in the open space. They crash together and dance uncontrollably in a circle while jumping up and down, fists punching the air. They part ways as quickly as they had convened, literally dancing back into the crowd with smiles and laughter. Not to be outdone, one young man runs right up to the wall of the Palazzo and throws himself onto the metal grating that protects one of its massive Gothic windows. For a full second, he hangs on through sheer determination, pumped with adrenaline, as if trying to scale a fence, until the police officer standing *right next to him* gently nudges him down. Soon thereafter, two teenage boys manifest their glee in another way, simply by *lying down on the paving stones* next to one another, holding their faces and looking to the sky in awed amazement. They remain almost motionless for several seconds while mentally absorbing the news, as if they had fainted. All the while, a cadre of news cameras and other photographers descend on them to digitally capture their moment of elation.

Buried farther back amidst the sea of humanity, various segments of onlookers suddenly rise up in celebration with a unified roar of ecstasy. Clusters of up to several hundred people at a time are enjoying unfettered bliss. Viewing from afar, one can detect their collective fists rising upwards in a frenzy, their combined voices emitting an impressive shout across Siena's grand public space, Piazza del Campo (often shortened to "the Campo"). One group becomes organized enough to boisterously sing a variation of Siena's most popular folk melodies, "Il Canto della Verbena" ("Song of Verbena"). Shouting the words across the open expanse, their arms rise in unison at key points for emphasis.

Regardless of how people's emotions are being displayed, everyone is reacting spontaneously to the very same thing; that is, a series of ten colored flags are being placed in deliberate succession on the upper façade of their beloved Palazzo Pubblico. To those who know better, these are not just any decorative flags attached to the Palazzo. Rather, their distinctive, artistic designs carry with them a set of deeply held cultural identities and shared community meanings. In fact, the banners represent ten of Siena's seventeen *contrade* (local neighborhoods or wards). Their collective histories date back to medieval times and (even more importantly) to the heady days of the Republic of Siena before its final capitulation to its Florentine neighbors around 1555.

Today in front of the Palazzo, however, the meaning of these ten flags is even more profound. The human ecstasy erupting without abandon is not unexpected. Indeed, their contrade have been drawn from a lottery to participate in a special horse race known as a Palio Straordinario (Extraordinary Palio; often shortened to "the Straordinario"). Aside from the city's two regularly scheduled Palio events held during July and August, the Senesi (residents of Siena; singular, Senese) have not seen the likes of a Straordinario in eighteen years. It turns out that these additional races are not held as frequently as in the city's storied past.

Normally, it is usually reason enough to celebrate when selected for either of the annual summer races. But to learn that your *contrada* (neighborhood) will be one of ten to join a rarely held third Palio will incite nothing less than mass hysteria. If you have not surmised by now, the Palio is a very big deal to all seventeen contrade and to Siena as a whole.

Legacy of the Republic

Let's back up a bit to get a better sense of the Siena landscape. For those largely unaware of the city's unseen social geography, the map below (Figure 1) reveals the location of all seventeen contrade and their respective territories within the historic city walls of Siena. Piazza del Campo is near the center of the map, appropriately representing the city's veritable beating heart and public focus. The shell-shaped *piazza* (town square) further serves as the intersection between the city's three dominant *terzi* (districts), each strung out densely along its own elevated ridge. As for the seventeen contrade, their *rioni* (territories) have remained virtually unchanged since the year 1729. However, an understanding of the history of the Republic of Siena (1125–1555) is critical to learn why there are now only seventeen contrade.

Figure 1. Map of Siena's seventeen contrade and the city's three districts (terzi). (Source: https://www.picturesfromitaly.com/tuscany)

Before the middle 1300s, historical accounts point to as many as sixty contrade scattered throughout a more densely packed city. One fundamental reason for subdividing the city in this way was military in nature. Each contrada was expected to voluntarily supply soldiers to defend the city. Today the most outward association between the contrade and their former military roles is found in the elegantly costumed *corteo storico* (historical procession) that precedes the Palio on race day. Episodes of war and plague reduced the population, culminating gravely with the unrelenting Black Death of 1348, which ravaged much of Europe. Within the span of several months, approximately a third to half of Siena's population had been unceremoniously carried away. Following that tragic episode, the verified number of contrade fell to forty-two for some time afterwards.[1] Though greatly diminished in number over the centuries, the seventeen remaining contrade provide a direct and intense local connection to the heyday of the Siena Republic. This so-called golden age is often defined as the years 1260 through its defeat approximately three centuries later.

What is so special about the year 1260? It happens to mark the most highly revered military victory of Siena's medieval past—the Battle of Montaperti—when the Senese army enjoyed an absolutely crushing victory over their rival Florentines. Not just incidentally, this was one of numerous crises that engendered Siena's centuries-long relationship with the Virgin Mary (the Madonna). There have been numerous times in Siena's complicated past when the people have petitioned the Virgin Mary for assistance with whatever predicament happened to be ailing them. The Battle of Montaperti is one of the earliest such events and remains the most significant. Leading up to that decisive battle, the Senesi had barely survived an unrelenting siege by the Florentine army. Knowing they were outnumbered and on the defensive, the Senesi prayed for assistance from the Virgin Mary. Even though the Senese army won due to their excellent military strategy, the Virgin Mary is still given the lion's share of credit for Siena's unqualified success in that battle.[2] It is no wonder that in relatively recent soccer (European football) matches between Siena and its neighbor to the north, quite serious placards and chants from the Senese faithful instructed their rival to "Remember Montaperti!"

Perhaps astonishingly to outsiders like me, all seventeen of today's contrade were already in existence well before the Republic of Siena's 1555 defeat at the hands of the Duchy of Florence in the fractious days before our modern nation-state system. Then in 1729, Siena's governess, the Princess Violante of Bavaria, settled various lingering boundary disputes by issuing a decree that finalized the contrada territories once and for all. With the very same declaration, six largely inactive contrade were summarily dissolved (or "suppressed"): those of the Bear, Strong Sword, Viper, Rooster, Lion, and Oak. It should be no surprise, then, that the deceptively modest flags flying on the Palazzo convey a distinct sense of place and a deeply rooted attachment to centuries-old communities that many outsiders may not fully understand.

All contrade come with the trappings of full-fledged, self-governing populations, but they also exist within the legal jurisdiction of the Siena municipality. Each contrada includes its own *società* (community center), symbolic public spaces, folk songs, a patriotic anthem, color schemes, an *oratorio* (chapel), a stable for the care and feeding of the horse during the days of the Palio, and—perhaps most importantly—democratically elected leaders. The elected head of the contrada is usually known as the *priore* (president), with two exceptions: the Goose contrada elects a *governatore* (governor) and the Caterpillar elects a *rettore* (rector).

Many of the contrade maintain official allies as well as a long-time rival. The most common origins of these rivalries were various historical boundary disputes between neighboring contrade, but sometimes they were inspired by antagonistic behaviors incited during the Palio. Interestingly, all the rival pairs share a common territorial boundary except for that of the Goose and Tower. As described by the respected scholars Alan Dundes and Alessandro Falassi, there are four possible relationships between two contrade: alliance, friendship, no relationship, and enmity (or rivalry).[3]

Those who have read my first book may recall some fascinating aspects of these relationships. One of my goals then was to better ascertain how seriously the *contradaioli* (residents of a contrada; singular, contradaiolo) consider their own rivalries outside of Palio time. Generally, I found that the Senesi can (often) all but ignore the rivalries throughout the year in favor of conducting business or maintaining friendships. After all, despite the incredibly strong identity felt for their own contrada, everyone is first and foremost a Senese. When faced with various adversity or challenges affecting the whole city, its residents unite under the black-and-white *balzana* (coat of arms) of Siena regardless of contrada affiliation. As one might imagine, however, it is during and around the emotionally intense days of the Palio when contrada rivalries manifest most dramatically. As the story about the Straordinario progresses below, we will uncover clear examples of how seriously these rivalries are considered, especially with respect to deciding which contrade compete.

There are currently six established rival pairs in Siena:

- Tower—Goose
- Porcupine—She-Wolf
- Snail—Turtle
- Shell—Ram
- Eagle—Panther
- Owl—Unicorn

One additional rivalry, between the Caterpillar and the Giraffe, was annulled with none other than a peace treaty in 1996. In another curiosity, the Wave contrada can be interpreted as a second rival to the Tower, though the Tower does not officially recognize this rivalry. Nonetheless, when it comes to influencing the outcome of the Palio, the Wave and the Goose are typically quite aligned in their interests against their common foe.

Basics of the Palio

Despite the advent of automobiles, suburbs, air-conditioned apartment flats, digital communication, global trade, and the all-consuming internet, it can seem as though the persistent march of time in Siena has effectively been suspended. Twice each year—on rare occasions, three times—the local population with its seventeen distinct communities rally around a startlingly brief event. On the scheduled days of July 2 and August 16, ten hopeful contrade attempt to win a horse race around the central square, Piazza del Campo. In modern times as in the distant past, both summer Palii (plural of Palio) are dedicated to the Virgin Mary, thereby inextricably linking the traditions of the Catholic Church with those of the Palio. Only three laps are required to determine the winner, usually no longer than 90 seconds from start to finish. However, what the race lacks in duration is more than compensated for by the collective emotional intensity and drama it elicits.

Not just another horse race, the Palio is characterized by some important eccentricities. Let's look at the big ones here for now. One is the direction in which the competitors race, which is clockwise around the harrowing track; nearly all Western horse races move counterclockwise. This necessitates special training for the horses, as they need to become accustomed to turning right instead of left. A specially designed practice track in the nearby town of Mociano purposely simulates the actual course in the Campo. As for the *fantini* (jockeys; singular *fantino*) who ride them, they rely on very little gear to support their effort. There is no saddle because they ride bareback, and there are no stirrups that might entangle them when they (quite possibly) might be thrown off the horse at one of several hair-raising turns. The only tool—or weapon—provided to jockeys during the actual race (but not for the preceding six trials) is the two-foot-long *nerbo*, a whip produced amusingly from the dried, stretched phallus of a calf. Whether jockeys use it to urge their own horse onward, to hold back another horse, or to beat up a nearby jockey remains entirely up to them. In no small amount of irony, the lot of ten fantini are screened for weapons just before the race, yet they are then each provided with a nerbo by a police officer as they enter onto the track.

Of course, the deployment of the nerbo is moot should the fantino fall from his horse. Falling occurs rather commonly during the actual race when the hooves meet the turf, so to speak. On their route around the Campo, there are two especially hazardous turns. The first is known as the curve of San Martino (the curve at the corner of the San Martino district), near the left side of the Palazzo Pubblico as one faces it. This spot is where contestants race downhill through a 95-degree turn to avoid the impressive Renaissance-era Cappella di Piazza (Chapel of the Square). This imposing marble structure was erected following the Black Death of 1348 in appreciation of that portion of the population that managed to survive. Its architectural merits aside, during the Palio it simply serves as a challenging and dangerous obstacle to navigate around.

The second-most hazardous turn is on the opposite, up-slope side of the Palazzo Pubblico, known as the turn at the Casato (the curve at Casato di Sotto, one of eleven streets leading into the Campo). A good percentage of accidents occur here, though not to the extent of the curve of San Martino. However, should an unfortunate jockey succumb to one of these curves or anywhere else for that matter, the contrada need not give up all hope. This is because of the curious fact that the horse can still win the Palio on its own accord, and it sometimes does precisely that upon unceremoniously throwing its fantino to the turf.

UNBRIDLED SPIRIT

For their part, the fantini are typically hired mercenaries—sometimes referred to as *assassini* (assassins)—from outside Siena. Most are not tied emotionally to a particular contrada, though exceptions do occur. All else being equal, a jockey is free to race for whatever contrada he prefers, assuming the contrada is likewise interested in him. This absence of loyalty is why contradaioli tend to dote lovingly on the horses and pamper them to no end while also assuring their safety to the extent possible. In contrast, they really couldn't care less about the fantini.

With this admittedly whirlwind background in mind, we are better prepared to comprehend today's passion-filled event in the Campo. Prior to any Palio, a lottery (drawing) is required to determine which fortunate contrade will be allowed to compete. Known locally as the *estrazione* (extraction) of the contrade, this event is vital because only ten horses and jockeys race in any given Palio. The extraction therefore determines which are in and which are out.

That said, there is a wrinkle thrown into the process. Curiously for unsuspecting visitors, the July and August Palii are considered separate annual events, completely independent of one another. While both are dedicated to the Virgin Mary (Madonna), they are distinct. Briefly for now, the July Palio is dedicated to the Madonna of Provenzano, referring to a local church with its own historical significance. In fact, the celebration for the victorious contrada following the July race occurs at this very church. On the flip side, the August Palio is perceived as a festival dedicated to the Madonna of the Assumption, which centuries ago had its origins in the annual Feast of the Assumption around August 15. The celebration and related events for that Palio occur at the Duomo (the main cathedral in the city). For this reason, even though the July and August races appear to be identical on the surface, they have little to do with one another.

Given this quirky practice, the wrinkle is thus: Determining which contrade will race on July 2 is largely based on those that did not race the previous July; likewise for the August event. In a quite logical and fair-minded approach for everyone, the rule is that the seven contrade that sat out the Palio the previous July or August are guaranteed a spot the following year. If the Shell did not run last July, for instance, it is guaranteed a place within the next consecutive July race. When the Senesi populate the Campo for the scheduled summer extractions, therefore, they go in already knowing seven of the contrade that will run. The only thing left to chance is the final set of three contrade, which are chosen by lottery to round out the final ten competitors.

An Unlikely Straordinario

The scenario above describes the customary process for the two summer Palii. Today, however, the state of affairs in the Campo was elevated to yet a new level of drama given that *all ten* contrade were extracted simultaneously to race in the Straordinario. This is simply because there was no precedent from the previous year to help determine the competitors. So why is this third, quite extraordinary Palio being held? As we will see later in more detail, Siena's population decides once in a great while to hold a third race, completely independent of its summer counterparts. The rationale for holding a Straordinario must be deemed very special indeed, and each case is carefully considered and vetted before it is officially approved. Typically, a Straordinario is organized to celebrate or commemorate a historically significant event. The turn of the millennium and the Apollo 11 lunar landing are two prominent examples. In this case, Siena will hold a Straordinario on Saturday, October 20, 2018, to specifically commemorate the end of World War I (known originally as la Grande Guerra, or the Great War).

The decision to hold such an unusual Palio is not taken lightly. Approval for a Straordinario must pass through a sequential process of decision making. This process is spelled out in precise detail within the official *Regolamento del Palio*, the municipality's overarching set of regulations governing how the Palio is run and organized.[4] One need not dig any further than Article 2 of the 45-page document, which directs that "Extraordinary Palii may be carried out on the occasion of absolutely exceptional circumstances or events." An original proposal for considering a Straordinario is either initiated directly by the mayor or city council, or provided as a proposal by an outside party directly to the mayor. If the proposal seems to be legitimate and worthy of further consideration, the matter is then handed over to the seventeen contrade to judge whether the proposed rationale is appropriately significant to warrant such an event.

Readers should understand one caveat in the interest of setting up the story herein. At least ten of the seventeen contrade need to vote in favor of a proposal to hold a Straordinario, and they need to vote completely independent of one another. If only nine or less contrade vote in favor, then the extra Palio will not be run. Each contrada can manage its own election the way it wishes. Should the proposal pass this fundamental test of contrada support, the decision then gets thrown back to the mayor and city council to either affirm or reverse the decision.

For those who are quick to presume—perhaps understandably—that the Senesi would simply embrace any reason to hold another Palio, it is notable that in this case the reverse was true. In fact, only ten contrade ultimately voted in favor of commemorating the conclusion of World War I in this way—precisely the minimum number required—meaning that seven contrade voted against the idea. Voting results in some contrade were quite close, including those that tilted in favor. Thus, had a few hundred members of even one contrada somehow changed their vote, this Straordinario would not be happening. I am therefore curious to learn why so many Senesi could not bring themselves to support it.

Beyond this elaborate voting process and its very close outcome, there is one further point of interest. Upon the event's final approval, the municipality provides five additional days for any contrada that initially voted "no" to reverse its decision. This process effectively allows a contrada to participate in the same Palio that it had *just officially voted against*. As we will see, this particular aspect of the process—the second vote—will provide no end of debate for many Senesi as preparation for this Palio continues to unfold.

What all of this amounted to was an extraction today in the Campo that commanded a serious level of local attention. Every contrada had an equal chance of being drawn, thereby providing for a dramatic surprise for everyone holding a stake in its outcome. And so it was, today at 5:30 p.m. on this September 30, 2018 when an unusual extraction took place in Piazza del Campo. Those ten contrade fortunate enough to be chosen will vie for a unique Palio victory on October 20, providing for an astonishingly short amount of time between now and then.

To better appreciate the constraints here, it is useful to consider the amount of time typically available for planning the July and August events. In those cases, seven of the ten chosen contrade already know they will participate a full year in advance. The final three chosen by lottery enjoy approximately six weeks to prepare. Among many other things, contracts with jockeys need to be negotiated and finalized, and the ever-complex *partiti* (back-room deal making) needs to be accomplished.

The Partiti

"Deal making?" readers might ask with a raised eyebrow or two. One must keep in mind that the Palio is more a game than it is a sport; it is essentially the one continuously surviving game in Siena that has withstood the so-called test of time since the Middle Ages. It is amazing enough that the Palio did not evaporate centuries ago, something that has commonly occurred with similar festivals elsewhere. Some festivals have been revived recently, but primarily as tourist attractions. Rather, Siena's Palio is a rare event in the Tuscan region that has not only survived but has increased in relevance for its local population.

Given that all aspects of the Palio are controlled by the Senesi, it follows that none of what occurs during or around the Palio is designed as a spectacle for outsiders. Rather, the festival represents an extremely localized community celebration that those from outside Siena are—quite understandably—hard-pressed to fully comprehend. Although visitors to the city may not be its primary audience, the Palio has provided a growing challenge for the city in recent decades. Its best-kept secret is becoming increasingly known to an online global viewership. Consequently, knowledge of the partiti that occurs behind the scenes—and sometimes even out in the open—can be difficult to stomach for those familiar with the rigorous standards and ethics that characterize organized sports elsewhere.

For me, the existence of clandestine partiti is perfectly fine. In Siena, visitors bear witness to what is essentially a medieval-era community game that somehow continues to thrive well into the twenty-first century. Such practices, therefore, will necessarily come with deeply engrained traditions and customs handed down through the ages. One of my favorite quotes regarding the practice of deal making comes from Dundes and Falassi, who argue, "The Palio simply would not be the Palio without partiti!" They further explain that the practice represents "man's attempt to control his fate through skillful diplomacy and manipulation."[5] It is important to remember that each of the seventeen contrade are always attempting to maintain some level of autonomy and self-determination, even at their smaller scale of operation. The Palio thus provides the perfect opportunity to practice such diplomacy and negotiation among these long-standing community organizations.

On a more official level, it is true that the governing regulations for the conduct of the Palio forbid any type of partiti or related agreements with intentions to alter the outcome of the race. However, the Senesi proceed with such agreements anyway, and everyone knows about them. It is simply expected, and it has been part of their approach for generations. I have decided to accept the complex practice as part of the cultural system already in place here. As an outsider, it is not for me to judge the process through my own cultural lens; given that the partiti have no impact outside Siena, I believe that its people can simply do whatever they want. All seventeen potential contestants exist on their own level playing field. Nobody is left out of the opportunity to conduct partiti in its various forms.

Uncharted Territory for the Senesi

The need to conduct the partiti is just one aspect of the Straordinario that reminds the Senesi that precious little time remains for all ten contrade to complete their planning. There is much to be accomplished within the incredibly short span of three weeks. Today's jubilation from those fortunate to be extracted will quickly transition now to a marathon of planning, strategizing, and—for the municipality—transforming Piazza del Campo into a veritable arena for the third time in 2018. All of this invites an array of questions as to how such an event will ultimately play out. I am particularly curious about how this Palio will differ from its summer counterparts, both in terms of its organization and scheduling. There is also another factor at play here—memory—because the last Straordinario was held some eighteen years ago at the turn of the millennium. What challenges are in store for successfully accomplishing such a complex event? It is likely that few people recall the details of organizing the last one. Beyond questions of logistics, to what extent are the Senesi actually supportive of the event? Perhaps most important, are they genuinely enthusiastic about its rationale, which is the commemoration of the end of World War I? Why or why not?

OCTOBER SKIES

One serious issue is the weather—you know, the seemingly random stuff that comes down at us from the sky. City leaders and media alike are focusing intently on possible weather scenarios while emphasizing the strangeness of a mid-October Palio. On seemingly everyone's mind is this fundamental question: What will October skies bring to a rather nervous Siena? One news article noted that—following today's emotional event in the Campo—the next big "Straordinario" deadline will arrive in about a week and a half. This is when the actual race comes into the range of the extended, ten-day weather forecast. Until then, there is little hope of predicting what the weather might do from one day to the next. And the weather here is not taken lightly; indeed, the Palio and its associated activities on and off the track are almost entirely dependent on the outdoors. One local news writer simply left the weather up to the gods: "Aside from superstition, optimists by nature, and pessimists regardless, the contrada of Giove Pluvio [Jove the Raingiver, or Jupiter] will be the one to run the next Palio, even if its flag is not exposed outside the triple windows." Implied here is that only the omnipotent god of the weather will be fully in charge here.[6]

Adding to the mystique surrounding the weather is another news story circulating about a previous Straordinario, none other than that of October 4, 1745. For readers curious as to the relevance here, this happens to have been the only previous example in the last few centuries of a Straordinario held as late as October. Won by the Panther with not a little controversy, the memory of that earlier race was somewhat kept alive through a newspaper article dating to 1896.[7] Flashing forward to 2018, the story was dug up yet again with no other purpose than to recognize the historical significance of Siena's only other October Straordinario. According to the account, the Panther's 1745 victory was owed specifically to a "fanatic Panterina"—a female Panther supporter who walloped the favored horse of the Forest contrada with a stick during the race. The Forest's horse lost its lead due to this alleged foul play, allowing the Panther's horse to slip by for the win. For her part, the Panterina was summarily arrested and taken to jail—for how long is anyone's guess. Also significant, the transgression inaugurated a century-long rivalry between the Panther and Forest. As for the weather that day? Nobody knows.

This story is now consequently serving as an intriguing local interest piece because the upcoming Palio will smash this previous record by occurring a full sixteen days later in the year. Who knows what kind of skies one might expect this late in October? Of course, this type of news coverage does little to reassure a local population clearly on edge about the meteorological fiasco that may await us all. No matter, three weeks from today the optimists and skeptics alike will have their answers regarding whether the whole affair has been worth it—answers that will not likely be entirely clear.

※ CHAPTER 2 ※

The Chosen Ones

GIVEN THE NECESSITY OF DRAWING ALL TEN CONTRADE AT THE EXTRACTION described above, the process for doing so varied somewhat from the normal summer routine. The actual drawing inside the Palazzo Pubblico is not visible to the thousands of onlookers awaiting the results in the Campo. Thus, local news reporters have provided educational overviews for those unfamiliar with Straordinario protocols. In many ways, the Senesi are learning this process all over again as well.

Extraction of the Contrade

Before today's extraction, the city's mayor, Luigi De Mossi, had summoned all seventeen contrada captains to the Palazzo Pubblico to assist with the drawing. During the so-called "days of the Palio"—namely the four sequential days leading up to and including the race—the leader of each contrada relinquishes all authority to the *capitano* (captain) and his *mangini* (assistants). It is therefore the captains who participate most directly in Palio decision making and events. With the captains all present for the drawing earlier today, the mayor kicked off the process by drawing the name of the first contrada to race in the upcoming Palio. In turn, the captain of that contrada drew the name of the second contrada, the captain of the second drew the third, and so on. Amusingly, it is entirely possible to draw one's own contrada. On the flip side, however, the captain also risks drawing the name of his rival contrada, which likely causes no end of visible consternation for said captain. Regardless, once the final ten are chosen to race, the remaining seven contrade are still drawn sequentially by the mayor to determine less dramatic decisions; for instance, the lineup order of the contrade and their *comparse* (delegations) for the historical procession or participation in the six upcoming *prove* (trials).

Overall, the process of extracting the contrade resembles that of the two summer events, but with one fundamental difference. For the July and August Palii, the mayor first draws the names of all three contrade from an urn, recalling that only three are typically extracted for those Palii. In turn, the captains of those three contrade pick sequentially from a second urn to determine which contrada will join the race.[8]

For its part, the public spectacle begins in tandem with the actual extraction inside the Palazzo Pubblico. In the words of one media piece written to prepare the Senesi for the event, "Then will come the display of the flags enshrined by the sound of the trumpets and, of course, the exultation of ten contrade in Piazza del Campo, which will undoubtedly be more crowded than ever."[9]

To clarify what the public actually witnesses, an initial trumpet fanfare announces the beginning of the extraction, played by six *trombettiere* (trumpet players) with their long-belled horns known as *chiarine* (clarions). The fanfare is performed out of an open window on the Palazzo's second floor (which is actually referred to by Italians as the *primo piano* or the first floor). Following a second brief fanfare, the flag of the first selected contrada is simply extended out the window and placed in a holder nearby. Upon instantly recognizing their flag, the representative contrada members erupt in collective glee, as we saw displayed on the Campo earlier today. Only a few seconds later, and usually with the first contrada still celebrating, the fanfare is played yet again. The second flag then appears and is placed next to the first. This process continues apace until all ten flags are eventually flying next to one another on the façade of the Palazzo.

Aside from the festive trumpets, the simple act of displaying the flags outside the window is a rather subdued, unpretentious affair. At one moment the flag is not there, and the next moment it is. This sober action is in direct contrast to the instant and dramatic reaction spawned down below as the flag emerges out the window. And today's event provided an additional level of drama above the norm—not only due to the novelty of holding a Straordinario in October, but also because of the additional need to select all ten contrade. Today, everyone had a chance to be a part of the chosen ten. It is no wonder that certain contrada members were nearly fainting on the ground or were—quite literally—climbing the walls. This was the "mother of all extractions," even by Siena's standards. And what of the members of the seven contrade not chosen to run? As described in the same article cited above, "for the remaining seven [not extracted] today, it will be winter."[10] Perhaps harsh, but true.

With the last flag planted on the wall of the Palazzo, the stage is now set for the latest October Straordinario in recorded history. In the order of their extraction, the contrade listed below will compete on October 20. The second column indicates whether the extracted contrade had initially voted in favor of, or against, the proposal to hold a Palio to commemorate the end of World War I.

Contrade Extracted	Initial Vote
1. Torre (Tower)	No
2. Lupa (She-Wolf)	No
3. Chiocciola (Snail)	No
4. Oca (Goose)	No
5. Drago (Dragon)	No
6. Tartuca (Turtle)	Yes
7. Selva (Forest)	Yes
8. Civetta (Owl)	Yes
9. Nicchio (Shell)	Yes
10. Giraffa (Giraffe)	Yes

It is difficult to not break a smile when noticing how many contrade were extracted that initially voted "no." As if that weren't enough, the first five contrade to be drawn were those that had voted against the proposal—a rather bizarre fact not going unnoticed by the oft-superstitious Senesi.

Most and Least Likely to Win

Readers might wonder if there are any favorites that might enjoy a better chance of winning. Although the question is certainly premature at this point, it is not entirely off base. One might be surprised at the possible scope of analysis that can be considered at this early stage. The Senesi are, no doubt, already beginning to intensely deliberate the possibilities themselves. So, let's try to think like a Senese for a moment.

One of the first factors to consider is the number of rival pairs included in the selected group of ten. Generally, those Palii with numerous rival pairs on the track will be more contentious and the rival onlookers more prickly, with more at stake for everyone. Each rival contrada is not only trying to win, but it is also plotting to somehow deny victory to its nemesis. As a rule of thumb, more pairs of rivals in the race can lead to a lengthier lineup process at the *mossa* (starting line). Before the beginning of the race, each jockey will try to secure an advantage to launch his horse quickly while hopefully catching his rival off guard. In the Palio, therefore, the concept of "jockeying for position" is not just a figure of speech. All are desperately attempting to do exactly that.

This process is all the more difficult because nobody knows precisely when the race will begin. The one who starts the race is actually the jockey assigned to the tenth position at the lineup, known as the *rincorsa* (run-in horse). While the other nine jockeys fuss with their squirmy steeds at the *canape* (rope), the rincorsa remains about a horse length behind the others on the outside of the track. When he sees that his allies have a decent chance to start successfully, he will initiate his gallop to begin the race. Should a jockey be caught in an awkward position when the rincorsa makes his move, that mistake could be enough to seal his fate.

For instance, four rival pairs (eight out of ten contrade) were included in the Palio held in July 2013. It came as no surprise to the experienced Senesi, therefore, that the starting lineup process involved a particularly hair-raising ordeal which required more than an hour because of all the fidgeting among the competitors at the mossa. As the Campo descended into darkness, probably no more than five or ten minutes remained before the entire race would have been cancelled for the night.

Returning to today's extraction, the selected ten contrade include two pairs of rivals, namely those of the Tower and Goose, and the Snail and Turtle. Though not considered a high number of rival pairs, these four will most certainly be gunning for their respective nemeses in one way or another. In turn, this may provide advantages to the other six competitors. Tradition holds that a contrada will necessarily have a harder time winning a Palio if its rival is also in the Campo. Each rival will attempt to somehow disrupt his counterpart, either directly during the race or in more subtle ways through off-track negotiations. Using this logic, the more fortunate contrade extracted today are those whose rivals were not chosen—namely, the She-Wolf (rival: Porcupine), the Owl (rival: Unicorn), and the Shell (rival: Ram).

The manner in which local media outlets emphasize the number of rivals indicates the seriousness of these rivalries. Following today's extraction, for instance, the second paragraph of one article read as follows:

> [Tonight's event] was witnessed in Piazza del Campo by about 20 thousand people, though there are others who swear that attendance reached 40 thousand. In the next race there are historical rivals like those between Goose and Tower, and Turtle and Snail. With the extraction complete, the strategies of the captains have begun, with only 16 days to determine the winning strategy [before the days of the Palio begin] on October 17.[11]

Another article simply provides a list of the ten contrade extracted, followed immediately with this: "Rivali in Piazza: Torre e Oca, Chiocciola e Tartuca" (Rivals in the Piazza: Tower and Goose, Snail and Turtle).[12] Having your rival contrada participate in the Palio is a big deal indeed. It is not something for the contradaioli to take lightly.

Beyond the rival pairs, however, are other potential forces of influence. It is possible and quite likely that a contrada will make clandestine deals with various allies, even those that may not even be fielding a horse in the Campo. Perhaps most fortunate in this case are those contrade that no longer have an official rival: the Dragon, Forest, and Giraffe. Specifically, the Forest has been known to sneak up from behind to win a Palio because the other rival pairs are focused intently on one another. Every so often, consequently, the wily Forest cruises under the radar as the "forgotten" contrada. They won not long ago, in August 2015.

Taking this speculation one step further, we should also consider those contrade that have most recently won a Palio. A victory can seriously drain a contrada's budget to the point where a recent victor may not try terribly hard to win any time soon. Will they accept and celebrate an unexpected victory should the fates allow? Most definitely. But should such a thing occur, they still need to seriously consider one curiosity about the Palio. Quite simply, it costs a lot of money to win, which is probably counterintuitive to those of us accustomed to seeing sports teams and their organizations receive a windfall of funds following a championship. In the world of Siena, however, a victorious contrada does not win money. Rather, its community ends up paying others who had agreed to help them. The winning contrada is obligated to settle any partiti that may have been agreed upon with their counterparts, not to mention paying the jockey's sizable commission and any additional bonus for winning. After these immediate payoffs have been settled, there will come a full year of celebration dinners, parties, publications, parades, and related functions that collectively add up to a small fortune. Entire yearbooks are sometimes generated by a contrada to document a victory and its successive celebration events. Essentially, in Siena, to win is to pay. Despite this reality, there is nothing much more satisfying in the life of a Senese than to win yet another Palio.

The only actual prize that a victorious contrada takes home is a rectangular piece of silk cloth known generally as the *palio* (banner). It is also commonly referred to as the *cencio* (rag) or more formally as the *drappellone* (drapery). I tend to favor this latter term. Decorated by either a local or internationally acclaimed artist for each specific Palio, the drappellone is paraded around the city on various occasions following a victory, after which it is lovingly placed permanently behind glass for display within the contrada's museum. More about the meaning and creation of the drappellone is presented later.

What all of this means is that it is wise to consider which contrade have not won a Palio in some time, perhaps a decade or longer. During lengthy droughts without a victory, a contrada can amass a sizable war chest. These contrade are generally the most desperate to win and enjoy an ample budget to help them do so. From my conversations in recent years, these contrada budgets devoted to the Palio can soar into the millions of euros. For how long have some contrade endured lately without a win? Sometimes the drought has lasted as long as two, three, or even four decades. In July 2016, we gleefully watched the despondent She-Wolf finally win the drappellone following its own drought of twenty-seven years. At that point, the Eagle was dubbed the *nonna* (grandmother), a derogatory if fun-loving term describing the contrada that has endured the longest time without a Palio win, including either the July or August races. This is the status that the Eagle regretfully retains to this day. The poor Eagle has not won a Palio since July 3, 1992—twenty-seven years and counting—and they will not win this Palio, either, because they were simply not extracted.

It follows that we can dare make some predictions regarding those contrade that are most likely to try hard to win. Considering this measure alone, the She-Wolf is the least likely candidate to push for victory. After finally shedding its own status as nonna in July 2016, that contrada went on to win the next Palio in August (known in Siena as a *cappotto*—two wins in the same year). Then, most recently in August 2018, they won yet again. Amusingly, the She-Wolf is still celebrating, now only a few months following that unplanned victory. However, their members, the Lupaioli, are reportedly less than pleased about having the upcoming Straordinario steal their thunder. In any case, this is not a contrada that is desperate for a win, as they are still grappling (albeit joyfully) with the last one. No, they are not likely to put up a big fight, either on or off the track.

Another contrada with a recent victory is the Dragon, which won in July 2018, just before the She-Wolf's August triumph. Likewise, the Giraffe is still basking dimly in its own success from precisely one year earlier. If one were to hazard a guess for the Straordinario, it would be relatively safe to presume that these three will not intently push for victory. Strangely, some of the others extracted today have also won relatively recently, including the Goose (2013), Owl (2014), Tower (2015), and Forest (2015). Of course, none of these contrade would refuse another victory, especially that of a Straordinario, should the drappellone come home to their museum.

As quite bitter rivals, the Tower and Goose will likely have it in for each other. However, the Owl will find itself without its bothersome rival, the Unicorn. This fact alone may give them an edge. As for the Turtle and Snail, neither has won recently—especially the Snail—so they will both be angling for a win while also attempting to disrupt one another. As for the pesky Forest—well, the Senesi know all too well about the Forest—they are always an unknown quantity. But are they particularly hungry? Probably not. Still, I always give pause when I see their flag up on the Palazzo Pubblico.

And what of the Shell? It is no secret among the Senesi that the rather sizable community from the city's *Terzo di San Martino* (District of San Martino, the southeastern section of the city) has been valiantly attempting to find a route to victory for some years now. In recent Palii, they have contracted with the top jockeys and have occasionally landed one of the strongest horses (more on this process later). Adding to this, the Shell also has not won a Palio for quite some time; their last victory was in August 1998. That's right, the Shell has not yet won a Palio in this century, just like the Eagle. They are consequently overdue, having likely amassed a sizable budget to make it happen. As mentioned earlier, their rival, the Ram, will be sitting this one out. It should be noted that in July 2015, the jockey for the Ram literally lunged for the Shell's jockey and pulled him off his horse just after the race began. Illegal? Yes. Effective? Very. Thus, for this race the Shell is undoubtedly thankful that it will be on its own, with plenty of allies to cheer them on. If one were to make a bold prediction fresh off the extraction today, the Shell will be the one to beat. We will see if my Senese acquaintances agree.

All speculation, analysis, and rumoring aside, however, it is wise to keep in mind that much can happen before race time on October 20. Whether any of these factors plays out on the ground is anyone's guess. And that's the fun I really look forward to seeing.

But first, we have to get there.

❖ CHAPTER 3 ❖

Transatlantic Journey

A FEW WEEKS BEFORE THE EXTRACTION, I SHARED A SIENA NEWS ARTICLE WITH Linda: "Wow, Siena actually decided to hold a special Palio next month, in October!" I added, "It's already the middle of September, so they only have a month to prepare. I really don't know how they are going to manage it that quickly."

"Huh, that's amazing. I would think they could wait until next year and plan ahead," Linda responded quite logically from across our living room.

"But maybe it wouldn't have the same impact next year. The Palio is supposed to commemorate the end of World War I in November 1918. Their 100th anniversary would actually be held on the 101st. I'm not sure they could sell that one," I said only half-jokingly, chuckling at my own thought.

"Well, I think people would understand if it was held a year later. It would still be honoring those who served. Who cares if it's this year or next year?" Linda asked rhetorically. Knowing Linda as I do, however, she was probably only a few small steps away from emailing Siena's mayor that very question.

"I don't know; this is really shocking. Maybe there are others who are thinking like you. From what I see, even the Senesi weren't expecting this." I followed this up with an anecdote for Linda's benefit: "When the proposal for this Palio made the news there, even Carlo just presumed they would do it next year in 2019. I had asked him if they would try for this October, and he said they would likely plan for the following year. So, he didn't seem to think it would even be possible next month." Readers of my book, *Living the Palio*, may remember Carlo as a friend from the Panther contrada. We had essentially met through dumb luck several years ago while purchasing contrada dinner tickets. We have stayed in touch ever since, and he is kind enough to keep this American outsider somewhat informed of happenings in his hometown.

An Impulsive Decision

Then Linda popped the question that would ultimately lead to the writing of this book. "Well, when did you say it's being held? Late October? Are you thinking of going?"

I responded instantly with nary a thought, "Ha! Gosh, no. I hadn't even considered it. We're in the middle of the semester, and we were just there in July." With that response, I brushed off the idea as being just this side of ludicrous. Nonetheless, Linda's innocent idea had taken root in my mind and blossomed quickly. Within days we were looking at airfares to see what options might exist while I toyed with rearranging my classes and related obligations.

Before I knew it, any lingering doubt turned into a dedicated resolve. Next month, we would return to Siena and head back into the Campo, stunning as it still seemed. It was hard to deny the obvious: A unique and fascinating story awaited us about the Extraordinary Palio—an event that had not occurred for eighteen years. Added to that, the intricately complex event would have to be organized in record time and would fall later in the year than any previously recorded Palio. Yes, indeed. I would have to see this with my own eyes.

Tempting Fate

If you are one of the more adventurous souls intent on tempting fate, just plan an international arrival only a few hours before your first scheduled event. Although October falls midway into a hectic university semester, I managed to creatively carve out ten days for our own adventure. The trip would be sandwiched by two weekends allowing for travel. The catch was that our ambitious itinerary would "thread the needle" with little wiggle room in our travel plans should something go awry. And this would be no relaxing vacation. My combined plans to converse with numerous people amidst a week's worth of Palio events would constitute a veritable marathon of personal activity. I would essentially be on one of my typically intense, academic missions—the type of which Linda is well aware. After accounting for travel time in both directions, we would enjoy no more than seven full days to speak with the Senesi to learn about this rare event. Thus, while suddenly whisking across the Atlantic in October may not be our craziest moment, I am confident that it easily makes the top-five list.

All that aside, I have not wavered once from my admittedly lofty goal, that of witnessing the initial public revelation of the victory drappellone. As one of the more obscure, lesser-known Palio events, the presentation ceremony is held in the inner courtyard of the Palazzo Pubblico precisely one week before the race. However, we are scheduled to arrive in Siena only a few hours before the presentation, so there is not much allowance for possible travel delays. Given a variety of past travel hassles, one might question my sanity to attempt an arrival only hours in advance of the presentation. Linda sure did. Still, I view the presentation as a fitting place to begin our Straordinario experience, when the tall, silk banner is made public for the first time.

Following what is hoped to be an on-time departure from the United States, our flight into Rome is expected to arrive around 9:00 Sunday morning, Italy time. Should all go miraculously well, our direct bus to Siena will dump us at Piazza Gramsci on the north side of the city around 2:00 p.m. So, why not tempt fate? At worst, our flight into Rome will be too late to catch the bus to Siena. The backup plan is to take the train on a roundabout route that will still get us there before the evening event.

Course Correction

Now in the international terminal of Philadelphia airport, it's "all systems go." Our earlier connecting flight went off without a hitch, so now it's dinner time before boarding around 6:30 p.m. We are comforted from our annual experience with similar round-trip flights, to the point where the trip so far is almost like an occasional (if lengthy) commute. We thus decide to enjoy rare access to Smashburger fare, including the obligatory chocolate shakes. Following dinner will come another planned hour of lounging with fellow travelers near the gate.

Upon our return to the waiting area to find seats, we all suddenly stop to listen to a new announcement. "For those traveling to Rome," *never a good sign when they begin this way*, "the flight will be delayed due to a mechanical issue on the plane that they are trying to fix. The latest expected departure time is now 8:00 p.m." *Well, rats.* Linda and I look at each other with our typical facial expressions that essentially say to one another, *Are you serious?* Without much emotion, I say in a somewhat deflated tone, "There goes our bus to Siena if they can't get us out until 8:00." For all to go well in Rome, we need to navigate through customs and get out of the airport by 10:30 a.m. to enjoy any confidence of making the bus to Siena. The only other direct bus departs from the airport after 6:00 p.m., making the train option much more reasonable.

However, we did happily discover one important time saver this past summer, that of traveling with no checked bags. With access to a nearby laundromat or our own small washing machine, we really did not need more than four days' worth of clothing. Everything managed to fit into two carry-on roller bags, my backpack, and Linda's purse. Tonight, we are traveling similarly and can therefore avoid the baggage claim ritual upon arrival.

Eventually, we start losing faith as the original boarding time comes and goes. As we casually watch a college football game at the open end of a bar establishment, I notice that two middle-aged couples are also cheering for my favored team, which happens to be playing right now. At some point, one of the two women walks off, but she returns and quickly agitates the group. She has overheard something from the check-in desk and blurts out, "The person at the counter says they are preparing to announce another delay!" I think, *Oh no, that's it for the bus, and if we don't leave until after 8:00 p.m., we may not make it in time for the presentation.* Of course, Linda can't resist joining the group and chiming in. After some banter that only accelerates the rumor mill, she looks back to me and thinks aloud, "Maybe they have other flights to Florence or something? It might be worth it to check." I have learned many times over that this type of diplomatic statement is really code for, *Please go check; this is not a suggestion.* She then turns her passport over to me. "Here, you may need this." Despite my growing disappointment, I am still of the mindset that it is too early to scout out alternative flight arrangements. Nonetheless, desperation sets in, and I begrudgingly think to myself, *Why not?* I can also try to verify what this woman thought she overheard at the counter.

The decision of when to visit a check-in desk of a delayed flight is probably not much different from trying to predict the swings of the stock market—not that I have much experience in that area. On the one hand, you can decide to beat the crowd and be the first in line to capture an alternative flight. But this risks not knowing whether your scheduled flight might still board and take off nearly on time. In this way, you might be pulling out of "the market" too early. The alternative, however, is to wait around like everyone else until we are certain of yet another delay, if not a cancellation. At that point, you are instantly too late. Those most desperate and—more importantly—nearest to the counter will beat you there and claim many of the available seats on other flights, not to mention you will spend a considerable amount of frustrating time in line. At that point, Linda would wisely direct us to call the airline in a vain attempt to "jump the line" electronically. Yes, indeed; I can see where all of this might go. Continuing with the same analogy, waiting too long to make the jump by phone means that "the market" may have instantly crashed before you could act.

At Linda's prodding, I arrive at the desk to find myself pleasantly alone, eventually attracting the attention of an employee. One woman proves to be especially kind, and I ask sheepishly if they might provide an update soon. She responds calmly, "Based on what I know, they have not resolved the issue yet, and that could lead to another delay." I sometimes think that airline employees who work with the public are trained like politicians who have mastered the skills of diplomacy and evasion. Of course, she is merely stating that she does not yet know the outcome, and neither do the mechanics. This is all perfectly fair, if still just as frustrating. I then decide to make the big ask of whether there might be alternative flights elsewhere into Italy—also making it very clear that we do not have checked bags. Successfully flying standby on domestic flights is more likely if your bags are not already sitting on the delayed flight, but for an international, trans-Atlantic journey? I'm not giving it much hope.

To my first surprise, she is not yet busy and decides to help by checking for other flights. During the requisite period of frantic typing and scowling at her screen, I valiantly attempt to read her eyes and body language—just as a pet dog would do when judging whether its owner is going to take the hopeful animal for a walk. She then responds, "Well, the connections to Florence don't seem to work, though we could get you there the next day." I kindly decline that idea and suggest that we try other airports in Italy. She then intensifies her search and even converses with her partner about options. I am already impressed that she is even willing to check. Part of me had presumed that she would just wave me off entirely after her first attempt.

She then tells me while reading her screen, "There is a flight to Venice that's about to leave, I could call them to see if there are seats." *Really?!* I think, responding, "Yes, please check." This news puts a new thought in my head. We could take a train from Venice to Siena as we have done before and still arrive by evening. Upon hanging up the phone, she tells me, "The flight to Venice is already mostly boarded, and they have two seats, but not together." Wow, this presents a serious choice to make. Thinking quickly for once, I ask her how much time we have to make a decision. Her answer is less than hopeful: "Ten minutes tops; five minutes is better." More excited now, I quickly say that I will confer with my wife and return immediately with the decision. As I racewalk back to our perch, Linda is still laughing it up with her new friends.

I return to find all five of them pressing me to share what I learned. They are betting that the flight has likely been delayed yet again. One of the women asks me intently, "What did you find out?"

With everyone's eyes set on me, I say, "There is likely another delay coming, but they're not sure because the mechanics on the plane aren't sure, either." While they consider this lack of definitive news, I add logically, "But it's already past boarding time for the new 8:00 departure, so I would bet that we'll be leaving later."

Still within earshot of our acquaintances, I pull Linda away from the joking to tell her about the serious offer of a flight to Venice. I make it clear that the seats aren't together, which I suspect could be a serious downside for her. And, I conclude with the final emphatic shock, "We only have maybe five minutes, as boarding is nearly complete. We need to get up there, like now."

She then throws it back to me, asking, "What do you think? Do you want to do it?" The choice is now on me, and it's down to the wire. Should we take the uncertain bet that our scheduled flight may not even get off the ground tonight? Venice is the sure bet at this point, as the flight has already boarded, and it's on schedule and waiting to depart.

Instantly filled with a rare sense of adventure amidst some rational logic, I look at her and respond, "I think we should do it. Let's go to Venice."

An Unexpected Companion

With that, Linda is up in a flash while grabbing her share of the bags. Now determined not to miss this unexpected opportunity, we wish our friends the best of luck with their flight and make a beeline for the counter. The employee recognizes me, and we inform her of our decision, asking hopefully, "Do they still have room on the Venice flight?" She quickly calls and happily confirms that they do, adding "You will need to move quickly, as they are completing their boarding process." Somehow, she magically prints out two tickets almost from thin air and says "Here you go!" *Is this for real?* I can't help but wonder. In yet another stroke of fortune, the Venice flight is located only two gates away, right down the hall. Upon arrival we quickly confirm that our previous "angel" behind the check-in desk was accurate. There is an eerie emptiness at our new gate, with the only remaining activity consisting of an airline employee completing her duties next to the empty jet bridge. Still, she seems to know who we are and why we are here, so she must have been at the other end of those phone calls. While thanking her profusely, she scans our tickets which are now only minutes old, and we disappear down the jet bridge. A sense of finality is settling in, and there is no turning back now. We are going to land at an Italian airport that we had not planned on seeing, with absolutely no advance guidance as to what might await at the other end.

Once on board, I scan the shockingly tranquil scene. I smirk and quietly realize that boarding last may actually be the best time to join an international flight. Everyone else is already seated and out of the way. I am further relieved to find copious amounts of room in the overhead bins. *This is no Canadair regional jet,* I consider. Designers of this Airbus A330 wide-body had wisely provided down-right cavernous spaces for everyone's cherished carry-on bags. The other passengers are already fussing with their pillows and blankets or their personalized entertainment screens. My seat (14B) is well ahead of the one Linda prefers near the window (35A), so I first go back with her to help acclimate, before returning to my aisle seat farther up.

Upon returning to row 14, however, it appears that something is amiss. I need to double check my ticket and location because the seat is not empty as promised, and I had not paid much attention while helping Linda. Rather, a woman is sitting here, still talking to a companion seated in front of her. At this point I am seriously second guessing whether our previous "angel" knew what she was doing. *She didn't overbook us by accident, I hope.* Upon screening my ticket, however, the woman occupying "our" seat quickly relents and claims some "confusion" with the seating. I suspect that she may be the one who is actually misplaced. Apologizing, she relinquishes the seat to me and stands a few rows up in the foyer to await assistance, all the while conferring anxiously with family members nearby. I am suspecting that she "jumped the gun" and found an empty seat more to her liking after the boarding process had supposedly finished. And then we showed up. *Oops.*

Before feeling too smug, however, I am still paying mild attention to the continuing confusion a few rows up, which (not just incidentally) still involves my presence at row 14. Perhaps not surprisingly, a flight attendant heads my way. She politely tells me that I am going to be reseated and apologizes for the confusion. Not wanting to become an unwitting social media star aboard an international flight, I happily relent and agree to go wherever she wishes. It turns out that we are headed back toward Linda's territory. If we head back much farther, I contemplate, I may be asked to help serve food from the rear galley. In fact, we pass through that very space as we move to the other side of the plane. Soon, my new home for eight hours is finalized. I am in the aisle seat in the last row on the right as one faces forward, immediately in front of the restroom towering behind me. At this point, however, none of this matters. I am grateful to have a seat dedicated to only me, and one that is presumably going to take off with everyone else. Moreover, I now enjoy a line of sight to Linda on the opposite side, a few rows ahead. All is well, and I shift attention to storing my gear.

Telling this story might normally border on the mundane were it not for my new seatmate. I typically refrain from conversations on planes, family members included. I may be one of those few strange people who enjoys the diminutive personal space on the plane to simply relax and let go. In this case, however, I quickly discern that this occasion might be different. While settling in, the young man next to me acknowledges my presence by removing his headphones and pulling his eyes from his laptop. Dressed simply in a comfortable T-shirt and shorts, I suspect that he is a college student beginning his journey for a study-abroad program. I continue to ignore him until he astonishes me with a question.

"Are you headed to Venice on vacation?" He opens. Just as I was sizing him up, he was doing likewise with an arguably logical presumption.

Still silently giddy about being on this flight, I shift quickly into politeness mode. "Actually, no. My wife and I are trying to get to Siena, Italy, so I can do some research." I really don't quite know what to explain first about this mission of mine. *Does he really want to know about the Palio?* I doubt it. I end with the appropriate tag, "So, why are you headed to Venice?"

He nearly shocks me with, "I'm being stationed at a military base," he states calmly, though with little confidence or enthusiasm.

I respond with my first thought: "Oh, so I guess you're going for longer than a week," I grin.

"Yes," he laughs. "It will be much longer."

I then wonder why he would be stationed near Venice, so I ask, "Does our military have a base near there? Is that where you are going?"

"Well, it's an Air Force base near some town called... Vi-senza," he struggles to pronounce it.

This immediately triggers a mental light bulb and I respond enthusiastically with, "Oh, *Vicenza!*" also helping him pronounce its Italian name. "Yes, I remember that there is an Air Force base near the town. We were there for two weeks a few years ago, and people were talking about the Americans stationed nearby." I continue with, "That's great, congratulations. Is this your first time?"

"Yeah, actually I've never been out of the United States," he says, nearly ashamed. He's probably trying to remain confident, but his anxiety is showing through—and for good reason. I still recall that heading off to college on my own was bad enough, but my parents had at least dropped me off before disappearing. This poor guy is on a plane to a foreign country with who knows what ahead of him.

"So, is someone picking you up at the airport?" I ask hopefully.

"No, and I really don't know how I'm supposed to get there. I guess I'll just figure it out," he chuckles. *Oh my,* I quickly think to myself. *This doesn't sound promising. Somebody just put this kid on a one-way flight to Italy and hoped for the best? And I worry about our own students?!* While conversing with my travel companion, I can't help but also realize the irony of sitting next to a rookie Air Force service member on his first tour of duty. Although admittedly looking forward to an off-cycle Palio, one of my primary interests is to genuinely learn more about Italy's role in World War I. This is a topic I confess to having spent little time investigating, let alone contemplating. Without Siena's sudden and deliberate decision to quickly stage this event, there is little chance I would have paid more than cursory attention to the war's history. It is a new and unexpected arena of knowledge that I look forward to exploring.

At about this time, the crew asks everyone not to be alarmed while the plane's power is shut down for about five minutes, apparently to reboot the computers. *OK, whatever.* This does mean that while the crew is "dinking around up there," as my former colleague, Helen, might say, we have more time to access cell service and the internet. A single thought comes to mind.

"Really? Are you going to take the train? Vicenza is probably an hour away from Venice," I say with some concern in my voice, "and I don't know where the base is."

"I guess, maybe. Is the train the best way?" He asks sheepishly.

I then move into mentoring mode. "Probably, yes. Look, we have more time here before taking off, so let me see if I can pull up the Italian train schedule. I've used this many times before." I quickly get out my phone and pull up the home page for *Trenitalia*, the Italian railroad operator. I am confident enough at this point to not even need the English language option. Almost to my own delight, I quickly see options appear for trains to Vicenza following our planned arrival in Venice.

I explain, "OK, you can easily take a train to Vicenza," I say, following up with some instruction about the Italian train system and ticketing. "The catch is that you can't take the train from the airport, from what I know. You will need to get the train from the nearby town of Mestre, which is the gateway to Venice on the mainland. I suggest that you find a taxi to Mestre, though there might be a shuttle bus. You'll need to ask at the information desk there. I need to find out the same thing, as we also need to get to the train station," I add.

I am inwardly pleased that my own experience can now assist this young man. He looks as surprised as he is appreciative. I doubt he expected some stranger to sit down and offer detailed instructions about Italian travel. After providing some additional information about currency exchange (he has no euros, of course), I give him a sense of what to expect at customs. Although his travel will certainly not be challenge-free, hopefully this crash course will provide a fair chance of success with minimal embarrassment.

My instruction ends with an overview of the helpful website, TripAdvisor. "The forums on this travel site can provide almost any information about how to travel from one place to another in Italy. We use it all the time," I offer, also warning him that his phone may not work there. He will probably need to purchase a SIM card, but perhaps all of that can be handled when he finally arrives at the base.

Absorbing it all, he says, "OK, thanks a lot. I had no idea about any of that. I'll see how it goes."

"Actually," I respond, "I need to find out the same thing—how to get to Mestre and take the train to Siena. We had not planned to be on this flight!" I chuckle. With that, I decide to sneak more internet time to find possible train options for ourselves. After a few minutes, I focus on a series of trains that could get us to Siena by around 4:00 p.m. if all goes well. The first train departs Mestre at 11:47 a.m. After that, our chances of arriving before the evening presentation are substantially reduced. *Oh well*, I sigh to myself, *I have enough information about the train schedule now and there is nothing else we can do until setting foot in the Mestre train station to purchase tickets. We will get there when we get there.* Until then, it's time to enjoy the flight. At least I now feel moderately prepared for what to expect on the flipside. Linda should be happy to know later, I suspect, that we will not be flying entirely blind upon arrival.

❈ CHAPTER 4 ❈

Presentation of the Drappellone

K NOWN AS THE PRESENTATION OF THE DRAPPELLONE, THIS ROUGHLY HOUR-long event occurs within the otherwise hidden Cortile del Podestà (the inner courtyard, or *cortile*, of the Palazzo Pubblico). This is the same courtyard where the horses and jockeys are staged in advance of all Palio events, including the six trials and the final race. Local news stories always promote the upcoming presentation, complete with flattering biographies and occasional interviews of the artist chosen to design the drappellone. It is also televised, of course, including by the ever-trusty Canale 3 Toscana (Tuscany Channel 3), which I lovingly refer to as the "Palio channel" around the time of these events.

This may be an appropriate time to further unpack the term "palio" and its dual meanings. In modern times, the formal "Palio" refers generally to the race event and its surrounding rituals; however the less formal "palio" is derived from the Latin *pallium*, meaning a rectangular piece of cloth. As Dundes and Falassi explain, a palio was typically used in the Middle Ages to honor a patron saint or perhaps as a prize for winning a tournament or other contest.[13] The victor would receive the palio to recognize the triumph, not unlike receiving a game trophy. Today as in centuries past, the palio banner constitutes the sole prize for winning the race in Siena, and it is always carefully preserved within the museum of the victorious contrada. As mentioned earlier, the banner can also be affectionately referred to as the *cencio* (rag), though *drappellone* (drapery) is more formal and is apparently favored by local media. I will continue to use this latter term to avoid confusion with the actual event known as the Palio.

PRESENTATION OF THE DRAPPELLONE

Evolution of Drappellone Design

The artistry of these colorful banners has shifted through the centuries. Today's banners are made of silk, a fact that provides no end of angst to artists struggling to paint or otherwise decorate this challenging medium. As for creative limitations, however, there are virtually none. The chosen artist must abide by only a few rules, as outlined in the general regulations of the Palio. First and foremost, the banner must include an image of the Virgin Mary. This is critical for the Senesi, who in centuries past had petitioned her to protect their independent republic (as noted earlier). Beyond this, keen observers will notice a subtle difference between the July and August banners. Namely, those representing the July races portray a "half Virgin," consisting appropriately of her head and neck. Those of August, in contrast, must depict Mary in full, from head to toe. However, Mary's appearance and characteristics are left to the imagination of the artist. Another important rule is that the ten contrade to compete in the Palio must be represented somewhere on the banner. Otherwise, selected artists are virtually free to express themselves as desired, typically featuring their distinctive skills and styles. This general freedom with the artistry of the Palio banners was instituted by the city in 1949, which is relatively recent in the history of the Palio.

The oldest surviving drappellone of the modern era dates back to 1719 and is preserved within the museum of the Eagle. This banner marked a cultural turning point for the design of Palio banners because they would henceforth take the form of rectangular cloths made of silk.[14] The earlier drappellone designs of that period are less dramatic by modern-day standards, though they are still greatly appreciated for reflecting their own historical period. While portraying either a half or whole Virgin Mary, these earlier banners exhibited a more rigid, standardized design with almost no creative artistic license. Amusingly, the Senesi affectionately refer to this earlier design mode as *Panfortesco* Style, which is deemed "more suitable for wrapping *panforti* [a local Senese dessert specialty] than for hanging on the wall."[15]

Beyond the city's new regulations of 1949, two additional shifts in approach are noteworthy. Specifically, the drappellone designed for the Straordinario of September 21, 1969 was dedicated to the conquest of space, represented by the first lunar landing. This banner, which is prominently displayed in the museum of the Goose, apparently marked the first blending of traditional Senese design with more contemporary graphics and photography. Having called our students' attention to this work multiple times, I can attest to its stunning layout and creative choice of hues. Giulia Maestrini went so far as to describe this drappellone as "an epoch-making turning point, breaking tradition and leaving space for a new, very personal interpretation of the artist."[16]

The mid-1980s ushered in the next noticeable artistic shift. At this time, the city began to solicit designs from internationally renowned artists, but only for the August Palio, which is dedicated to the Madonna of the Assumption. In contrast, the banners for the July Palio are designed by a local or regional artist, a distinction that remains as of this writing. More curiously, not all artists are always itching to be selected. Some have even declined the invitation, either because of the challenges endemic to working on silk or the very real concern of being met with some measure of disapproval when their hard-earned product is officially revealed. Siena is notorious for not providing the most gracious of audiences, regardless of one's level of international artistic fame. Reactions from the Senesi at the presentation ceremony and well afterwards can range from unconstrained approval to tepid applause or worse, with collective boos and jeers directed at the artist. They can be a tough crowd.

Consequently, one would be wise these days to expect the unexpected. Banner designs of late have probably never been more distinctive or unpredictable. The recent drappellone of August 2018 provides a case in point. Causing not just a little local controversy, even the archbishop of Siena refused to officially bless the banner, primarily because Mary was holding a horse rather than Baby Jesus. Nor was he pleased, I further suspect, with the zombie-like, horror-movie character that was supposed to represent Mary. Before this example, other less-frightening banners have emerged with three-dimensional elements attached, such as the gigantic, eye-catching *bàrberi* (wooden balls colored to represent each contrada) projecting out from the drappellone of August 2003. This one ultimately came to represent the Caterpillar's first Palio victory of the new millennium.

Of course, such mysterious unpredictability is arguably what drives the high level of drama surrounding the presentation ceremony. Each event

PRESENTATION OF THE DRAPPELLONE

promises packed-in throngs who can instantly express their collective approval or consternation as the featured banner comes into view. During the public "reveal," those in attendance essentially play the role of an instant, crowd-sourced art critic.

Beyond the artistic realm, the presentation is analogous in one respect to the opening ceremonies of the Olympics, albeit on a much-reduced scale. Both officially kick off the sequence of festivities or events that follow. A telling and poetic account by Giulia Maestrini published by *La Nazione* (*The Nation*, Tuscany's premier daily newspaper) in 2004 reveals as much:

> When the sun goes down and the heat is boiling from the bricks of Piazza del Campo, hundreds of people, sweating and anxious, push themselves and huddle together, waiting to see a piece of colored cloth that from that moment on, for six very long days, will embody the supreme object of desire for the ten [competing contrade] ... The moment in which the cencio is presented in Siena is, for the artist who painted it and for the whole city, perhaps the most intense and most awaited: thus begin the dances, finally opening the curtain on the feast.[17]

It follows that, to experience the entire Palio as an interwoven sequence of cultural events, one should not ignore the presentation of the drappellone.

The Bersaglieri

After a flurry of unpacking and grocery shopping with Linda, I set out from our bed-and-breakfast lodging on the western side of town, aiming for the Campo. Now at around 3:30 p.m., the October sun remains strong, if not intense as in summer, and I immediately notice that the natural lighting along Via di Città is remarkably striking. The shadows are deep, and the low sun angle seems to highlight everything it hits even more so than in July. Combined with the almost eerie silence of nearly empty streets, my walk down to the Campo is one of surprising starkness and solitude.

Typically, the two Palio events of the summer often take place around the 7:00 p.m. hour and include the presentation of the drappellone the first day, the evening trials next, and the final race on the last day. The rationale for this timing is clear; this hour is the "sweet spot" that balances the remaining daylight with the onset of cooler evening conditions. One of the fundamental changes for this week's events is a consolidated time schedule to accommodate a sun that sets nearly two hours earlier in October. Tonight's presentation, therefore, will begin at 5:15 p.m. rather than the standard 7:00. The ensuing evening trials and final race will begin similarly.

My own personal goal is to arrive by 4:30, and I am grateful as I realize that I've made it on time. Last week, I had learned that an additional musical event would be held on the Campo before the presentation. A group unfamiliar to me, the Bersaglieri, would perform some sort of fanfare with their own unique variation of a marching band. Given that the city was already deviating from its standard Palio traditions by inviting the Bersaglieri, I felt compelled to add this performance to my planned itinerary. It was not a stretch to presume that the group is connected somehow to the history of World War I.

It turns out that the Bersaglieri are an infantry division of the Italian Army. The term "bersaglieri" translates as marksmen or sharpshooters. They have been around since before the unification of Italy, which occurred in the early 1860s.

This storied infantry division enjoys a unique place in Italian history and combat, the intrigue of which matches that of their distinctive uniforms. Formed as early as 1836 to serve the Kingdom of Sardinia, the Bersaglieri were absorbed into the Royal Italian Army after the peninsula was unified in the 1860s. As specially trained marksmen and skirmishers, this highly mobile unit of soldiers could move quickly and independently on their feet, without the standard military orders and centralized control that was required of other military units. Rather than central commands, the Bersaglieri relied more on an intricate system of bugle calls to communicate across the battlefield. Perhaps not surprisingly, given their presence at this evening's important kick-off event, they were deeply involved in the Italian theater of World War I. In fact, some twenty-one regiments of the Bersaglieri were assigned to the Italian front in northeastern Italy in their ongoing battles with the Austro-Hungarians, and—like the Italians overall—they sustained heavy casualties. By one count, more than 30,000 Bersaglieri were ultimately killed, and almost twice as many were injured.

PRESENTATION OF THE DRAPPELLONE

A portion of its members also served during the war in the bicycle infantry, following the advent of safety bicycles in the late nineteenth century. Despite the temptation to envision hapless soldiers trying to stabilize their bikes over rocky trails as children might do, bicycle troops became a serious tactical arm of the military. The bicycles themselves could replace horses without needing to feed or rest. They further proved to be faster than foot soldiers, did not require extensive roads, and could carry more equipment. The Bersaglieri used them through the conclusion of World War I.

Sometimes the Bersaglieri are compared to the specialized Army Rangers, Green Berets, or Navy Seals of the United States military with respect to their unique role and high standards of training. Most visible in modern days are the Bersaglieri uniforms, the most iconic item of which consists of a wide-brimmed hat with an attached plume of some 400 *capercaillie* (grouse) feathers flowing down one side. Mostly decorative today, they served a military purpose in the past, to shade the eyes of the marksmen when shooting and to provide camouflage.[18] In contemporary times, the unique helmet plumes provide a distinct identity for the crack military unit as they perform in parades and elsewhere for the public, not unlike the nationally popular military bands of America's armed forces.

There is no doubt that their most intriguing claim to fame involves a distinctively fast-paced jog while simultaneously playing their instruments in various parade events. It is no wonder, then, that Siena invited them to perform on the dirt track in advance of the Palio. As for this evening, local media outlets have announced plans for the Bersaglieri to provide a brief introductory concert in the Campo just before the presentation.

Making my way down into the Campo, I arrive to spy two clusters of people already gathered near the front of the Palazzo. At the center of one cluster is a cohort of uniformed soldiers wearing their distinctively plumed helmets. Curious to view this group more closely, I linger around the circle of humanity that has enclosed the sixty or so performers. Perhaps less than a minute after my arrival, they raise their instruments and play a song quite recognizable to both the Senesi and me. I chuckle at their rather unique musical arrangement, a variation on Siena's timeless "Il Canto della Verbena," which all contrada members sing relentlessly during the Palio and other appropriate times of the year. The song serves as a veritable anthem for the Senesi. Its lyrics focus on the beauty of the city and their collective emotional attachment to Piazza del Campo, where the herb of verbena once grew between its brick pavers.

Strangely, however, the Bersaglieri are essentially playing the song at themselves, having formed their own closed circle to face inward. Around the periphery of their backside is a modest circle of onlookers, but it is two or three people deep. For these reasons, the visibility of anyone outside the circle is greatly hampered. While reminding myself to remain nonjudgmental while experiencing a foreign culture, I can't help but wonder why they are not set up in a more traditional concert formation that projects better into the Campo. Perhaps they are just having fun in a more informal setting for this evening. Whatever their rationale, I enjoy studying their helmet plumes of grouse feathers as they play their next number, the familiar "March of the Palio." This is the primary song played during the corteo storico (historical procession), which winds its way from the Duomo to the Campo on the day of the Palio. The crack outfit has certainly learned how to pull at the emotional strings of the Senesi!

A Palazzo Entrance Strategy

Enthralled as I am with the Bersaglieri, I am also aware of the increasing density of people gathering around the Palazzo's main entrance. For all the effort required to be here right now, it would be unfortunate indeed if I missed the opportunity to gain a prime viewing spot for the presentation. Hastily abandoning the performers, I thus make my way to the entrance to join others who are acting similarly in preparation. Before entering, however, I purposely walk up to a woman distributing something free of charge for anybody smart enough to stick out a hand. Smiling as I receive mine, the handout is no longer a mystery, thanks to my past experiences here. Before the presentation, the city provides creative, multicolored cards that provide useful information about the ten contrade that will race in the upcoming Palio. More than just a simple piece of cardstock, however, these come complete with an insert that can be pulled or pushed from the bottom. Doing so provides information about each contrada in small viewing windows, such as the contrada captain and its most recent victory. On the back side of the

PRESENTATION OF THE DRAPPELLONE

card are empty lines that allow enthusiasts to list the names of the horses that will participate in the *tratta* (test runs) a few days from now.

After receiving my card, I turn back to the entrance and find it is a bit disheartening to see so many people crowded around the double-door entry into the Palazzo's cortile. *Is the interior space already filled up?* I wonder as the crowd squeezes through. I finally breathe a sigh of relief after pushing through this bottleneck of humanity to find a half-empty courtyard area. I suppose people just naturally enjoy hanging around entryways to converse with acquaintances, whether in Italy, America, or elsewhere. Upon entry, I instinctively know to turn left in search of my favored viewing area.

This latter decision should not be taken lightly. A few years ago, one of my friends from the Panther contrada, Carmina, alerted me to the existence of this event. To say the least, her suggestion did not disappoint. Of course, my first-time attendance came attached with a requisite learning curve. The main lesson involved my spontaneous choice to turn right upon entering the courtyard. Though seemingly innocuous, this decision can mean the difference between seeing the drappellone with one's own eyes versus having it blocked from view. Veterans of this event understand that the new drappellone will emerge from a door in the back-right corner of the courtyard as one faces it from the entrance. Its caretaker then displays it permanently in that same corner for the remainder of the ceremony. This placement renders the banner virtually invisible, however, to those on the right side whose view is unwittingly blocked by the unforgiving line of the courtyard's brick support columns.

Therefore, although counterintuitive, one can stand on the opposite (left) side to enjoy a direct line of sight to the banner. Of course, all of this matters only if one desires an immediate view of the drappellone upon its first arrival into the courtyard. Otherwise, people tend to come and go during the litany of successive speeches, at which time one can shuffle into a more successful viewing location. Not all is ultimately lost.

About halfway around the left side, I find a suitable place to park for the duration of the event. Others are doing the same around me. A few shorter people cluster in front of me, but they provide no bother. Had someone wanted to provide a fairer viewing approach for everyone, they might have considered temporary benches or stands to allow shorter people to enjoy a better view. Here as in the Campo for the Palio, however, people must deal with existing conditions to the best of their abilities, whether vertically challenged (like Linda) or not. As our crowd packs into the courtyard in the lead up to the ceremony, we all become fused in place with any additional wiggle room now completely gone. Still, everyone seems to be rather patient while making the best of their position. Soon the periphery of the courtyard becomes packed so tightly that it would be next to impossible to shift elsewhere through the crowd.

Within the open center of the courtyard, the human condition is much different. A table is reserved for city officials and dignitaries, including the mayor and the drappellone artist. This lengthy table, from which various speeches will emanate, serves as the focus of the ceremony. A sea of temporary plastic chairs occupies the remainder of the open space, reserved for specially invited guests and, I presume, family members of the artist and others speaking this afternoon. While those of us on the periphery are now summarily locked in place, those in the center are still lingering and socializing with their neighbors, some of whom remain standing before the ceremony. Now with some time to think and observe, I mentally take stock of the intelligent strategy of timing for this event. The interior courtyard is open to the elements, which this evening includes a soft orange glow of diffuse sunlight that provides for almost an ethereal setting.

Eventually, the bulk of dignitaries and guests in the center take their seats, reacting to some cue unknown to me. Then a few of Siena's famed trombettiere emerge to stand behind the table. At this point, I am doing my best to juggle two things in my cramped hands: my smartphone camera and that large information card provided earlier. It doesn't fit well in my pocket, so I finally stuff it partially in the back of my pants. Others around me are doing similarly while trying to determine their own individual strategies to digitally capture the event. A still wiser set of onlookers is not bothering with cameras at all; rather, they are content to simply watch and enjoy the "reveal." They know that close-ups of the banner will be available online in a matter of minutes after it is brought into public view. Or, they can linger patiently until the anxious crowd disperses to acquire some quality photos of their own.

Soon, the bar-like din of conversation begins to give way to a revered silence as those at the head table take their seats. Aside from witnessing the event directly, I am eager to see how the chosen artist will represent the intersection between the World War I, Siena, and the Palio. The artist has

PRESENTATION OF THE DRAPPELLONE

enjoyed even more freedom than usual for this particular drappellone because the typical rule requiring a portrayal of the Virgin Mary does not apply to a Straordinario. Tonight's artist is the renowned Gian Marco Montesano, originally from Torino (Turin). Among his numerous artistic accomplishments, he is particularly known for transforming images from historical photographs into meaningfully painted works of art.[19] Beyond his accomplishments as a well-known painter since the 1970s, Montesano has further succeeded as a theater director, producing shows throughout Italy, Paris, and Hungary.

It is reasonable to presume that Montesano has not enjoyed much sleep of late. Interestingly, Siena's recently elected mayor, Luigi De Mossi, personally chose Montesano to design the banner, and the famed artist officially accepted the mayor's invitation less than one month ago, on September 18.[20] Montesano's first deadline was to submit potential sketches only two days following the mayor's decision to select him for the honor. If that was not enough pressure, the artist's scanner was broken, forcing him to be resourceful in finding another machine on short notice. Once submitted, the mayor chose his preferred sketch.

When asked during an interview what he knew about Siena, Montesano admitted being completely unfamiliar with the city aside from its reputation as a beautiful place. In response, the polite interviewer allowed that it would be "better this way; the impact will be more surprising." Little did anyone know to what extent this would be true. Regardless, the interviewer further uncovered Montesano's self-proclaimed claustrophobia, which explained why the famed artist could never imagine himself standing in the center of the congested Campo to watch the Palio. He did, however, agree to provide some personal thoughts about World War I and its implications for Italy:

> [The war was] a fundamental watershed in the history of Europe. Four empires fall, the ancient world is shattered, a different world is born. For Italy it is the accomplishment of the Risorgimento [unification movement]. The Italians, strangers among themselves so far, fight together, die together, suffer together. Rich, poor, illiterate, southern, Piedmontese, they find themselves on the same side.[21]

I would learn later that this brand of response represents a relatively positive one compared to more somber and cynical answers to the same question. Though technically ending with an Italian victory, there was in reality very little for the Kingdom of Italy to celebrate.

Montesano's Drappellone

There is no introductory speech. Instead, the musicians take their places behind the head table, the long-belled trumpets simply rise, and a fanfare is played. It is instructive to note how Siena uses the universal language of music to announce the beginning of such events rather than more typical human words. Immediately afterward, the city's elegant red banner is brought forward. The banner features the city's striking black-and-white balzana with smaller images of the 17 contrada logos displayed below it. This banner admittedly once had me quite confused and can be one of Siena's subtle jokes for outsiders like me. Upon seeing it for the first time a few years earlier, I presumed it to be the actual drappellone. My first thought was, *Wow, this one is very plain and elegant—and short.* With no reaction from the crowd, the joke was on me. The real star of the evening was still yet to appear.

Amidst the crowd's anticipatory silence, the fanfare is played a second time. Soon thereafter, a tall pole and attached banner emerge gingerly through the rear doorway. The drappellone for the 2018 Palio Straordinario is arriving. Its sheer bulkiness means that it cannot be hidden from view any longer. It is placed to the right side of the head table, and everyone's eyes are now focused like lasers on the colored piece of silk.

Only a split-second glance is required to discern the banner's main feature, that of two human subjects filling the bottom half, surrounded by a sky-blue background. The banner's top half features the city's balzana, appropriately surrounded by icons of the ten contrade that will compete one week from today. As expected, there is no Virgin Mary. Fortunately—given my own limited artistic training—there is nothing abstract about it. An Italian soldier sporting his army-green uniform is bending over to kiss the hand of a young woman, who is wearing a white dress similar in style to a ball gown. The intended symbolic storyline is probably no more complicated than that of a despondent young man saying goodbye to his girlfriend or fiancé as he heads off to war. There is no wedding ring on her left hand, which dangles by her side in plain sight. In the soldier's right hand is an object that I am failing to identify.

The overall composition is what I would initially describe as elegantly simple, perhaps demonstrating the human side (and toll) of both soldier and family left behind. Within a few short seconds, our audience provides its first collective reaction with rather mild if still enthusiastic applause. While joining in, I cannot help but notice one thing. The young woman is curiously emotionless, and she is apparently not even looking at the love of her life. Rather, she glances straight ahead, or perhaps dismissively off to her left. There are no tears or outward signs of angst. One might almost suggest that she is bored, if not completely indifferent. Is this how a young woman typically reacts when saying goodbye to a beloved companion she may never see again? Additionally, for what reason is he merely kissing her hand, and why is she dressed like that? As Paul McCartney sings in his own timeless song, "Penny Lane," the scene is "very strange" indeed.

Within about a minute after the unveiling, the crowd settles down. The mayor then rises to provide an impressively emotional speech that includes comments related to the significance of World War I (Figure 2). Although I can generally catch the meaning of his well-spoken Italian, I am further impressed that he is not relying on any script or notes. His speech is nonetheless very well polished and smoothly delivered. A second thing grabs my attention. The clear and powerful speaker system is having quite the difficulty competing with the incessant chatter emerging from our peripheral crowd. It seems that nobody in my vicinity is actually listening, and it is only the rare person like me who continues to stand still. Rather, people are shuffling around intently to either earn a better view of the drappellone, gain the attention of friends or family nearby, or weasel their way back out into the Campo. The invitees in the center, however, along with the various television cameras, continue to pay close attention to the ceremony.

Figure 2. The presentation of the drappellone. (Photo: Author)

The Masgalano

The mayor does end up talking for quite some time, after which a representative of the artist provides a speech of her own. While the audience continues to buzz about the drappellone, a second, lesser known unveiling is now taking place. Many visitors don't realize that another contest occurs on the day of the Palio, in this case between all seventeen contrade. First held centuries ago, the *masgalano* (derived from Spanish, meaning "most elegant") award was originally awarded to the contrada that demonstrated the highest level of elegance, skill, and overall appearance during the corteo storico. The tradition was discontinued for some time until 1950, when the masgalano was reinstated with the goal of elevating the level of prestige and skill of each contrada's *comparsa* (contingent), which marches and performs in the historical procession before the race.[22]

Unlike the drappellone, which reflects the victory of one specific Palio race, the masgalano prize is awarded to the contrada that achieves the highest total combined score from both the July and August events. The entire comparsa of each contrada may be responsible for its collective score, but it is

PRESENTATION OF THE DRAPPELLONE

the performance of the two *alfieri* (flag bearers) that primarily determines the outcome of the contest.[23] There is, consequently, only one masgalano prize awarded each year, taking both Palio performances into account. The prize typically consists of a large plate-sized object with some or all material consisting of silver. Like the drappellone, its design and production are commissioned to a specific artist by the city administration.

Because there is but one extraordinary Palio this year, the masgalano unveiled this evening will reflect only the top performance for this particular event. As is custom, a separate masgalano was created for the combined Palii of July and August of 2018, and it has already been presented to the Shell. Although certainly not as desirable as winning the Palio itself, the masgalano awards are likewise displayed proudly within the contrada museums. Since 1950, all seventeen contrade have earned a masgalano at least once. It so happens that the Giraffe contrada has won the most often, with ten awards. Also notable are the Snail and Shell, which have each won nine times. In contrast, the unfortunate Ram has only won once, as far back as 1959. The newest masgalano award is now being presented in front of our eyes, having been commissioned to artist Sara Cafarelli, a resident of the Giraffe contrada. Among other accomplishments, Cafarelli's work has been featured as far away as Miami and at New York's Museum of Modern Art. As it finally becomes visible in front of our remaining crowd, it is—in no fewer words—absolutely stunning, consisting of concentric, sleek rings of metal. Whatever museum is fortunate enough to display this award will no doubt be measurably improved.

Beware the Internet

To speedily exit the courtyard with untold hundreds of cramped attendees is easier said than done. As the ceremony winds down, the bulk of us begin to shuffle toward the one entrance and exit available, leading directly out to the Campo. The otherwise expansive double door creates a strangling bottleneck, and this is not the time for anyone caught here to fret about personal space. Making matters worse is an unconstrained rush of people from outside who wish to view the drappellone for themselves. All one can do is be patient and go with the flow which, as might be expected, is moving at a snail's pace. I can't help but wonder if some simple traffic control outside the doorway might expedite things a bit. Regardless, the people around me are generally patient, so nobody really raises a stink about the crowd. The Senesi most certainly know the drill here.

Having finally escaped the bottleneck in one piece, I emerge onto a more darkened Campo and begin my walk back to reconnect with Linda. As I barrel up through the Panther contrada on Via Stalloreggi, I decide to stop in to see our friend, Silvia, say hello, and ask if she has yet seen the recently revealed Palio banner online.

After catching up a bit, I mention that I had just attended the presentation ceremony. She speaks excellent English, largely self-taught. I ask, "Has the banner been posted yet?"

Looking back to her computer, she states unemotionally, "Yes. Hmm, compared to the one in August, this one is much better—both symbolically and artistically. I give this one a B."

I chuckle at the thought of grading the design, so I follow up with, "Do you like the simplicity?"

"No, I guess it seems too simplistic." Then she notices something else, adding, "What is the soldier holding in his right hand?" She moves in closer to scrutinize the image. Silvia doesn't miss much.

I laugh, "I don't know either." I had been wondering the same thing since the ceremony.

She responds, "I think they are flowers."

"Oh, that would make sense," I offer, adding with a chuckle, "I was thinking they might be bàrberi or even a cat." Although the cat would not make much logical sense, the thought had certainly come to mind when viewing it from afar.

Silvia laughs, continuing her analysis: "I know the artist did not have a lot of time to create the banner, but it still seems too simplistic. But he had, what, fifteen days?" She sympathizes while gesturing toward the screen.

I am curious about any chatter that might already be on social media. I ask, "Have you seen other people's reactions yet? Are people talking about it?"

"Yes, some are writing. The reaction seems to be mixed." This is probably not the resounding endorsement that Montesano would have preferred. My empathetic side can certainly appreciate the emotional stress involved with this challenging assignment, that of rendering a meaningful and appropriate image of a complicated war, all on very short notice. Talk about a losing

PRESENTATION OF THE DRAPPELLONE

proposition! That said, Montesano did make the decision to take on the challenge. After bidding Silvia farewell for now, I am feeling even more satisfied at having witnessed the ceremony in person.

Within an hour of visiting Silvia, local media outlets are providing their own perspectives on the drappellone. To their credit, the articles I see are giving the artist and his work the benefit of the doubt, sometimes with almost lavish praise. One writer provided the complimentary example included below, complete with gushing romanticism, as translated from its original Italian:

> [There is] no obvious reference to the battlefields. Montesano did not need it. The simulacrum of war is all there. The soldier who gives flowers to a beautiful girl while he greets and kisses her hand. He is the infantryman of the [Battle of the] Piave, a veteran of duty. A duty that is expressed here in the kindness of the homage given to beauty, to the rediscovered peace and to love. A form of prayer addressed to the figure of an absolute femininity in the universal heavens above.[24]

The writer further suggests that the artwork provides a "dialogue without words" that is "loaded with symbols." One case involves the artist's supposedly intentional effort to point the index finger of the woman to the blue shield embedded with the word, "Libertas"—a not-so-subtle nod to the emblem of the former Republic of Siena. Perhaps so. Or, is that simply how the hand is typically shaped in its dangling position? One might further be tempted to note that her finger could have just as easily been pointing to any of the three shields, simply dependent upon how they were arranged. Despite these initial thoughts, I responsibly admit that we all serve as armchair art critics, regardless of what the artist actually had in mind.

For all attempts at positivity, it turns out that Silvia's initial screening of mixed reviews would only represent the tip of a very large—and growing—iceberg. To set up this budding story, the next morning Linda and I head to the TIM (Telecom Italia) cell phone store to purchase the obligatory SIM cards, which will convert our phones to make use of the Italian cell service. Having grown weary of hearing me rave about this all-but-magical chip, Linda has become convinced to try one of her own. A few people are ahead of us in line, and soon a younger couple arrives behind us. The woman is clearly expecting, and soon. This is all Linda needs to make her acquaintance, asking when the baby is due. Within minutes she is probably no more than two steps away from being invited to the baby shower.

In fact, the couple is not only from Siena, but they are of the Turtle contrada. Upon discovering this, I wish them "good luck" in the upcoming Palio, for what it's worth. The Turtle has not yet won a race on our watch here in Siena. In return, both light up and reveal their ability to speak decent (if broken) English. They also quickly peg both of us as either British or American. The Senesi can easily discern this much, though they are typically stymied as to which side of the Atlantic we belong. It does not take long for my own embarrassment to kick in. Linda not only announces our intent to see the Palio, but that I am planning to write a book about it. This is not something I would tell people on the street, as it is usually helpful to earn some credibility first. However, they fortunately seem intrigued, so we consequently enjoy an impromptu conversation while waiting in line.

Then I mention my attendance at the presentation of the drappellone last night. This innocent comment triggers an instant, dramatic reaction from the soon-to-be father, catching me off guard. He is irreversibly agitated and pulls out his smartphone. He asks, "Did you see what the artist did?!" Now confused, I confess that I most likely had not. "Take a look at this!" He quickly shows us a social media post on his phone while his companion chuckles beside him. "The image he painted is copied from a photo!" *No way! Way.* He continues, "And the soldier isn't even Italian—he's German!" Startled, I glance at the post to witness the source of his distress. The scene is admittedly stunning. I gasp in shock and we stare at each other like two gossiping teenagers. He continues, now on a roll, "They said the artist intended to have her finger pointing toward the shield to represent the city, but nobody believes that now. Even the [woman's] dress isn't from that era. He just copied it from the photo!" Our SIM cards now long forgotten, we are all laughing at the discovery like old friends—not the actual strangers who had met only five minutes earlier. I am already contemplating, *This is how information can go viral quickly, both online and by word-of-mouth!*

The post, or meme, in question reveals two images side by side. One is the artistic depiction of a presumably romantic couple on the drappellone, placed adjacent to a nearly identical, photographed image. Although the artist

PRESENTATION OF THE DRAPPELLONE

has wisely replaced the German helmet with an Italian one, there is no question about what I am seeing. The comparison is uncanny and is certainly not a coincidence. Perhaps less surprising is that online sleuths have already discovered the alleged source of the author's original inspiration. This is 2018, after all; very little in the world remains private, much less hard to find. Within only a few daylight hours since the presentation, the entire city is already plunging headlong into its next Palio controversy. I can't escape one particular piece of irony: *The original soldier was German? Oh, my.*

At about the time of our impromptu discussion with the couple from the Turtle, the local media was already revising its originally positive assessment. The drappellone of the artist Montesano had become embroiled in a "social storm," according to one online news article, referring to the artwork as a "copy and paste."[25] Its writer further acknowledged the ease with which the alleged source photo was found online. Even the woman's hand is nearly identical in both depictions, the article noted, and "the controversy has gone crazy on social media, especially on Facebook." As one might expect, a variety of creative and sarcastic posts were circulating online, including "Find the differences," and "Poor palio," to "It seems the painter of this palio was very original." In a valiant effort to remain balanced, however, this article also noted some comments that defended the artist. Samples included, "[The artist] needed to be inspired by something," and "There was little time [to complete the banner]."

Perhaps the most lucid observation consisted of a comment repeated many times over: "The palio? I will also take it white."[26] This latter phrase is well known in Siena, and it serves in part to unite the seventeen contrade. To win the Palio remains the paramount quest, regardless of the artwork portrayed on the victory banner.[27] The subjective quality of artwork will do little to dampen the unbridled spirit of the contradaioli, who will still be overjoyed to preserve their prize for eternity. Thus, within a few days the controversy will likely take a back seat to the more important business of winning a rather rare Palio and, if necessary, the victor will be perfectly happy to receive the drappellone "in white" (literally, a blank piece of white silk)—whether emblazoned with a disguised German soldier or not.

PART II:
PERSPECTIVES

❈ CHAPTER 5 ❈

Dario's World

WITH THE PRESENTATION AND ITS ENSUING DRAMA BEHIND US AND OUR smartphones happily "speaking Italian," there is barely enough time for me to regroup at our lodging before setting out again into Siena's medieval streets. My self-proclaimed "Listening Tour" kicks off today as I seek to better understand the historical context of the World War I, the Straordinario being held in its name, and Senese perspectives on any or all of it. Having admittedly paid little focused attention to a history of the war, I am looking forward to a conversation tonight with one of the city's foremost historical experts on the conflict.

However, before I piece together the war's historical context this evening, I have scheduled an early afternoon lunch with a familiar friend and author—none other than Dario Castagno. Aside from his role as a proud member of the Caterpillar contrada, Dario has impressively become known in the English-speaking world for his ever-expanding authorship of enjoyable books related to the Chianti region and the more expansive Tuscan realm. In fact, I had barely managed to acquire his latest book, *The Year of the Chicory*, before our departure for Siena, and it kept me suitably entertained until we landed in Venice. Alas, we arrived too soon, as I had only managed to read half of it.

While once again contemplating Dario's personalized stories from Chianti, I am reminded of something important prior to meeting with him. That is, I probably need to mentally slow down my hurried pace before our lunch today. It was only yesterday that Linda and I were landing at an unplanned airport and navigating the train system, determined as I was to view the first event of the week. In marked contrast to my typical habit of scurrying around, however, Dario seems to effortlessly transport his companions into a slower-paced lifestyle. As I bolt out on my latest mission to find Dario in the *rione* (territory) of the Caterpillar, I therefore coach myself to take a deep breath and prepare to transition into the stress-free, more relaxed ways of Dario's world.

Return to the Caterpillar

On my way to meet Dario, I make a first stop at the contrada's fountain hidden in a grotto beneath Via dei Rossi to more closely inspect the statue of Francesco d'Agnolo—known affectionately by the contrada as Barbicone—who rises out of the water pointing his sword. For his part, Barbicone is revered even today as a fourteenth-century hero of the Caterpillar. Not only did he lead the contrada's military contingent to defend the city against the militias of King Charles IV of Bohemia, but he further led a popular uprising against the Senese government in 1371 in a fight for better working and living conditions. It is therefore no surprise that the local hero is honored with an artistic statue adorning the baptismal fountain.[28]

Unfortunately, the fountain has endured multiple recent acts of vandalism lately, which is mirroring the citywide increase in such desecration and thefts of local property. After the third recent incident with this particular fountain, a foreign student finally admitted to the crime. He had apparently neglected to see the surveillance camera nearby. Now squinting into the fountain's sheltered cove, I try to determine whether all has been restored. The sword and all of Barbicone's body parts seem to be in their proper places, so it appears that the contrada has once again made him whole. It is also a shame that my first thought about the fountain was whether it was back in one piece.

Moving beyond Barbicone, I have been instructed by Dario to make my way to the Società L'alba (the Caterpillar's community center) on my own. Fortunately, the route is now old hat for me, as I have accomplished this numerous times either with a contingent of students in tow or in search of contrada dinner tickets. Each of the seventeen contrade manages its own società that serves as a welcoming hub and hangout for contradaioli. Dario should be finishing up with one of his characteristic contrada tours around 1:00 p.m., after which he is supposed to meet me there. Then we will head to lunch—or something. A little voice in my head reminds me to expect the unexpected as I make my way down Via del Comune to find the nondescript entrance to the società.

Despite my past experiences here, I am already second guessing the location of the entrance. Upon stumbling down about a third of the street, I counsel myself to not venture much farther. Bypassing the entrance would necessitate a return up the steep slope once again. With no immediate success, I eventually relent and dive further down the street to finally spy the telltale tiled symbol and entryway, which today is closed and locked up. I lean back onto a building façade across the street and retreat into my phone. Despite some personal pride in being a part of the last generation not entirely dependent upon the smartphone, I must also admit to its welcome source of global news and connections. It does keep me occupied while loitering in the midst of an otherwise empty contrada street.

Immersed as I am in global connectivity, I fail to notice that Dario has emerged onto the street several buildings up. In fact, he calls out for me rather than the reverse. Also unexpected is the apparent company he is keeping, that of a middle-aged man and woman. Rather than finding him with numerous students as usual, this fortunate pair is enjoying Dario's undivided attention.

"Tom, we're up here!" Dario yells down the street. He has already shut and locked the door from which they exited, so I conclude there are no more people to follow.

"Dario, ciao!" I enthusiastically say as we shake hands. He immediately introduces me to his acquaintances, Jack and Jill (*who went up the Via del Comune hill... never mind*, I muse). I add, "I was expecting a large group of students to be following you out!"

"Ha, no, they are getting an exclusive tour." I quickly learn that the tour has not yet concluded, either. Dario adds, "Come along with us. We have a few stops to make." Without any protest from me, I instantly become the fourth member of our small cohort as we gradually retreat up the veritable mountainside of Via del Comune. Dario points out the alley leading to the Caterpillar's stable, where its cherished horse resides during the days of the Palio. After this, even our small group splits into its own cohorts as Jack and I drop back to begin a conversation of our own. Jill scoots ahead to enjoy any lingering comments that Dario may offer as we make our way toward the historic center.

DARIO'S WORLD

With some surprise I learn quickly that Jack is an independent movie producer, and he and his wife both hailed originally from my own home state of Connecticut. It never fails to amaze me how often someone from this smallish U.S. state asks, "What town did you grow up in?" This happens more frequently than probabilities might otherwise forecast. All the while enjoying his company, I am eyeballing Dario and Jill, who have migrated farther ahead along the bustling Via dei Rossi. *Where is he going? I ask myself. No matter, time will tell, as it always does. Just go along for the ride.* At this point, I am presuming that we will be joined for lunch.

Somehow, we manage to wind our way into the Goose contrada, of all places, where I silently recognize its steep streets leading down to the ancient water supply, Fontebranda, and the complex of monuments that honor Santa Catarina (Saint Catherine). This is the neighborhood where we lived during our first two summers here and where we also enjoyed an unlikely Goose victory celebration to boot. We turn into the entry of a corner restaurant, and Dario slips in to talk with the proprietor. The place is swamped, and nearly every table seems to be occupied. *Is he trying to find a place for lunch? Why here?* I ask myself while mentally preparing to share some time with Dario's guests as well. But then Dario emerges just as quickly and motions for Jack and Jill to enter the busy place. A host briskly welcomes them, and they say their goodbyes to Dario. Just like that, we lose them as they dive into the crowded restaurant lunch scene. I never see them again.

Still, it turns out that my own impromptu tour with Dario is not yet concluded. He calmly suggests, "Let's head back toward the Campo, as I need to pay someone for Palio tickets that I promised some visitors. Do you happen to need tickets?" With this question he admittedly catches me off guard as we stroll up toward Piazza Indipendenza from the Goose contrada.

"Well, we hadn't planned to pay for bleacher tickets again. I might just go into the center for this one," I claim truthfully, as I still had not discussed other options with Linda. Given the costs of finding airfare and lodging only weeks earlier, acquiring Palio tickets was the least of our concerns. Oh, and there was the additional issue of the unpredictable October weather. This factor discouraged us from making too many outdoor plans in advance. Further, we are scheduled to depart Siena by bus around 3:00 p.m. the day after the Palio. Should we acquire tickets now, *a hundred things could go wrong with that stunt,* I had thought to myself. Pour enough rain over the track on

Palio day, or experience any number of other unfortunate delays, and we would miss the actual race entirely.

Despite all of this, I manage to ask, "Just out of curiosity, what is the cost of tickets right now?" I await a response as we dodge other pedestrians buried in their phones, paying little attention to people around them.

"Two hundered-eighty euro," Dario responds nonchalantly, adding, "Since it's October, not nearly as many visitors will be in town for the Palio. It's hard to tell whether the bleachers or the inside of the Campo will even fill up."

"OK, thanks. I'm definitely curious to see how many people attend," I say, adding, "I will talk to Linda about it." While honest, I am not yet convinced this is the deal of the century. Yes, these tickets are decidedly cheaper than summer bleacher tickets—almost half price in some cases. Still, the price is more than US$300 per ticket, and it's not a big leap to imagine that Linda would want to join me. Either way, the price does provide an early indication of how this Palio may contrast with its summer counterparts. That precious bleacher tickets are still available so close to October 20 suggests that viewership may be down for the upcoming event.

Without knowing our immediate destination, I dutifully keep up with Dario as we dart into one of the tunneled alleys and down into the Campo. The Palio bleachers are already assembled, making the effort to reach various restaurant establishments akin to walking through catacombs underneath the seats. Dario remains confident with his wayfinding skills, of course, and negotiates the narrow paths below the bleachers and along building façades. It is almost as if he is naturally enjoying his own personalized gerbil tube. We ultimately end up at the building entry to one of the Campo's numerous popular restaurants. Now standing in their patio area, he looks around for the person he is scheduled to meet. Then he grabs my attention and points to an energetic restaurant hostess who has not stopped moving since we arrived. She has been dutifully bolting around to greet patrons or check on tables.

"Do you see that woman?" Dario begins, though given our proximity within ten feet or so, I become nervous that she will notice our collective stares. But her attention is focused elsewhere as she multitasks both inside and outside the building. "She is the fiancé of one of the more successful jockeys now, Andrea Mari," he tells me in his typically undramatic fashion. "Brio," he adds, to remind me of the jockey's nickname.

I can't help but express my instant surprise. "Really! Brio! Wow, that's great." I grin, thinking of the jockey we saw win the Palio for the Tower in 2015. He had also been the one to make a surprise, comeback win for the Panther in 2006. I am admittedly somewhat starstruck. Andrea Mari is racking up the victories lately in an impressive fashion, having now won six Palio races in Siena. Most recently he brought victory to the Dragon in July 2018. Along with Tittia, Scompiglio, Trecciolino, and maybe Gingillo, Brio has found himself on the list of a handful of jockeys who are now highly sought after by multiple contrade to run for them. Then Dario tells me more of the story.

"They were supposed to get married last week," he chuckles, "but the Straordinario forced them to delay their plans. The wedding will be two weeks from now." The obvious implication here is left unsaid by both of us; Brio is planning to compete as one of the jockeys this coming Saturday, a goal which has likely led to a flurry of training, preparations, and negotiations on his part. With a historic Palio underway, the wedding can wait. After this bit of news, Dario identifies a balding man who also apparently works here in some capacity. I remain plastered to the wall as the two of them conduct their business.

Cow's Stomach and Wild Boar

With Dario's errands complete, it is time for a lunch of our own. I am silently relieved when he directs us away from this particularly posh establishment, given my recollection that I had not yet loaded my wallet with much cash. We navigate through the light street traffic as we return to Piazza Indipendenza. Although a bustling public space of its own, the modest piazza is relatively unseen and hidden away from much of the daily tourist traffic just off the Campo. Linda still occasionally asks which of the numerous side streets leads to Piazza Indipendenza. Despite my own years of experience here, I still need to double check my memory now and then. It is here where one finds a secondary hub of taxis, an entry street into the Goose, and my favorite bypass route to scoot up to Piazza Gramsci to catch a bus or obtain groceries in the northern part of the city. In fact, Dario is now pointing us up this very path of Via dei Termini and mentions his suggested place for lunch.

I react with some surprise, as I have rushed past this place on foot countless times without paying it much attention. We have arrived at the humble entrance of Prètto Prosciutteria e Convivio. Being quite the mouthful in its own right, the name is nearly too wide to fit on its narrow storefront. Upon first glance I am relieved to see its relaxed, informal character, in contrast to more stuffy restaurants with real tablecloths. This type of place is, in two words, perfectly comfortable. Moreover, the signage indicates that the place prides itself on serving only *prodotti tipici Toscani* (locally produced, typical products that arrive from the nearby Tuscan countryside).

"Let's try to eat here. I have someone I would like you to meet," suggests Dario, which piques my interest, of course. He explains further, "Since you have been reading my most recent book, one of the operators of this restaurant used to be the owner of The Irish, the pub where I met Jonathan." Dario is referring to one of his book's main characters. "You might recall, the Irish was Jonathan's favorite hangout here in Siena. Of course, the pub no longer exists."

"Yes, of course!" I respond with my eyes opened wider now, having just made my first physical connection to Dario's most recent publication, *The Year of the Chicory*. I had told him while we walked that I had managed to read the first half of the book on the plane. My compliment continued by explaining that his book was really the only thing I had accomplished on the flight beyond the obligatory eating and sleeping. Even the inflight movies were not particularly appealing this time.

Upon entering the compact yet bustling seating area, Dario pulls one of the wait staff aside. He returns to report that the former employee of The Irish is not working today. *Oh well, that's fine.* (We would learn later that his friend had sold the place, adequately explaining his absence.) We settle into our seats at a small table set for two near the front counter. We are provided with two menus, as expected. My initial confidence quickly gives way to uncertainty, however, as I flip back and forth quizzically through the numerous pages. Despite my relative pride at having conquered most Italian menu formats, this one presents a new challenge. Not only is it rather square-shaped with laminated pages and tabs, but I am not discerning the typical breakdown of *antipasti* (starters), *primi piatti* (first plates), *secondi* (main courses), and *contorni* (vegetables), let alone the expected pizzas. *Where are the pizzas that I can fall back on?* I wonder. My first strategy is usually to identify the primi piatti to help me navigate the rest of the menu. In this case, it is more like someone had placed a completely foreign menu in front of me.

Indeed, some parts of it are almost written as a narrative, in paragraph form. *Really?* This truly defies any pattern I have ever seen.

With mild embarrassment, I finally surrender and ask Dario to help me find the primi piatti, desperately seeking any kind of recognizable pasta dishes. Somewhat relieving my stress is the fact that Dario is likewise perplexed. He asks our *cameriere* (waiter) whether they have primi piatti. He motions to the chalkboard on the wall, which I am fortunately facing. OK, I have seen this practice before, whereby a more specialized establishment provides its standard offerings by writing them out on a chalkboard or on a disposable paper menu. The practice never disappoints, however, because it typically indicates that you have found a more specialized, informal family-run restaurant. Sometimes one can even find handwritten menus of the day placed outside their entryways. Humorously, sometimes the penmanship approaches the illegibility of my own. At this moment, however, my time is up to make a decision without further ado. In Italian I say, "I would like the *pappardelle al cinghiale*, please," asking for a popular Senese dish of flat pasta noodles with wild boar sauce. It's a safe bet, and I am much less concerned with my menu decision than I am with learning from Dario's perspectives.

As if determined to make our meat-eating binge complete, Dario orders *lampredotto*, perhaps the actual reason we are here today. After ordering, I indicate my confusion about this particular cuisine. He explains, "It's a typical Fiorentino dish that I adore, and this is the only place in Siena that serves it. It's made out of a cow's second stomach." *All righty then.*

Origins of the Straordinario

With the necessities out of the way, our conversation turns to the upcoming Palio. First, I am curious about the origin of the proposal for the Straordinario, so Dario logically begins there.

"The proposal for the Palio came to City Hall quite late in the year, August 28," he begins in his typically reserved tone. "It came from the Assoarma, an umbrella group that oversees all of the military organizations in Italy." I ask him to spell the group's name for me. While copying, he continues, "The Senesi didn't take it seriously at first. The reason the proposal came so late, it seems, was to take advantage of the recently elected mayor and his new administration, rather than take a chance with the previous mayor who was likely on his way out. The new mayor likely wants to show everyone that the city can organize and run a Palio on short notice." He grins cynically.

"Oh wow," I react to this thought. "I guess it makes sense that there would be some political rationale for holding the event." I begin to contemplate the possibility that the recent mayoral election this past summer is connected somehow to the proposal and decision to run the Palio. I will be very interested to verify this with others later this week.

"And the new mayor is a Shell contradaiolo," Dario adds for contemplative effect. "He would not publicly promote the contrada or his personal ties to it, though he is certainly interested in seeing the Shell have another chance at winning a Palio."

"The contrade had to vote for the Palio on their own, though, right? So, the decision was not entirely up to the mayor?" I press for more information about the decision-making process.

"Yes, so, each contrada held an initial vote during a general assembly, known as an *assemblea generale*, the typical name for a contrada's public business meetings. The rule is that at least ten of the seventeen contrade need to approve a proposal for a Palio Straordinario by a simple majority vote. And the vote is based on who shows up at the meeting," he explains confidently.

"Do all contrade vote in the same manner, or do they have different voting processes?" I ask, curious to learn whether a standard approach exists for all contrade.

"Each contrada can do it differently if it wants. With us in the Bruco, the vote was conducted with a simple show of hands, 'yes' or 'no.' The result was heavily in favor; about 90 percent of those who voted were in support of the Palio."

"So, what was the turnout for the vote, and were there any generational differences? I had seen some hints of that online last week," I say, hoping to verify what I had read.

"The turnout in the Bruco was decent, with about 600 or 700 people. Yes, we noticed that the younger members were the most enthusiastic. The minimum voting age in the contrada is 16, so that certainly contributed to the vote of support," Dario offered.

Dario's plate of lampredotto is still rather full, I notice, largely because I have kept him talking. I thus purposely slow down my own rate of consumption to better match his own.

DARIO'S WORLD

Dario continues his educational overview, unphased by the food left on his plate. "Aside from the Bruco, only nine other contrade voted in favor of the Palio, while the other seven voted 'no.' Had one more contrada voted 'no,' there would be no Palio this coming Saturday."

"Yes, I was surprised the decision was that close," I say. "I saw that those who initially voted against were allowed to reverse their vote, is that correct?"

"Yes, and this is one of the more interesting things. Now that Siena had voted to hold the Straordinario, the seven contrade which originally voted against it were given five days to reverse their vote and join the race. Of course, all of them voted 'yes.' Why would a contrada vote 'no' and risk the chance of their rival racing alone?"

"Do you agree with that policy?" I jump in, especially curious about this approach. "I mean, a good number of those contrade that originally voted 'no' were actually extracted to race!" I exclaim, adding, "It seems that some contrade that were not very interested in running were chosen, while other, highly motivated contrade were left out—like the Bruco!"

"Yes, like the Bruco." Dario admits quietly with a slight grimace as he glances down at his plate. He continues, almost exasperated. "I knew it was going to happen, but this was worse than one could imagine. The first five extracted had all voted 'no': Tower, She-Wolf, Snail, Goose, and Dragon." Dario looks into the air while thinking through the order in which they were chosen by lottery. "And then the next five chosen had all voted 'yes.' What are the chances of that?" He shakes his head and grins, though clearly displeased. His nonverbal gestures tell me he believes the whole affair has been nothing short of ridiculous.

I respond, "OK, so what were the reasons that some contrade voted 'no' originally? I have to say it was hard to miss the fact that several of the recent Palio winners voted to stay out of this one. Are they concerned about costs?"

"Sure, of course," he allows, confirming my observation as rather obvious. "The Dragon and She-Wolf both won this past summer, and they are still celebrating. They did not have a strong motive to join the Straordinario. The She-Wolf has won three times since 2016. Everything has been lining up for them recently—winning as rincorsa this past August, for example, the tenth spot in the lineup. As you know, it's very difficult to win from there." I am recalling my own surprise when I learned about this feat two months ago. He continues, "So, when it came time to vote 'yes' or 'no' for the Straordinario, the She-Wolf voted 'no' because the contrada is financially broke. They are still hosting celebration dinners this month," Dario laughs and takes a rare bite. "And yet they still get picked for the Straordinario. It's just their time right now, whether they wanted it or not." Another smile appears on Dario's face, looking down contemplatively at the floor. I cannot help but also acknowledge his hint of Senese superstition with respect to the She-Wolf, given his comment that it's "just their time." Still, given the impressive run of luck, or fate, or whatever is happening with that contrada lately, one would be hard-pressed to disagree.

Though not revealing my own surprise, this is the first indication I have received that the decision of whether to hold the Straordinario may have involved factors beyond that of commemorating World War I. Rather, more practical and financial reasons influenced some (if not all) contrade to vote one way or the other. Given that the war still provided the original rationale for this Palio, I now turn to this particular topic. I am not letting him off the hook just yet.

Reflections on World War I

"Do you think that World War I was an appropriate rationale for holding a Palio?" I open this new line of conversation.

"Well, the war was disastrous for the Italians. More than half a million Italians were killed, with many battles lost. When the Austrians finally did break through, they were spread across this plain and didn't really know what to do next. It didn't take long for the Italians to finally surround and defeat them. But by then, there really wasn't much reason to celebrate."

I interpret this as less than a resounding endorsement of holding a Palio in the war's name. I respond, "Is the memory of the war important to the Senese, regardless of the Palio?"

"Oh yes. Every contrada has its own memorial of the war. The Bruco memorial is in our chapel and includes about 15 or 20 names of soldiers who lost their lives. The primary monument for Siena is up near Piazza Gramsci. Do you know where the Garibaldi statue is located? It's near there."

"That sounds interesting. I'll head up there this week to look for it. I never really studied that war, so I'm interested to learn how the Senesi were involved," I respond, which reminds me about an event hosted by the Panther yesterday, before our arrival. "I noticed that the Panther contrada held an educational event this past weekend," I add. "Are there other educational efforts taking place this week?" Even if the war was not foremost on people's minds during the contrada votes, I remain optimistic that the official reason for the Palio still provides an educational opportunity for locals and outsiders alike.

Dario explains, "Well, the Bruco has not held anything specific this week, though a variety of events were held around the city a few years ago to reflect on Italy's entrance into the war." He continues with not a little pride, "The Bruco was one of the first contrade to organize a commemoration of the war in 2015. It was dedicated to the fallen of the contrada. I still have the contrada medallion from that event," he says with a smile.

What I am hearing is that the Senesi wish to keep alive the memory and history of the war, with a Straordinario or not. Then Dario shifts the topic to something a bit less solemn, which admittedly causes my face to light up.

He asks with a subtle smirk, "Did you attend the presentation of the Palio banner last night?"

"Yes, I did! I was determined to make it to Siena in time for that event," I laugh. "What do you think of the drappellone?" I don't let on yet about the impromptu conversation Linda and I enjoyed this morning.

"Well, you heard the audience clapping last night. I couldn't believe it. They actually booed the one [drappellone] in August, so I was surprised this time. The August one was absolutely terrible, but it was entirely expected coming from that artist. I was actually pleased that the archbishop refused to bless it, though it was mainly because the required Madonna was holding a horse instead of Jesus. His issue wasn't with the actual art, I guess," he laughs. "So, this one deserved the same negative reaction, in my opinion." He stops here, I suppose to reflect and also to sneak a bite of lampredotto.

"Wow! So, what are your main problems with it?" I wonder if he agrees with other perspectives we've heard thus far.

"Well, first, the theme of the banner—it's just too general. It could have shown more of a connection with Siena. There's nothing about Siena on it. And what do you think of this?" He now turns to his phone, scrolls a bit, then hands it to me. I can't help but grin because I know exactly what he is going to reveal. I look, nonetheless.

"Yup!" I emit a quick laugh. "Wow, this is really getting around the internet," I add, returning his phone after glancing at the same comparative images from the couple we encountered this morning.

Dario continues in his understated tone, "The art is obviously copied from that photo, and the soldier in the original photo is German, so the artist just changed the helmet style. And the dress worn by the woman is not even from that era. And yet they were clapping last night." *Of course*, I remind myself, *the viewers had yet to learn about the so-called "copy and paste" issue.* Nonetheless, I can appreciate why the artwork perhaps should not have earned such generous applause.

I react with, "Well, my own initial thought was that it was elegantly simple, apparently representing a soldier kissing his sweetheart goodbye, perhaps for good," sharing my own first impression. "Since we know it was copied from that photo, though, it really loses the intended meaning," I confess with some disappointment. "And I do see your point about the lack of connection to Siena. That would have made the art much more meaningful to the city." Dario gives a nod in agreement and puts his phone away.

This reminds me of another topic related to the presentation. "Can you explain what the Bersaglieri band is all about? Why are they here in Siena?"

Dario responds with another question, "Did you see them yesterday at the presentation? They were supposed to perform before the ceremony."

"Well, I tried to see them," I begin with a chuckle. "When I arrived in the Campo prior to the presentation they were playing an informal concert. I have to say it was kind of strangely set up," I add, deciding to share an outsider's observation. "Their group had formed a closed circle, facing in toward themselves, so the sound was not projecting very well." I laugh. "I guess I notice these things because of my own experience as a band member. Not only that, but a throng of people were clustered around their circle, so I could not have gotten near them had I tried. So, anyway, I enjoyed the music nearby but didn't really see the group."

"Well, you might get a second chance, if you will be in the Campo for the Palio," he explains with a grin. "They are going to perform on the track before the race, and I believe for the *prova generale* [final evening trial] as well." At which point, Dario signals me to wait as he returns to his phone. After a few swipes he finds a website and turns the sound up. As he hands me the phone again, a fast-paced march plays for probably everyone in the restaurant and kitchen area to hear. Though I quickly glance side to side with some concern, Dario is satisfied, and I silently tell myself that this is for educational purposes. I watch the short video as the Bersaglieri band performs their trademark jog along a parade street while valiantly attempting to play an Italian march.

"That is definitely impressive," I say, with memories of my own marching band days swimming in my head. I add, "I don't understand how they can actually play while jogging up and down like that. It's not easy to play while moving, and your mouth can really take a beating. I nearly lost some teeth one time!" Dario laughs at the thought. I can't resist explaining more. "In our college marching band, we were taught a 'high-step' and were trained specifically how to plant our feet so that our upper body moved as little as possible. The result was that we looked like we were floating down the field," I explain, a bit nostalgically. "Even then, it was very difficult for me to play the trumpet with a decent sound. So, it's amazing that this group can manage at all."

"Well, we will see how they do on the dirt track." He then adds, "You know how the Carabinieri [mounted calvary] perform their traditional routine on horses before the prova generale and Palio? They are still planning to do that, but I think without the fast-paced charge this time. I actually think it would be more meaningful for the Straordinario if the city would change the tradition this time and have the Bersaglieri perform on their own, without the Carabinieri." This makes me consider what challenges might exist for completely changing the traditional routine of the Palio.

The Carabinieri to which Dario refers is considered one of Italy's four armed forces, designated as such since 2001. Like the Bersaglieri, the Carabinieri can be traced back to the Kingdom of Sardinia. Its name is actually of French derivation, referring to soldiers who carried carbines. Its mounted calvary unit typically performs prior to both the prova generale and the Palio race, complete with full regalia. They typically make one slow lap around the track, followed by a heart-stopping, full-gallop charge with swords pointing into the air. This time, however, the group will share some time with their Bersaglieri counterparts, as Dario mentioned.

An Increasingly Rare Occasion

At this point, our meat-heavy meals have virtually disappeared, and I ask for the bill. In Italy, however, this does not mean that we get chased out just yet. Thankfully, Dario is in no big rush, and I don't have any pressing appointments until dinner. I am therefore content to let our lunch play out naturally, and I do have one more topic I am eager to broach.

"Do you think it was a good idea to hold a Palio this time of year, in late October?"

After contemplating how to respond, he begins, "It's a lot more complicated to hold a Straordinario now. And the city hasn't done one since the change of the millennium in 2000. Back in the 1960s and 70s, it was a lot simpler to organize a Palio, and less costly. One concern is the horses. They are essentially done with training for the season and are now back in their stables. So, they're not well prepared to run a race right now. Not only that, but now there are complicated regulations about preparing the horses, including the veterinary assessments, and so forth. And we should remember that even this Palio was narrowly approved. It almost didn't happen. So, it's not a common thing to do anymore."

After absorbing this information, I respond with, "Yes, it seems that the frequency of these events has decreased. I noticed in the Palio statistics that there were sometimes three or four of them per decade! I couldn't believe how common they were," I exclaim.

Before our arrival here, I visited my favorite website for Palio statistics, ilpalio.org. Given the site's incomparable array of data on all things Palio, it was not a far reach to expect a special category for this type of event.[29] Once found, I first discovered that a total of forty-eight such events have occurred between the years 1712 and 2000. The forty-ninth Straordinario will consequently be held later this week. Curiously, six of them actually ran only the horses, with no jockeys on their backs—all between the years 1809 and 1907. And, three Straordinarii (plural of Straordinario) allowed all seventeen contrade to run, one of them with horses only.

Beyond these fun facts, one trend jumped out. Namely, these special events were held much more frequently during the twentieth century than they are now, as Dario noted earlier. For instance, two such events were held during each decade of the 1940s, 1950s, and 1980s, averaging one every five years. Only one Straordinario was held during the 1970s, but no less than four occurred during the 1960s alone—the fourth celebrating none other than the first lunar landing in 1969.

Compared to these earlier decades, then, only one other Straordinario has been held between 1986 and now, and it celebrated the new millennium. Even the author of a local news piece, Massimo Biliorsi, eloquently indicated the significance of this fact, writing just prior to the extraction of the contrade last month, "The Straordinario is itself an event that disrupts the sensations of the contradaioli, moves the hands of time, fits into days reserved for other [purposes], pursues dreams that summer has not allowed us to achieve . . . An extraordinary show in every sense. It will take us back in time, when running in September happened much more often than today."[30]

Dario nods in agreement but then throws in a surprise I had not yet considered. "Yes, that's true. However, there have been other proposals since 2000." My eyebrows go up with this news. "They were not approved for various reasons. Around 2008, a proposal was made to have a Straordinario to commemorate the 750th anniversary of the Battle of Montaperti. The anniversary was coming up in 2010." I can't help but chuckle at hearing such a high anniversary number. Dario explains, "I believe it was turned down because the '50' anniversary number was too generalized, so it wasn't really meaningful." Then Dario offers a suggestion for the future, with a slight grin. "I think we should hold a Straordinario every fifty years to commemorate the battle. Just institute it and you can plan for it ahead of time."

"Yes, that would definitely be cool," I agree with a smile. The 800th anniversary is thus relatively close, so with Dario's suggestion we could start planning for the year 2060. Returning to reality from this far-out scenario, I inquire about the financing for this event. "How does the city intend to pay for this Palio, since they cannot depend upon the bank like they once did?" I am referring to the venerable Banca Monte dei Paschi, or "Babbo [Daddy] Monte" as locals have traditionally referred to the influential banking institution. Having served Siena and Tuscany since the 1470s, it only recently succumbed to the global economic recession after 2008 and is no longer locally owned. Much of the Palio, along with numerous other organizations and events, had benefited directly from the bank's lucrative, locally controlled foundation until around 2013. Lately the city and contrade have been forced to search for alternative funding sources.

Dario once again surprises me with a response I had not expected. "There is a rumor going around," he begins. "Not long ago there was a Netflix television show filmed in the Campo and along some of the streets."

"Do you know what it's called?" I quickly ask.

"I don't know the name of the show, but it is definitely American. And I believe the lead actor is fairly famous. The rumor is that the Comune [municipal government] was paid around 400,000 euro to allow for the filming here. There's a lot of money involved when a studio wants to film somewhere like Siena, sort of like that [James] Bond film, *Quantum of Solace*."

This latter film is one of the few that included scenes from Siena and the Palio. The city guards the traditions and media coverage of the Palio very closely, and each proposed project requires serious scrutiny before it is often rejected. Even the opening scenes of *Quantum of Solace*, filmed as they were during a recent Palio race, remain particularly controversial here.

Dario continues with the rest of his story. "To organize and set up for a Palio costs almost as much these days as what the city was paid for the Netflix filming. So, the rumor is that the Comune is using that money to pay for the Straordinario."

I respond quite naturally with a typical question, given my social science background. "That's amazing! Is there any evidence to support the rumor at this point?"

"Well, not right now, but it will have to show up in the city's expense report at the end of the year," he offers. "The city is getting the money from somewhere. These days it costs a lot of money to pay for the dirt track, the set-up labor, and especially the security. These costs were much cheaper in the past."

Dario then returns to his phone once more and pulls up a short video. I almost cover my mouth with my hand, reacting with raw surprise as a sports car appears to careen carelessly into the Campo and spin around one of the cement pedestals. My first question is how the driver managed to avoid hitting these important, if numerous, features that ring the entire public space. Of course, I am watching a scripted chase scene for the Netflix show. The scene cuts to another chase taking place on one of Siena's streets outside the Campo. I believe that I briefly detect the street leading down to the Church of Provenzano in the Giraffe contrada.

DARIO'S WORLD

"I would not be surprised," reflects Dario, "if the city allows for more filming during the upcoming events this week, given how much money is at stake."

"We'll see soon enough!" I respond, as we wrap up our lunch and settle the bill. I then ask, "Where are you going to watch the Palio?"

"That's the funny thing," he says, "I won't even be here in Siena, as I've already made plans elsewhere. Nobody really saw this coming, so there might be a noticeable drop in attendance." Thus, not even Dario will be hosting guests in the bleachers for this race.

We bid farewell to the staff and step outside once again. As we adjust to the warm October weather that continues to bless the city, Dario looks to the sky and suggests, "You know, I have always believed that October would be the perfect time to hold a Palio—every year. The weather is generally much better like it is today; there is no sweating or high humidity, and it rarely rains with downpours as it does in July and August. It just makes good sense."

Still, as noted earlier, the extreme level of concern about the weather should not be underestimated. One only need point to the special weather station recently installed somewhere near—or on—Palazzo Berlinghieri to provide real time weather information for the upcoming Palio.[31] Equally science-oriented (if somewhat amusing) is the news that the Comune laid down a four meter-by-four meter patch of sample racetrack turf in the parking lot of Piazza Mercato on September 20, directly behind Palazzo Pubblico. According to the journalist capturing the moment, the scene provided for a "strange impression" this time of year. With the sample turf quickly fenced in for safekeeping, the goal of this science project was to expose the turf to the characteristic humidity of autumn. Quite wisely, the Comune is not assuming that the special blend of dirt commonly used in July and August will be sufficient to assure the safety of the horses in October.[32]

Having bid Dario farewell, I now return to our lodging to reconnect with Linda. In addition to relaying Dario's anecdotes to her, I also recount his rare optimism about holding a Palio in October and his revelation about the recent filming for Netflix. This latter point is all the prompting Linda needs to quickly set to work. She immediately gets online to hopefully identify the Netflix production. Given the miracle that is the internet, she discovers within minutes that the film in question will be titled *6 Underground*, starring Ryan Reynolds of *Deadpool* fame. Initial filming began not long ago in July

2018 in a variety of cities including Siena, Florence, Rome, and Taranto, Italy, along with the more predictable Los Angeles. Given this background, at least this part of Dario's information proves to be accurate. With approximately $150 million to spend on the production, according to one online source, it does not require a giant leap to presume that Siena was well compensated for its troubles.

Whether the Straordinario is funded by an arm of Hollywood or not will be of little consequence should an unforgiving tempest arrive to ruin all the fun.

✣ CHAPTER 6 ✣

Mutilated Victory

D URING OUR FIRST SUMMER IN SIENA, WE WERE INTRODUCED TO THE ITALIAN tradition of *aperitivo*. While often disappointed that Senese restaurants rarely served dinner before 7:00 p.m., there is a cultural reason for this. Italians do not generally eat dinner until much later than Americans, although they do offer something akin to what we would call "happy hour." The Italian version, known as aperitivo, is less about alcoholic drinks, however, and more about opening up the evening with good conversation and preparing the taste buds for dinner. The term derives from Latin, which loosely means "to open."[33] Linda and I once wondered what all of those people were doing while seated at patio tables that seemed to have spilled from the doors of every eating establishment. We had longingly hoped that they were eating actual meals, indicating that we could follow suit. Upon further scrutiny, however, they were merely enjoying light fare and drinks in those hours roughly between 5:00 and 7:00 p.m. Depending upon the situation, our choices were usually twofold: either return to our apartment and cook (if possible) or wait out the Italians and return somewhere later in the evening—often to open up the place at 7:00 sharp as their first (obviously American) customers.

Aperitivo on the Campo

Eventually, we would learn about the Italian pre-dinner tradition of aperitivo. This early evening event to "whet the appetite" or to "get the juices flowing" is delightfully focused more on the food but also involves low-alcohol drinks, such as aromatized wines or bitter liqueurs often served with carbonated water. Establishments typically use one of two approaches to distribute the lighter foods of aperitivo. Some employ a restaurant-style approach, whereby a waiter brings out one or more trays of food that might include combinations of nuts, bruschetta, cold cuts, bread, bean salad, olives, and various cheeses. The other approach is buffet style, where patrons are ushered into the restaurant to choose their own fare. Either way, I must confess more than once to having successfully assembled a rather satisfying meal on these items alone.

It is the buffet style of aperitivo that I am enjoying this evening at Bar Il Palio on the Campo with my two companions, Mike and Gabriele.

Mike is an American friend and colleague who now lives in Siena, and he helped arrange this get-together a week ago. Additionally, he has been kind enough to introduce me to Gabriele Maccianti, a well-known local historian who specializes in the study of World War I. After mentioning my intent to learn more about the war, Mike graciously offered to invite Gabriele to better explain the war's background and how it affected Siena. I am grateful that Mike is joining us as well, not only for his good company, but because he can help translate whatever Gabriele throws at me in Italian. Confident as I am now with basic Italian language skills, trying to comprehend historical concepts related to a world war is something altogether different.

Upon arriving at our designated meeting spot, I find Mike and Gabriele already settled at a small round table under the restaurant's expansive awnings. Following introductions, I tell Gabriele about my interest in the war and Siena's role during that time. Mike then moves effortlessly into translation mode. Upon the arrival of our waiter, we briefly disband to indulge in the aperitivo buffet inside.

Learning about World War I

As we begin to nibble, Gabriele begins quite appropriately with a general comment. "Most people focus on the Second World War and its aftermath, since it is more recent and still in the minds of survivors and their families. But in some ways Italians are more sentimental and emotionally connected to the First World War." I nod with a serious expression on my face, trying to soak up all the information our resident historian is willing to offer. He continues, "Today, every family in Siena has stories about World War I and how it affected them. Although there are no surviving veterans, the event is still vivid in the collective memory of the Senesi, and Italians generally. This memory is actually more unified and less divisive than discussions about World War II."

"Oh, interesting. What are the reasons for that?" I ask curiously.

"Well, people were generally embarrassed about Italy's role in World War II, due mostly to the influence of fascism here." I nod once again as a light bulb clicks on in my head. "Italians were highly polarized, with many participating in serious resistance against the fascist government. Fascism was closely associated with the war effort, and so it was not fashionable to discuss it publicly. A lot of people were concerned that if they spoke passionately in some way about the second war, they would be considered a fascist sympathizer. This continued right through the 1960s. Only more recently has it become more acceptable to discuss World War II again."

"OK, that makes a lot of sense," I respond.

Gabriele thinks again and shares a statistic to drive home his point. "It's kind of interesting also that Italy's government provided some 80 percent of its national budget to support World War I, while that figure was only about 64 percent for the Second World War."

I ask a follow-up question: "How many people served in the first war compared with the second? Was there a big difference with that as well?

"OK, well, I will start by saying that there were actually more servicemen in the first war than in the second. About six million men were called up. Of those, about five million went into service, with the other million used for backup and support in various ways. Four million actually saw action on the battlefields. Of those, about a half million, or 500,000, perished. Twice that many were wounded in some way." I shake my head while trying to comprehend the sheer scale of the losses.

To clarify, I ask, "So, you said they were 'called up.' Was there an expectation that young males would serve in the military during that time?"

"Oh yes, and this was actually the first major war in which soldiers were conscripted through a mandatory draft," Gabriele states, but follows up like a true historian with, "although technically the first time was when Italy invaded Libya in 1911." He continues to explain some history of the draft itself. "Italy actually had a draft in place since the 1870s, soon after the peninsula had been unified under the new Italian kingdom. So, Italy was already familiar with the idea of a draft. Of course, people were not very pleased with it during wartime! Compulsory service of some kind actually continued here until the 1990s. Still, all previous wars throughout much of history had relied upon professional armies. They had always expected to be paid!" We chuckle at this. "So, the Great War was the first major conflict that made use of conscripted troops in Italy."

"How did the Italian government determine who was eligible for the draft?" I ask.

"Well, there was a wide range of ages involved, and it wasn't always applied fairly. During the war, those born between 1874 and 1900 were eligible for the draft. Those who had already been drafted in 1913 or 1914 were forced to extend their tours beyond the typical three years of service. This sometimes meant that some served as many as six or seven years, presuming they stayed alive."

"Did the soldiers come from all over Italy, or were certain cities or regions more affected than others for some reason? For instance, how was Siena affected by the wartime draft?"

"The role of Siena during the war was similar to other cities around Italy, even though all the fighting was in the extreme northeastern part of the country. So, a city's geographic location didn't matter. What mattered much more was whether the conscripted troops were coming from rural or urban areas—the countryside versus the city."

"Oh, that's interesting. Were urban residents affected more because they weren't involved with agriculture?" This is my best logical guess at the moment.

"Actually, it was exactly the opposite," he smiles as I reveal some surprise. "For cities like Siena, the number of wartime casualties was proportionally lower than for those coming from the countryside. The working class of the city often specialized in certain skills or trades. They were employed as carpenters, masons, machinists, and so forth. The army made good use of their skills during the war, so they were less likely to see battle on the front lines. However, peasant farmers from the countryside were less fortunate, usually having no additional skills besides farming. So, naturally they were the ones trained to use weapons, and they were involved in a disproportionate amount of the fighting as infantrymen."

Italy Enters the War

"So, what was the reason Italy entered the war? Was the country being threatened?" I turn to a new direction of thought.

Upon translation from Mike, Gabriele contemplates how to respond to this American newcomer. "Italy had actually been aligned with Germany and Austria-Hungary—the Central Powers—for many years, since the 1880s. But for Italy it was more of a defensive agreement. When Austria-Hungary attacked Serbia to start the war, Italy did not feel an obligation to participate in support of that effort."

"Are you saying that they tried to remain neutral? How did they switch sides to favor the Allies?" I ask with some confusion.

"Well, for some time the Triple Entente—Britain, France, and Russia, also referred to as the Allies—courted the Italians, thinking that their loose alignment with the Central Powers could be broken. They were right. In 1915, the then-secret Treaty of London was signed by the Triple Entente and the Kingdom of Italy, with the Italians promising to enter the war against Austria-Hungary and Germany. Italy joined the war officially one month later, in May. However, the treaty didn't become public knowledge until 1917."

I follow up with the logical question, "So, why did Italy suddenly change course and join the Allies?

"Italy entered the war with a double purpose. The first was an explicit one, to hopefully unify the numerous Italian-speaking populations on the peninsula under one national purpose for the first time. The second was more implicit, less public, which emerged from the Treaty of London. The Allies had promised Italy lots of additional territory, especially large chunks of Austria-Hungary to the north and much of the Dalmatian coastal strip on the eastern side of the Adriatic Sea. Many of the urban centers there were already inhabited predominantly by Italian-speaking populations. The rural areas were more Slavic. So, presuming that the Allies would win the war, Italy stood to add vast swaths of territory to its north and east. Essentially the Adriatic would for the first time ever become an Italian sea."

"Wow, that's amazing, especially that the public didn't know about those promises when they entered the war." I contemplate his answer and then ask, "What was the public sentiment about entering the war? How did the Senesi take the news, for instance?"

"When Italy entered the war in 1915, the Campanone, or bell on the Torre del Mangia [the Palazzo's bell tower] rang to announce Italy's entrance into the war. This was a system that had been in place for centuries to announce news to the public. This in turn triggered other bells in the city and throughout the countryside."

"Wow, so the bells were still used to communicate even into the twentieth century. That's fascinating." I immediately think of a comparison to modern times and say as much, "It must have been kind of like today's cell towers, sending direct signals to other towers around it."

He responds and chuckles, "Yes, I suppose so. It's the way that information was spread in the days before phones and computers." He continues to explain Siena's reaction to joining the war. "The Italians were divided over the idea of entering the conflict, and Siena was no different. One faction was pro-war, the so-called Hawks, who were happy to join. These people were the interventionists on the right-wing side of politics in Italy. Siena was actually a hub of hawkish activities before and during the war."

"Oh, interesting. Why was that?" I express my surprise once again.

"The University of Siena." He responds nonchalantly.

"Hmm, so are you referring to the students, faculty, or both? In America most universities are known historically for their antiwar protests," I explain, showing some confusion once again. I am also wondering if I was misinterpreting his comment and its meaning due to a translation issue.

"Oh, sure, I understand," he reacts to my thought. "Here in Siena, the students generally promoted the war. We have to remember that most students at that time were wealthy, essentially members of the elite, and their social class was known for promoting the glory of war and heroism. They also followed various leaders and proponents at the time, such as a poet named Gabriele D'Annunzio. He heavily promoted the war nationally through his writing."

"Did the students reflect the general sentiment of Siena's population overall?" I ask to clarify to what extent the Senesi and Italians supported the war.

"No, the university was definitely more hawkish than the general population. The majority of citizens were actually neutralists, which is true throughout much of Italy. Then there were the 'dove-ish' factions who railed against the war. However, they could never get their act together to mount a sustained protest or resistance as they would do during World War II. This segment of the population was in itself quite fractured. They included socialists, moderates, Catholics, and others who just were not able to organize into a sustained movement. Even the socialists, who were most prone to leading demonstrations or strikes, could not organize themselves due to internal strife and factions. This is why there was never a strike led against the war in Italy. Generally, the moderates and socialists seem to have accepted their fate."

"Now that's fascinating!" I exclaim, while wrapping my head around the historical context. Then he quizzes me about a certain author.

A Farewell to Arms

"Are you familiar with one of the most famous antiwar Americans who served with the Italians?" He quizzes me with a smile.

Thinking quickly, I confess that I cannot conjure up a specific individual from that time period. I regrettably tell him as much.

"Back then he was a little-known individual named Ernest Hemingway. After his service and a bad injury to go with it, he went on to write a book called *A Farewell to Arms*. It doesn't take much effort to realize that his main character—based on himself—is not exactly a proponent of the war!" Gabriele laughs.

"Oh wow, I'm familiar with Hemingway, and I have heard the title. I did not know his story was connected to World War I, let alone the Italian front."

"Well, it brought a lot of attention to the conditions on the Italian front lines. Like his main character, he was an ambulance driver, not an infantryman. But he still gained first-hand experience with the Italians. Most of the attention about the war has focused on the western front, between the Germans and the Allies. The Italians became more of an afterthought."

"Yes, I need to get that book and catch up myself," I respond. "I confess to being one of those people who have not learned much about the Italian involvement with the war. It was challenging enough to encourage my generation to learn about the Second World War, let alone the first." Gabriele nods sympathetically.

Those generally familiar with Ernest Hemingway may recall especially his later accomplishments, including the Nobel Prize for Literature in 1954.

Only one year earlier, he published *The Old Man and the Sea*, which led to the Pulitzer Prize. However, it was arguably the publication of a much earlier novel in 1929, *A Farewell to Arms*, that established Hemingway as one of America's greatest writers and solidified his future writing career.[34]

For those unfamiliar with the novel's central story, the protagonist is Lieutenant Frederic Henry, who in 1916 finds himself on the Italian front during World War I as a driver for the Italian ambulance corps. His first experience in battle occurs while eating what passes for dinner. He and fellow ambulance drivers are hit by a mortar shell, which severely damages Henry's leg. He is eventually taken to an American hospital for treatment, during which time he is reacquainted with a nurse, Catherine Barkley. They fall in love and remain together that summer, though he is eventually forced to return to the front lines. No sooner does he arrive when the combined forces of the Germans and Austrians break through the Italian defenses, necessitating a massive Italian retreat from Caporetto back to the Piave River (which is historically accurate).

Much of the story then focuses on Henry's dramatic attempt to reunite with Catherine, who is expecting their first child. After nearly getting himself killed during the Italian retreat, they successfully flee by night to Switzerland. It is here that Hemingway brings the tragic tale of love and war to a close. As one who has read this book only recently for the first time, I must caution that *A Farewell to Arms* is no Disney fairytale. Indeed, Hemingway did not write such things. Rather, his antiwar sentiments are peppered throughout the book, perhaps most prominently in the novel's title. Beyond the story's dour roots in the tragedy of war, however, one can learn to appreciate Hemingway's brilliant and critically acclaimed mastery of the English language and the profound symbolism he employs throughout the story. As his grandson noted in a later commemorative edition of the work, the author became known for writing on the principle of the iceberg—that is, with minimalist text on the surface and seven-eighths more beneath the water.[35] After all, Hemingway did not win the Nobel Prize for nothing.

While much of the story's plotline was inspired by his own experiences, Hemingway did not actually arrive on the Italian front until well after the infamous retreat from Caporetto. Despite multiple attempts in early 1918 to enlist with various American armed services, Hemingway had been rejected by all of them because of his poor eyesight. He ultimately responded to a recruiting campaign and signed on as an ambulance driver for the Red Cross, and thereby made his way to the Italian front by June 1918.[36] The war would officially end only some five months later. Still, in similar fashion to his novel's main character, both of Hemingway's legs were severely wounded by mortar fire in early July, though he still managed to bring fellow Italian soldiers to safety following the attack. For this, he received the Italian Silver Medal for Bravery. After initial surgeries and recovery, he was transferred to the Red Cross hospital in Milan, where he convalesced for six months. As for the novel itself—strangely published on the very day of the 1929 stock market crash—*A Farewell to Arms* ultimately became accepted as the "best American novel to emerge from World War I."[37] If Gabriele has anything to say about it, the seminal work retains a special place in the collective hearts of the Italians to this day.

Along the Italian Front

Focusing more on Siena, I ask, "It appears the city cancelled the Palio for a few years during the war. Was that out of respect for the soldiers, or for other, more economic reasons?"

"Part of it was the timing of when the Italians declared war against the Austro-Hungarians, which happened in May 1915. Similar to today, the extraction of the contrade would have occurred just after that, so they suspended the extraction and the July Palio. Those who remained in the city proposed that a race be organized for ticket holders only, the idea being to benefit the war effort. But it was voted down, because it could have been viewed as discourteous to those already killed or wounded."

"OK, so the city did not want to dishonor those who were fighting. That makes sense," I say.

"Yes, and there was a lot of public discontent from Italians during the war. Unlike the other national powers that were generally enthusiastic, Italy was not, and there was very little good news coming from the front. On the political right was the church, for instance, which was never going to support the attack of a fellow Catholic power such as Austria. The pope was intensely opposed to the war. As for the socialist left, they never bought into the nationalist argument, that of using the war to unite the Italian peninsula. So, unlike many of the other national powers, Italy never really became enthusiastic, either before or during the fighting."

This brings up a question for me about whether Italy ever considered itself victorious. I ask, "I recall reading that Austria-Hungary finally capitulated and surrendered, which brought the war to an end. Wasn't the victory something to celebrate?"

Gabriele understands my confusion and responds in a matter-of-fact manner. "Before that final offensive effort by the Italians, virtually nothing had gone well for them. It was one disaster after another. Many viewed the war as a complete waste of human life." He continues to explain the progression of the war effort, which I would supplement later for my own better understanding.

After signing the clandestine Treaty of London, Italy declared war against Austria-Hungary, and fighting between the two national powers began shortly thereafter. The Isonzo region of northeastern Italy would serve as the general theater of engagement throughout the war. Although the Austro-Hungarians were heavily outnumbered, they held the high ground in the mountains, overlooking the more numerous but poorly led Italian troops. Between 1915 and 1917, the Italians undertook no less than eleven poorly designed assaults on the Austro-Hungarian line but gained nothing more than a few kilometers of ground to show for it. Already by the end of 1915, more than 60,000 Italians had been killed. By the conclusion of the eleventh fruitless offensive, more than 130,000 lives had been lost on the Italian side alone. Morale plummeted, as did Italian support nationwide. Around this time, Pope Benedict XV—already an outspoken critic—referred to the war as a "useless massacre" and a "horrible carnage that dishonours Europe."[38] Not surprisingly, desertions in the army continued to increase, peaking at around 60,000 by 1917. It is difficult to imagine a worse outcome than this, though what happened next would eclipse anything the young Kingdom of Italy had yet witnessed.

Following the eleventh failed offensive, the Italian commander attempted a different strategy. Knowing that the Germans were now providing support to the Austro-Hungarians, he decided to build up defenses to prepare for a presumed offensive by the Central Powers. And this is precisely what occurred.[39] Known as the Battle of Caporetto, the attack on the Italian lines began on October 24, 1917, and lasted nearly a month. Despite being outnumbered nearly two to one by the Italians, the Central Powers swept down, outflanked the Italian lines, and surrounded them.

On the first day alone, the Germans advanced as far as 23 kilometers.[40] At the battle's conclusion in mid-November, some 11,000 more Italians had been killed, and a quarter million had been taken prisoner. An untold number of them had voluntarily surrendered. The territory and military hardware lost to the Central Powers was likewise appalling. Once the Italians had stabilized along the Piave River, they had retreated more than 150 kilometers and lost some 20,000 square kilometers of territory to their adversary.[41] The Battle of Caporetto was appropriately labeled an "unmitigated disaster," and it further earned the notorious status as one of the worst military defeats of the entire war.[42]

With the Italians finally dug in along the Piave, something was finally turning in their favor. The Austro-Hungarian troops had become utterly disheartened and exhausted from fighting continuously along separate fronts, with the Italians to their west and the Russians to their east. Still, in June 1918 they decided to run an offensive of their own to break the Italian lines along the Piave. By this time, however, the Allies had also managed to reinforce the remaining Italian troops. In short, what was dubbed the Battle of the Piave River proved disastrous this time for the Central Powers. While the Italians held strong, the Austro-Hungarians lost nearly 12,000 soldiers, with more than 80,000 injured. More than 25,000 were captured.[43]

General Armando Diaz, who had been placed in charge of the Italian front to implement drastic changes in strategy shortly after the Battle of Caporetto, rejected the calls of his allied counterparts to launch an immediate offensive against the reeling Austro-Hungarian army. Rather, he deliberately took time to construct a careful and thorough battle plan while the Italian lines were being reinforced. He was determined to assure the best possible success by remaining patient and by moving methodically and intentionally. Ultimately, the strategy would become one for the books. On October 24, 1918, what became known as the Battle of Vittorio Veneto was launched. This time, the Italians and their allied reinforcements advanced swiftly until Austria-Hungary could take no more. By November 3, when the Austro-Hungarians finally capitulated, the Italians had finally earned the rout they had been seeking all along.

MUTILATED VICTORY

One day later, on November 4, Austria-Hungary signed an armistice, effectively ending the war on the Italian front. After watching the full surrender of their main partner, the Germans were forced to do the same only one week later. Suddenly—and quite eerily, according to witnesses—all guns went silent, and the war ended practically overnight. Despite this final, long-awaited success, however, few Italians were declaring victory. Throughout the war, more than 650,000 Italian soldiers had been killed and more than a million had been seriously wounded. Beyond the direct military toll, another half million civilians had perished, many as a result of famine caused by failing harvests. Italy then found itself economically bankrupt with inflation skyrocketing more than 400 percent.[44] Many would question for decades—as well as through the current day—whether the dual motives of national unity and promised territorial expansion were ultimately worth the toll.

The Paris Peace Conference

One might still be tempted to ask whether Italy ever received the territories promised in the secret Treaty of London. This is the next question I ask.

Gabriele begins to explain the tragic situation. He starts by saying, "It became known as the mutilated victory, or the *Vittoria Mutilata*. The phrase was actually first written by the Italian poet mentioned earlier, Gabriele D'Annunzio. His original words were somewhat different: 'Victory will not be mutilated.' He wrote that on the very day when the Italian armies launched the final offensive of Vittorio Veneto. His intent was to affirm that the Italian negotiations from the Treaty of London deserved to be accepted. Unfortunately, that did not happen."

Trying to make sense of this, I ask, "Do you mean that the Allies refused the Italians what they had been promised for joining the war?"

"Most of it, yes."

"How can that happen? Had they blatantly lied about it earlier, or was it a case of making grand promises that they ultimately could not keep?"

After thinking a bit, Gabriele responds, "There was a combination of factors—including the American President, Woodrow Wilson. You may have heard of Wilson's Fourteen Points related to the war?" I respond affirmatively, though I had not studied them for some time. He continues,

"Well, his first point was very clear, that no international pacts should be made in secret."

I smile in recognition. "Ah, so there goes the original Treaty of London?"

"Exactly," responds Gabriele. "Wilson refused to recognize that original pact, considering it null and void."

"That's kind of ironic, I suppose," I said, thinking through this information. "America did not even enter the war until well after it began, and only after they were begrudgingly forced into it. And here is Wilson discrediting the earlier agreements," I summarize, shaking my head with a chuckle.

"Yes, I suppose there is some irony to it. Not only that, but Wilson had received a letter from the British foreign secretary that disapproved of awarding Italy with the territory on the eastern side of the Adriatic Sea. He essentially convinced Wilson that transferring the former Slavic region to Italy would only cause more problems. Beyond that, Britain felt no true animosity toward Austria-Hungary in the first place, so they did not see a need to shift their territories to the Italians."

"And thus was born the new state of Yugoslavia—the land of the South Slavs," I recall from teaching Human Geography some years earlier.

Gabriele takes up where I left off: "And with that, Italy's expansionist leaders were denied their dream of completely surrounding the Adriatic and essentially turning it into an Italian waterbody. They had especially expected to be awarded the Dalmatian Coast and Fiume, but this was not granted. Beyond that, Italy was further denied a range of colonial territories that they had also been promised."

"This was all decided at the Treaty of Versailles, right?" I ask.

He corrects me a bit, responding, "The actual signing of the treaty occurred at Versailles, but all of the difficult negotiations required six months to finalize. All of that occurred in Paris, so it was known as the Paris Peace Conference."

"Huh, we certainly didn't learn that in high school," I joke. Following this line of thinking, I ask, "So, who did the Italians generally blame when they were refused what was promised?"

Gabriele becomes more animated now, as I must have hit a nerve. Thinking with a sigh, he explains, "The general consensus of blame—greatly simplified—fell on the incapacity of the Italian negotiators at the peace conference. At one point, Italy's premier, Vittorio Orlando, was so furious that he walked out of the negotiations, though he later returned. Even during the talks, it was clear that the Italians were not being taken seriously. The deck was already stacked against them. Britain and France were both less supportive of Italy's territorial demands, partly because they had been compelled to reinforce the Italian troops later in the war."

To be sure I'm understanding this correctly, I offer, "So, this was the 'mutilated victory'? The Italian negotiators failed to receive the territorial concessions promised if the Allies won the war, correct?"

"Yes. Because the negotiators represented the pro-war leftist government at the time, the general consensus was that the liberal ruling class was incompetent and had failed to deliver what was owed to Italy. In the eyes of more moderate public opinion, it was the left that had dragged Italy into the war in the first place. Thus, the liberal state seemed to be unacceptably weak coming out of the war, and the Paris Peace Conference only reinforced that perception. Members of the bourgeoisie and the aristocracy felt resentment against the left. Generally, the Italians felt bitter and disgraced following the Treaty of Versailles." Gabriele takes a breath, and another bite.

Aftermath of the War

Then something else comes to Gabriele's mind. He asks, "Are you aware of what happened next in Italian politics?" He challenges me once again, to my delight.

"At some point we see the rise of Benito Mussolini, right?" I offer.

"Exactly. There was a strong cause-effect relationship between the public's bitter disapproval at the end of the war and the very rapid rise of Fascism. This is probably the greatest irony. Since the liberal ruling class was widely discredited, this opened the door for Fascism to take root. Only three years after the peace treaty, Mussolini's Fascist dictatorship began. The interesting thing is that Mussolini had been a steadfast socialist in his younger years and vehemently against the war. And later, he even served in the Italian army and was wounded. He was a Bersagliere!"

"No kidding, that's amazing," I quip, thinking of what I had already learned about that unit of crack sharpshooters.

Gabriele continues the story. "Eventually, Mussolini completely shifted his position and denounced the socialists. He used the war and its aftermath to his political advantage, greatly fomenting the cause of nationalism to make up for the war's unsatisfactory results. Essentially, Mussolini created a one-party dictatorship and advocated strongly for the creation of an Italian empire. Although somewhat begrudgingly, many Italians went along with his nationalistic message and supported him at the outset. So, the lack of success at the peace conference essentially encouraged the country to move headlong toward Fascism.

Simply astounded, I reflect, "Wow, I never realized how closely Fascism was related to the war. Talk about unintended consequences!" I then make the next logical, if disturbing, connection. "And this would in turn contribute to Italy's next human disaster known as World War II."

Given that our aperitivo plates are nearly empty, we both decide to postpone a discussion about World War II for another time. Our attention turns back to Siena and the Palio. I ask how the war affected the Palio itself.

Gabriele begins, "Since the war concluded officially on November 4, 1918, the first Palio was held the following July of 1919. For that Palio, the bleachers in front of Palazzo Pubblico—you know, where the children sit during the trials—were reserved for wounded soldiers or veterans who had spent time in the hospital." He adds, "And are you familiar with the festive flag-waving ritual of the seventeen contrade that occurs at the conclusion of the corteo storico?"

"Yes, in fact I've been curious about that, thinking it's a sign of good sportsmanship or something," I offer as a guess.

"Well, that is one example of the flag-waving and drum routines known in Siena as the *sbandierata*. It was actually performed for the first time during the July 1919 Palio to honor the soldiers after World War I. The tradition has remained ever since." This specific event is held after the entire corteo storico has made its way around the Campo, just prior to the Palio race. Alfieri from all seventeen contrade line up along the track in front of Palazzo Pubblico and toss their respective flags into the air in immediate succession, one after the other. This aerial performance never fails to impress the crowd.

"OK, so it's like a living memorial," I suggest, to which he ponders briefly and nods. At this news my mouth is hanging open at the thought of an actual

Palio ritual designed to commemorate the war's end. There is no doubt that the festive performance before each race will now have more meaning.

My "living memorial" comment triggers a discussion about a related topic. Gabriele opens with, "The creation of memorials and monuments of various kinds after the war is actually a story in itself. The creation of the first monuments began in 1922. The Siena Province has some 260 monuments devoted to World War I alone." To this impressive number, he adds a caveat. "Some of them were mandated by the national government under the rule of Mussolini, but others were supported more traditionally by family members of the victims to memorialize them."

"So, are you saying that his government was building memorials for political aims?" I respond logically, but with some disappointment.

"Sure, the socialists generally opposed the apparent glorification of the war that was taking place through the building of monuments. Many of the state-sponsored memorials doubled as a celebration of nationalism," Gabriele explains.

The scholar Vanda Wilcox has written further on the extent to which the Fascist regime promoted its agenda of national unification. War memorials and monuments were strategically constructed within the cities and territory where the battles occurred. One prominent example was in the newly Italian town of Caporetto, where the central government constructed a massive monument in 1938. For its part, Caporetto is now called Kobarid and is part of the newly independent nation of Slovenia. Having been occupied by the Germans during World War II, the community was awarded by the Allies to communist Yugoslavia following the war, which in turn was dissolved and broken up in 1991. (Are you following all of this?)

Beyond the traditional memorials, the government went so far as to launch an extensive effort to relocate the interred bodies of the war dead from their original, localized graveyards to more centralized *ossuari* (ossuaries, which were special facilities for storing collective human remains, mainly bones). Dozens of such ossuaries were created throughout the 1930s where the fallen were reinterred. In addition to the pragmatic goal of improving hygiene at the original burial sites, a primary motive of the massive government program was to create "a more homogenous, fascist-sanctioned national memory rather than retaining individual local cemeteries with diverse presentations of the war."[45] Overall, the style and wording of monuments erected during this era reveal a shift from their earlier focus on mourning the casualties to a more "celebrative, triumphalist rhetoric."[46] The main intent was, of course, to glorify the sacrifices of war in the name of national greatness. In fewer words, Mussolini's propaganda-rich Fascist era was off and running.

Victory Speech

With our aperitivo treats long completed, Gabriele offers, "Do you have some time? There is something at Palazzo Pubblico that might interest you." I immediately think, *A bonus field trip? Of course, I have time!* I tell him as much, and we bid the staff farewell.

As the three of us casually walk downslope across the Campo, Gabriele asks, "Have you seen Siena's memorials of the war?"

"No, not yet," I admit, "though I would like to do so if I can find them," I tease, continuing, "I was informed that there is one near Piazza Gramsci by the Garibaldi statue."

He responds, "Yes, that's true. The other one is inside the Church of San Domenico." This throws me off a bit.

"They placed a memorial in a church?" I ask with some surprise. "I was only inside there once before, so I will need to make another visit!" This is the same church—officially a basilica—where the purported physical remains of Santa Caterina are displayed.

With Gabriele steering the way, we find ourselves outside the service entrance to Palazzo Pubblico. This is one of two main entrances to the Palazzo, on the side opposite the Cortile del Podestà, where the presentation of the drappellone was held. Despite numerous, lengthy visits to Siena, this will be my first time entering here. Occasionally we find ourselves in the right place at the right time to see the occasional wedding party emerge from this very portal. At this moment, the entrance area is rather dense with people darting in or out, with some lingering to socialize either immediately inside or outside. Given the entryway's cavernous opening, people are apparently free to come and go as they like.

We take a few steps beyond the threshold of the entryway, and Gabriele motions for us to stop. Nobody seems to be paying attention to our presence, as people are still maneuvering around us or simply standing nearby. While

MUTILATED VICTORY

attempting to stand our ground, he points up above our heads to something on the wall to our left. I glance upward to see a massive, nearly black and poorly lit plaque that is clearly constructed of heavy metal. A substantial amount of Italian text fills up the plaque's imposing face. My first thought is admittedly bizarre: *Why did they put it up there, and inside this darkened entryway?* It is almost as if the Senesi were unsure about where to display it.

Gabriele explains, "This is the victory speech—or the *Bollettino della Vittoria*—from the commanding general, Armando Diaz. He originally gave the speech on 4 November 1918, the day following the last battle of the Italian front, when the Austro-Hungarians laid down their weapons and surrendered for good. The armistice went into effect the next day, when this speech was given."

"Oh, wow. This was the decisive victory for the Italians and Allies, correct?" I ask to confirm.

"Yes, and it is known as the Battle of Vittorio Veneto." Under the command of Diaz, it was this final offensive that led to the surrender of Austria-Hungary. It marked the end of the Austro-Hungarian Empire and caused Germany to surrender one week later to end the entire war," he concludes, then also adds thoughtfully, "Of course, the Italians were still reeling from all of the failed and poorly led offensives before that. So, the central government was desperate to demonstrate how this final success led to Italy's decisive victory in the war. But the reality was bittersweet."

"This is really remarkable," I react, staring upward with my mouth open. "But why is this here in Siena?" I can't help but wonder how this massive plaque ended up in one of Italy's smaller cities.

"Well, these plaques were copied and sent to every Italian city. They were even placed into schools, and children were expected to memorize the speech." Then with a grin, he adds, "As one final insult to the enemy, the plaques were apparently forged with metal melted down from captured Austrian military equipment."

"Well, of course! I wouldn't expect any less," I smile sarcastically, referring to the creative if arrogant reuse of enemy hardware. I then add, "Having children memorize the speech seems similar to our own Pledge of Allegiance in the United States. Although, our pledge is much shorter! I can't imagine anyone memorizing this whole thing. Whoever wrote this speech was on a roll," I joke.

At this point, Gabriele, Mike, and I decide to part ways for the evening after I offer my sincere gratitude for spending so much time with me to improve my fuzzy understanding.

As for the victory speech, it consists of a rather unexpectedly detailed—if grossly hyperbolic—account of the final Italian offensive of Vittorio Veneto and its conclusion. It is not difficult to imagine General Diaz gloating smugly as he concluded with his final line:

> The remnants of what was one of the world's most powerful armies are returning in hopelessness and chaos up the valleys from which they had descended with boastful confidence.

Perhaps such pomposity is understandable, given the raw passion and pent-up frustration that Diaz was undoubtedly channeling from the armed forces as the fighting wound down. It is the first line of his speech, however, that may have served as a more appropriate, somewhat less bombastic conclusion to this tragic chapter in Italian history. To that end, those summative words are offered here to conclude this chapter:

> The war against Austria-Hungary, which the Italian Army, inferior in number and equipment, began on 24 May 1915 under the leadership of His Majesty and supreme leader the King and conducted with unwavering faith and tenacious bravery without rest for 41 months, is won.

CHAPTER 7

Generations Apart

THE NEXT MORNING, I TAKE A PLASTIC CHAIR OPPOSITE ANTONIO IN HIS SMALL office. I hardly need to ask my friend about the Straordinario; he is already reading my mind. For his part, Antonio practically embodies the collective spirit of the Goose contrada, living and breathing it every day in the shadow of Fontebranda. We had met a few years ago, during a visit with our students to the contrada museum and oratorio. Beyond his excellent command of English, he is a natural teacher and enjoys expounding on the Palio and contrada to those he believes are genuinely interested. Fortunately, I had met his standard. He once told me that he does not invite just anyone or any group into the contrada, and he has found an easy customer with me, someone who is never hesitant to hear his latest stories and perspectives. When I find him in his office this morning, he needs only a few seconds to move beyond the pleasantries and get down to talking about the Straordinario. I quickly discover that there is a lot on his mind right now.

A Myriad of Concerns

"This situation is very strange," Antonio begins simply, though in a serious tone. "Nobody was expecting to hold a Palio this soon. The contracts with the jockeys end in August, after the second Palio," he explains. "There are a lot of complications now, as there are no previous negotiations with the jockeys, which we would normally have. So, we have to begin negotiations all over again." Antonio throws up his hands in mild frustration and looks directly at me. "Normally, we would make the decision to hold a Straordinario in May or June, so we could all plan for the entire year."

"Oh, I see," I tell him and nod in understanding. Antonio is verifying Dario's earlier comment regarding the short amount of time available to plan.

GENERATIONS APART

I ask, "So, how is it different for the preparations in the contrada now that the Goose is going to run?"

"Well, what is very strange is that our people are not talking about the Palio as much because we can't discuss the horses and jockeys as we normally would do," he reflects. "Fewer people will likely come to the dinners because the excitement has not been built up in advance. Plus, a lot of people used their vacation time for the summer races, so more people have to work this week. And the children have school, so weekly schedules will be keeping people away."

"Hmm, that makes sense," I say out loud as I start to understand the complexities. "So, what you are saying is that the contrada dinners are important for generating enthusiasm?"

"Well, of course!" Antonio has no problem being direct with me. "The dinners are very important to create excitement around the Palio. Without the dinners, the Palio is much less meaningful. They create a social—how do you say, festive—atmosphere that brings the contrada together. So, these dinners won't provide the same feeling. And if the weather is cold, fewer people will come, even with the tents. We have tents set up, but not everybody will be able to hear the head table speeches, and there aren't as many seats available."

This last topic surprises me a bit, though it really shouldn't. I had certainly wondered how the contrade would plan for dinners in mid-October with uncertain weather and temperatures. We nearly froze to death in the Panther two years earlier, and that was on July 1 with an atypical cold front moving through. It seems that the Goose and other contrade are investing in circus-type tents to shelter their cautious attendees. They would otherwise be exposed to the elements for several hours on these rapidly cooling autumn nights.

What intrigues me more, however, is how the contrada dinners play such a significant role in fostering a social atmosphere. This makes inherent sense, though I had never heard anyone mention this direct connection. The Palio is an opportunity for socialization and community building, and it happens to conclude with an admittedly hair-raising ninety-second race.

Antonio briefly glances at some paperwork, then starts again. "Another concern is about the horses, because they are not used to training or racing this time of year."

"Oh, I hadn't thought about the training schedule. So, it's not easy to prepare the horses quickly?" I ask.

"No, not at all, it's very complicated." He then adds, "Did you notice, there are fewer horses that were checked out by the veterinarian last week? Fewer horses were provided by their owners for this Palio than usual, and so there were not as many horses assessed by the veterinarian. This must mean that owners have concerns about entering their horses for various reasons."

City leadership has likewise been apprehensive about the training of horses at this time of year. One online news story highlighted the municipality's dilemma with the "physical condition of the horses," especially with respect to their extra training, "given that almost all of them had slowed down after the Assumption," referring to the August Palio.[47] Even the practice track in Mociano, typically used to train the horses for the summer Palii, is a point of concern. That track is usually closed for the season by September. Recently, inspectors revisited the site to assess its viability to remain open a few days a week; hopefully, they are allowing owners and jockeys to use the facility.

Beyond re-opening the practice track, a fundamental problem revolves around the protection of the erodible dirt track in the Campo from inclement weather. During the summer, approximately one week before the race, the Campo is transformed almost overnight from a romantic public space to an intimidating racetrack. A relentless circuit of dump trucks deposits a carefully prepared mixture of turf around the perimeter of the Campo. Steamrollers quickly follow to uniformly tamp down the fresh earth. Much of this conversion of the Campo occurs almost magically overnight, to the point where I have told Linda that "Santa Claus showed up last night." Over a multiyear period, I have occasionally managed to find myself in the path of the dump-truck parade along Via Pantaneto or I've positioned myself along the barriers in the Campo to watch the steamrollers do their work. In the typical case of warm and dry weather, the steamrollers are followed in turn with employees bearing water hoses to better pack down the turf. During this time, no one is permitted to walk on the track, so mobility in and around the Campo is severely impeded. After the turf is laid down, the mixture is carefully monitored for consistent composition and moisture content. The Palio turf is more than just any old dirt that was scooped up and thrown in a truck; it is a special blend of materials deemed ideal for this purpose, scrupulously tended to until race day.

Among numerous other things, how to protect the track from typical October weather has likewise given city officials reason to pause.[48] Of course, the track's condition holds important implications for the safety of the horses. For instance, a debate has raged for years in Siena about whether the track should be covered with a protective tarp. The topic has understandably surfaced especially during Palio seasons that prove rainier than average. A few years ago, it became necessary to truck in additional turf to replace some of the original track, which was being unceremoniously washed down into the sewers. To "walk" through the Campo became a serious exercise in mud control, making for a colossal mess following several days of solid rain.

Now, for this Straordinario, the debate over covering the turf has arisen once again. Soon after the official approval to hold the event, city leaders and personnel began considering the feasibility of various options to protect the track. Those with opinions on the subject have typically fallen into two broad camps—those who believe that any type of cover would violate sacrosanct traditions, and those who argue for some kind of protection, given recent hassles with Mother Nature. According to the local media, the municipality is taking this issue very seriously, first by exploring the wide variety of options that might exist. Numerous technical issues have likewise been considered, not the least being the type and form of tarp to use, such as those deployed on top of soccer fields. In contrast, various less invasive and differently colored solutions have been considered. More technical approaches have also been discussed, such as an inflatable rollers, which spread across the track when necessary and can be retracted. The apparent tradeoff is their bulkiness, necessitating the follow-up decision of where to place them. Beyond that, questions arise about whether the entire track should be covered, or only the more treacherous curves. At this point, all prior discussion may be moot, anyway. No such covers have made an appearance in the Campo this week.

Choosing the Horses

One might wonder how horses are chosen for the Palio. Antonio's comment about the veterinarian refers to the first step of a rather complex process. As directed by the city's rigorous protocols for the treatment and training of horses, the first stop for any owner who wishes to submit a horse for consideration is at the *previsite* (veterinary assessments). These initial tests occur at the city's approved veterinary clinic, Il Ceppo, at least several weeks before the race. Horses can and do get rejected at this phase, even before they touch the turf in the Campo. The number of horses registered for the previsite can surpass 100, as with the 106 steeds that were assessed for the most recent, August 2018 Palio. In comparison, only 45 were registered this time, a notable reduction for the Straordinario, as Antonio has indicated.

Then Antonio says something even more telling. "Did you see the prove regolamentate this morning?" He is referring to the next step in testing the horses that have been approved by the veterinarian. This is the first time that the Senesi have a chance to see the potential horses trot around the track in the Campo.

I respond regretfully, "No, I had to miss it due to another appointment. How did it go?"

"Well, you're not the only one," he says comfortingly, though in a tone signaling some frustration. "There were barely any people in the Campo; it was nearly empty. It was not festive or emotional like normal," he observes, then quickly adds an afterthought, "and it was later in the morning this time. It's not like it was held at sunrise!"

"Yes, that's true," I reflect. "I've attended that event when it was very early in the morning! I was surprised how late it was today, though I imagine it was pushed back for the shorter day length."

The prove regolamentate were known up until recently as the *prove di notte* (night trials), and are still occasionally referred to as such. The summer versions are held at an annoyingly early time of day, between 6:00 and 7:00 a.m., just as dawn is starting to break across Siena. Despite my sleepy eyes, I have managed to drag myself to at least two of these events out of sheer curiosity, if nothing else. Horse owners and jockeys use the track to practice various skills without the stress of the actual racing conditions. Not long ago, the night trials lived up to their name. Jockeys brought horses to the Campo in secrecy to run the track in the dead of night, hoping not to publicly divulge any special skills a particular horse might bring to the Palio.

My first experience with the 6:00 a.m. edition a few years ago proved startling for two reasons. First, the streets of Siena were still pin-drop silent around that time in the calm, muggy (if pleasantly chilly) morning air.

GENERATIONS APART

Immediately upon turning into the Campo from a side street, however, it seemed as though I had suddenly entered an alternate universe and time zone. The mood turned instantly from tranquil to festive, with an accompanying human energy level more typical of daytime. People more awake than me were already in the bleachers, while others in the center of the Campo were conversing and peripherally screening the action. It was one of the most surreal scenes I have ever witnessed.

My second observation was that many of the younger people in attendance were clearly inebriated from challenging themselves to pull "all-nighters" before the trials began at sunrise. Because many of them were up beyond midnight already, their logic was to stay awake for a few hours longer until the first Palio event. The result, I somewhat shockingly discovered, was a tired Campo littered high with various trash, beer cans, and wine bottles. The scene looked like the aftermath of a small tornado with its devastating trail of debris.

However, it is also quite possible that I had unwittingly witnessed Siena's very last occurrence of this questionable tradition. My follow-up experience one year later found a much cleaner Campo with a greater police presence. I suspect that the city administration had lost its patience with having their esteemed public space defiled by the overnight trash of idealistic youth.

Although they still occur one day before the standard four days of the Palio, the prove regolamentate still tend to attract a good number of Senesi. Some tourists will also hang around to check out the latest pool of steeds. The circling of the Campo by the horses provides the first truly emotional indication that the Palio has finally arrived at the city's doorstep.

Of the forty-five horses assessed at Il Ceppo last week, thirty-four were approved to continue in the selection process. Of these, six advanced straight to the tratta, which means they were already accepted as semifinalists and were consequently allowed to skip this morning's prove regolamentate. All six have raced at least one previous Palio, so they are considered experienced enough to move on to the next round of testing. Of those six, however, only one has ever claimed a Palio victory—the now-legendary Porto Alabe. Designated recently with the lighthearted recognition as Siena's 2018 *Horse of the Year*, Porto Alabe has won the last two August Palii in a row. This included, as Dario discussed earlier, the most recent victory for the She-Wolf contrada.

With some presumed assistance by its jockey, Giussepe Zedde (nicknamed Gingillo), Porto Alabe not only won the race, but he did so even though he was the rincorsa, or tenth position. This feat is something rarely accomplished and requires an especially strong animal. As the only horse in contention that has won a Palio—let alone two—there is no question that Porto Alabe will be the star attraction and most desired competitor should he be chosen after the prove regolamentate.

As for the remaining twenty-eight horses approved by the veterinarian, they were more thoroughly tested this morning to determine which ones would move on to tomorrow's *tratta* with Porto Alabe and his friends. Essentially kicking off the days of the Palio, tomorrow's tratta will test the remaining horses that advance from today's prove regolamentate. Media outlets are predicting that approximately twenty-five horses will be involved in the tratta, which is also uncharacteristically low. Following the tratta, the captains of all ten contrade running in the Palio will make their collective final decision on which ten horses will race, thereby completing a dizzying array of tests.

To summarize this elaborate process, horses must advance through three testing phases—the previsite, the prove regolamentate, and the tratta—before being selected to race. The process is quite involved, perhaps not entirely unlike America's March Madness for the annual college basketball tournament. Few visitors to Siena likely realize these behind-the-scenes efforts when they see the final ten horses race the Palio.

Voting for the Straordinario

Beyond Antonio's concerns about attendance, I shift our focus to the original rationale for holding this week's Palio. I ask, "Given the challenges with October at this point, do you think it was a bad idea to hold a Palio to commemorate the Great War?"

After thinking a bit, he offers, "The reason for holding the Palio—to commemorate the end of the war—is actually worth it, I believe. Siena has always taken that war very seriously, and the city and contrade have monuments to remember the people who played a role. In fact, are you aware of the sbandierata that is held before the race in the Campo?"

"Oh, yes. I have seen it, and I was told about it yesterday. It was added to commemorate the end of the war, right?"

"Sure, exactly," he confirms. "All seventeen contrade are represented, and they perform flag routines. Like you said, this was added at the end of the war to recognize and honor the veterans. It is typically very difficult to change Palio traditions, but they did it for this. It then became popular, so the city continues the practice today. I think this is evidence that the city is intent on remembering the war. So, no, it's not a bad idea in itself," he concludes.

Then he reflects further. "The reasons for concern are more practical right now. I already mentioned the concerns with training the horses. Also, Siena has never held a Palio in late October, and the city has not even organized a Straordinario in the past eighteen years. It takes a lot of time to organize, and taking chances on the weather is really risky," he states with some visible seriousness.

Antonio's perspectives on the October timeframe are contrary to those of Dario, who believed that October would be the ideal month. Of course, this is a matter of opinion, depending upon one's preference for summer versus autumn. Regardless, I ask, "So, was this the reason why the Goose voted against it?" I have absolutely no forewarning that Antonio is about to launch into the topics of contrada politics and strategizing.

He begins, "Sure, the weather was an issue, but there were other arguments being made against the Palio. The Goose typically votes against such events. We are generally one of the more conservative, right-wing contrade in Siena. Now, our rival, the Tower, tends to be more left-wing. Unlike us, the Tower tends to vote in favor of these. Although, even the Tower voted 'no' this time, but their vote was very close—I believe decided by not many votes at all," he says rather analytically.

Now he has me intrigued, yet more confused. "Why do the politics matter with respect to voting trends?" I ask hopefully.

"So, basically the Tower is more interested in trying to win. This is not to—how do you say, boast—but the history of Palio wins is heavily in favor of the Goose right now. For much of the last century, we have won maybe twenty Palii, and the Tower maybe four or five." He glances upward to reflect on victory numbers. "We have more to lose if our rival wins a Straordinario, so we vote more conservatively. This time, our captain and other leaders discouraged the members from voting in favor, and they explained why. They had numerous reasons, but basically they did not want to give the Tower a chance. And you might remember that the Tower did in fact win most recently in 2015. So, to give them another chance would not be a good thing for our contrada."

Wow, I think to myself while indicting that I understand. *The contrada rivalries are a factor in the voting that I had not considered.*

Antonio continues, almost as an afterthought, "Then there were the other practical reasons. For example, we are not in negotiations with a jockey right now. And the weather, the training of the horses, and those types of things." He waves them off.

"That's fascinating—that you are concerned about your rival's chances. What was the final vote in the contrada, if I may ask?"

"Roughly 2 to 1, about 246 against to 150 in favor," he recalls.

"So, who were the people who voted in favor—and against the wishes of your leaders?" I chuckle.

He responds immediately, "The young people. The voting age is sixteen, so they were interested in having the ... *festa*—the party," he says definitively. A lot of them do not understand the practical reasons and what all is involved." *Wow*, I think again. Antonio is suggesting a generational divide of some kind.

A Generational Paradox

I must now ask the big question that is on my mind. "Do you think the rationale of the Great War was a factor for some who voted 'yes' or 'no'?"

"No, it didn't matter," he says conclusively, as I let out a laugh at this candid response. Likely also detecting the expression of wonder on my face, he continues. "The result was the opposite of what you might think. The older generation is more inclined to appreciate the rationale for the Straordinario, since their grandparents were involved in the war, and there is more of an emotional connection. Also, Siena held an event recently when the letters from soldiers and families were read aloud at a ceremony. It was all very emotional. So, Siena already holds events like this to help remember World War I, and older people did not feel we needed a Palio to do the same thing."

While I absorb all of this, he adds, "But then there are the younger people who are less emotionally connected to the war. To them, the war seems to be

GENERATIONS APART

much more distant and further in the past, and so they can't comprehend its significance as clearly. And yet, they were the ones who generally voted for the Straordinario!" He laughs and shakes his head. "This is the opposite of what you might expect," he concludes. "I really don't understand it."

With this insight, the proverbial light bulb triggers in my head. Perhaps without realizing it, Antonio just identified a significant paradox associated with the decision to hold the Palio. It appears for now that the contradaioli with the closest emotional connection to the war were primarily the ones to vote against it, while those most emotionally distant—the younger people—voted more in favor of the idea.

I respond, "So, do you believe that your leaders and their arguments actually influenced the vote within the contrada? I mean, do people tend to listen to them?" I chuckle, essentially asking to what extent their leadership can influence the larger population.

"Oh yes, I think a lot of us agreed with them about the possible problems involved with organizing a Palio in such a short period of time," he confirms. "And we did not want to give the Tower a chance. I am happy that our leaders took responsibility for explaining their reasons to everyone." Now more animated, Antonio continues along this train of thought. "I know that other captains and leaders in other contrade did not explain their concerns to their people. Why would they be against it and not explain their reasons? Even though they voiced opposition to the idea, they just stood aside and said nothing." Antonio's hands are waving in the air now with shoulders shrugging. "Why would they not explain such things? The people just voted the way they wanted anyway, so the leaders were not doing their job." As if wrapping up a closing argument in court, he concludes, "You need to use your head, if you're a captain or leader. Explain to your people what the issues are, so they can make a better decision that makes sense. Without direction, the people voted 'yes.'"

After absorbing this perspective, I provide a hypothetical situation, quite off the top of my head. "What if only the captains and contrada leadership were able to vote, without the general public? Do you think the Palio would have been approved?" Rather than stumping him as I expected, he provides a definitive answer.

"Seventeen to nothing, against. They all vote 'no.'" he asserts, while slapping a hand on the desk.

"Really, wow!" I react, with nothing more intelligent to say, aside from my blank stare.

He continues, "Sure, none of the leaders that I know were in favor of it. And of course, only ten contrade actually voted 'yes,' so the whole thing came very close to not being approved."

"So, whether Siena really wants it or not, you're getting a Palio!" I proclaim facetiously with a sly grin. "With so many unknowns, maybe it will be fun," I add, attempting to lighten his skeptical mood.

My own optimism aside, additional evidence exists to support Antonio's generational observations. One influential Senese was recently interviewed about his thoughts on the Straordinario, none other than former mayor Pierluigi Piccini, who presided over the city during its most recent Straordinario on September 9, 2000.[49] As a point of historical interest, he confirmed that the 2000 race was the last ever to use thoroughbred horses. Early in 2001, a new regulation was approved to only allow half-bred horses to compete, with the main goal of reducing equine injuries. Thoroughbred horses are considered more fragile and less capable of negotiating the hazardous track unharmed. Thus, the very next Palio, in July 2001, was the first to deploy only half-bred horses that were stronger and more suitable for the challenging circuit. During Piccini's time in office, the city council had further worked to improve the standard ingredients and conditions required for the turf. Such revelations only confirm that the Palio, with all of its cherished traditions, still evolves and grows with the times.

Beyond reminiscing, Piccini reflected on his own concerns for the future of Siena's prized event. He believed, for instance, that "the climate has changed toward the Palio," as his interviewer quoted him. He explained, "I think this is becoming a race with less ritual, and this needs to be reintroduced as the norm. If there are no ritual processes, then this merely becomes a festival." Piccini further compared the planning for this current Straordinario with that of the year 2000. He recalled that work began during the previous February to plan ahead with all interested parties involved. There was a unified belief, he continued, that everyone needed to know about the Straordinario well in advance and that it should be run no later than September. "These, in my opinion, are the normal procedures, and are the correct ones, because the Palii are run in the summer. It is necessary that the contrade know about this before the two normal Palii, from my point of view."

GENERATIONS APART

This was certainly no ringing endorsement for how the current Straordinario is being handled. Not only was the late decision highly irregular, he believed, but it was also inappropriate for this later time of year.

Perhaps more controversial was a speech that Piccini delivered and later published on the Internet. In his "Extraordinary Palio: Emblem of a Populist Drift," he laid out a cautionary statement about the potential future of the Palio. Piccini believed that the Palio was is in danger of becoming less a meaningful tradition and more a product for consumption, and it was primarily the younger generation that was driving this trend. He argued, in part "The Palio . . . is reduced to simple goods to consume, provided as a meal not only to tourists but also to the Senesi." From his perspective, the Palio—with this upcoming Straordinario a case in point—was at risk of being reduced to a mere diversion, an event that "loses its value" and "becomes a meaningless race."

If those sentiments were not enough to spawn local debate, his next statement about the upcoming Straordinario would ultimately do the trick. He claimed, "This is why the administration itself has emphasized, positively, the presence of many 'young people' to vote, a new generation that looks little to the future but [relies upon] an empty tradition, looking for some reassurance. In reality, it is this generation that has become, certainly not just for local responsibilities, a consumer."[50] As one might imagine, little time was required for a flurry of counterarguments to appear on social media, especially from younger Senesi who found Piccini's comments offensive to their generation.

Whatever one's perspective on the future of the Palio, it is now readily apparent that the Senesi do not simply rise in one collective voice in favor of a Straordinario whenever somebody proposes one. It might be tempting to presume that any excuse for another Palio would be met with cheering and fists in the air across Siena. Rather, the opposite appears to be true. Dario had already indicated that previous proposals for such events had also been rejected, and this one nearly met the same fate. What this tells me is that Siena takes its Palii—and the reasons for holding them—very seriously. The existence of a possible generational shift, whether real or imagined, or—more likely—somewhere in between, is only adding to the intrigue of Siena's ongoing community discussion.

Dissecting the Vote

After shuffling a few papers and checking a text message, Antonio mentions almost out of the blue, "I really don't understand why other contrade voted 'yes.'" Somewhat perplexed, I am thinking that he already explained this; certain leaders apparently preferred a hands-off approach and did not interfere with the wishes of their constituents. Beyond this factor, however, he is thinking more about Palio strategy rather than moral or practical reasoning. "Look at the Panther," he offers, my ears perking up at his attention to the contrada I know best. "They are risking a lot because they are giving the Eagle a chance to win a Palio that they didn't have before. The Eagle is the nonna!" Antonio emphasizes, applying the derogatory title given to the contrada that has endured the longest time without a Palio win.

Antonio continues, looking me in the eye. "Why would the Panther want to do that? A rival like the Eagle has a lot of money at its disposal because it hasn't won for so long. So, the rival has the advantage, and the Panther is weak in comparison. Why is their leadership not explaining this to the people?" While shrugging my shoulders, I make a mental note to ask this very question when I meet with various Panterini (members of the Panther contrada) later this week. Antonio then turns his focus to others. "And the Turtle—why vote 'yes'? They are also giving a chance to its rival, the Snail, which hasn't won in about twenty years. This makes no sense to me."

It strikes me as fascinating that a rival contrada's status might be one of the more important factors in a decision about whether to hold a Straordinario. Until today, I had naively believed that each contrada would vote primarily based on whether the idea to commemorate World War I was appropriate. I should have considered, however, that the factors collectively contributing to a contrada's decision are multifaceted and complex.

However, this discussion would not be complete without an analysis of the second, follow-up vote that was held. I can't resist asking Antonio about his thoughts about this part of the decision process. "I am aware that there was a second vote allowed for those contrade that voted 'no,'" I begin. "Do you believe the second vote was a good idea?"

"Well, it was basically meaningless," he surprises me yet again. "The seven that voted 'no' felt compelled to join the Palio anyway. Once the Palio was officially approved by the ten contrade that voted 'yes,' the ones that voted 'no' were given five days to change their vote. Now that they knew the Straordinario would in fact be held, of course they reversed their decision and voted to be a part of it," he grins.

Still admittedly confused as to the logic here, I press onward. "Why did they feel compelled to join? If the She-Wolf or Dragon wanted to remain out of the race due to their recent victories or lack of funds, why not continue to vote 'no'?" I am basically curious as to why those initial concerns would no longer matter.

Antonio provides a scenario to help me understand. "OK, if you are the She-Wolf, or even us, the Goose, which first voted 'no,' and you know that the Straordinario will be run, what happens if you vote 'no' again? You might be the only contrada to do so, because you don't know how the other ones are voting. You will be left out of the pick (extraction). You are giving your rival a chance to win, without you in the Campo to possibly disrupt them. The She-Wolf is in a good place right now, with three recent victories. The last thing they want to do is give the Porcupine a chance after the She-Wolf just won in August. The same is true with us. We don't want to give the Tower a chance, knowing that we will not have the same opportunity. And for us it worked out OK, because both the Goose and Tower were picked to run. We each have a chance to win and also to disrupt each other."

Reflecting on this logic, I confirm, "So, what you are saying is that there is no good reason to vote 'no' the second time?"

"Yes, that is correct. The only way for a contrada to vote 'no' the second time would be to contact its rival and ask *them* to vote 'no.' This comes from a position of weakness. And there is no guarantee that the rival will agree. And if they do agree, your contrada's leadership has to explain to the people why you negotiated with the rival and are giving up your chance. The whole process would be very difficult. We had to vote 'yes.'"

What I am learning here, it seems, is that the contrada rivalries can hold a significant influence on whether to hold a Straordinario. Still, as Antonio pondered aloud, this is not necessarily the leading factor for all contrade. Others—like the Panther, Turtle, and Owl—voted "yes" the first time, even though their rivals have not won a Palio recently and are more desperate to do so. Something else must be persuading these other contrade to embrace the idea.

With that, I offer my gratitude to Antonio for sharing his time and knowledge, and I leave him to his business. From here, I decide to walk down to Fontebranda, curious to see how the Goose is protecting their outdoor dinner area from inclement weather. During the warmth and humidity of summer, one typically approaches this special place to find a sea of green- and red-colored tablecloths in advance of the nightly contrada dinners.

As I clomp down the steeply pitched Via di Santa Caterina where we celebrated with the Goose six years earlier, my eyes light up at the strangeness of the scene. *Oh my word*, I think, *Antonio was not kidding*. A collection of circus-type tents unfolds in front of me. I count at least four tents of various sizes and orientations, which completely alter the normal landscape around Fontebranda (Figure 3). One of the tents is located across the street, presumably for cooking and preparations. The Goose has clearly not left anything to chance. I now understand why the contrade are generally concerned about their respective dinner plans this week. The infrastructure for the traditional dinners alone is—to hazard an expression—over the top. This scene would simply be unthinkable during the summer, when thousands of contrada members gather together in the open air.

Speaking of food and dinners, the timing of my arrival here is auspicious. Just to the opposite side of the Goose's tent city awaits a most important event—lunch.

Figure 3. Dinner tents for the Goose contrada, adjacent to Siena's ancient water supply of Fontebranda. (Photo: Author)

Lunch in the Goose

In a setting that might seem somewhat strange for a medieval city, I am meeting two friends today at a restaurant called La Cricca Quattro, found within a more modern, standalone structure just off Via di Fontebranda. What it lacks in historic charm is more than compensated for by its sense of community and friendly atmosphere. Its management and clientele alike tend to hail from the Goose, not a big surprise given its location across from Fontebranda. This is a place for local contrada members to eat some lunch or dinner while catching up with friends. The owner and his staff are often seen conversing with patrons, many of whom they likely know well.

For these reasons, I applaud the decision of my friend, Donald, to alight here for an early afternoon meal. Don is an American who spends probably half of each year living and working in Siena while leading student groups in various capacities, so he is not fully an expatriate. Our respective programs in recent years are what initially brought us together. We are joined by another mutual friend, Alessandro (Alex), a middle-aged, lifelong member of the Wave contrada.

It is already early afternoon, and I'm hungry enough for a heaping pasta dish rather than the typically lighter salad. We thus all choose similar primi piatti as Don and Alex chat with the waiter, whom I believe also owns the place. With orders settled, I open with, "I really wasn't planning to come back to Siena so soon!" They chuckle in response to my sarcasm. I follow with, "Did anyone here in Siena know about the Straordinario before September?"

"Ha—nobody knew," responds Don. "The proposal for the Palio arrived from the Assoarma to City Hall on August 28. It went through a series of approvals, but it's all been very recent."

His response triggers discussion of a larger issue. "So, what I don't understand is why a national military organization would know anything about the Palio here, let alone want Siena to hold one," I mention quizzically.

Don replies without hesitation. "It was definitely political."

"Really? On who's part?" I prod.

"The city administration—the mayor. You were here in July, right? He was recently elected, and he happens to be the first right-wing mayor here since World War II—the first time ever in democratic Italy. I think he and his administration want to show that they can organize a Palio on short notice."

"That's interesting," I say with raised eyebrows. "It seems like there is a lot of risk involved, should something not work out well," I add.

"Yes, that could be, though it seems that they wanted to take the risk. Around the time of the original proposal, somebody found an email message that showed how someone from City Hall made a suggestion to the Assoarma to propose a Palio. It was in the media for a few days."

"Oh, wow, that's something else. That would explain the sudden proposal, however," I admit with a grin.

"Well, it got more suspicious when the email was redacted later and then explained away as a mistake." All three of us laugh. "Whatever the truth is, the idea is out there now, so people I know are just assuming that it was a political motive to hold the Palio."

While considering this revelation, I turn to Alex, who is as dedicated to the Wave contrada as Antonio is to the Goose. Fortunately, both the Wave and

GENERATIONS APART

Goose are friendly to one another because they share a common rival: the Tower contrada. I ask, "What was the voting process in the Wave? Was it a close vote to hold the Straordinario?"

"No, the Wave was highly opposed to the Palio," Alex begins. "The vote was something like eighty percent against to twenty percent in favor."

I react, "Wow, so you had five days to change your minds, right?"

"Well, yes. But the Wave and the Snail actually held our two votes on the same night—first, to decide on the Palio. And second, if the Palio is approved, should we include ourselves in it. Usually these are separate meetings, but in this case, they were included in the same night. So, we voted 'no,' then 'yes.'" We all laugh at his simplified summary.

I then ask them the same question I asked Antonio earlier today, regarding the various anxieties about holding the Palio. Don responds first. "There are big concerns with the horses and track." He then provides a fresh insight I had not yet considered. "We need to think of the horses as athletes. They have a training season, similar to humans." My eyebrows rise with this comparison, which seems to confirm what Antonio was saying earlier. He further explains, "They even have special diets that change with the seasons, and there is an off-season during winter. For example, there is one horse owned by someone I know that is fifteen kilograms heavier than it was this summer." I snicker while imagining a racehorse becoming a couch potato and kicking back a pint of gelato. He continues, "Some owners are not even willing to offer their horses for this event because there is too much risk and too little time to prepare. Some of the horses might even be ridden by the jockeys who own them, to make up for the lack of participation."

Alex jumps in with a related thought, in this case about weather conditions. "What happens if it rains and the track stays wet at night? This time of year, there is less daylight and less daytime heating to dry it out in time for the next morning. In summer, this is not so much a problem as the dirt can dry quickly."

"Yes, of course! That makes sense," I say excitedly, reminded of my education in climatology. I add in agreement, "There is less chance for evaporation to occur at night when it cools down so much."

Alex continues his train of thought. "Right, and even without the rain, there is a lot more dew on the ground this time of year, so that would impact the track in the morning. If you can't run the tratta, then how are you going to hold the drawing of the horses immediately after that?" Thanks to Alex's logic, I am now considering why typical climate conditions may not be the most ideal for an October Palio after all.

The apparent end to a discussion about moisture provides an opening to ask a favorite question. "With these concerns, who were the people who voted 'yes' in the Wave?"

Alex says without thinking, "It was the younger people mostly. They were excited about holding another Palio." This corroborates the earlier claims of both Antonio and Dario.

I follow up with, "So, do you think there is a generational change taking place? Is the younger generation likely to favor such events in the future, do you think?"

Don jumps in first. "I don't think it's an actual generational change that's taking place. It's more that the young people just simply don't get it." We laugh collectively at this blunt assertion. "But this is to be expected. They don't consider the potential factors and challenges involved with such a complex event. They tend to be more idealistic, so they aren't thinking practically." Don is suggesting that there is less of an actual cultural shift occurring as some might believe. Rather, a more natural contrast is at play here, between the wisdom that comes with age and the idealism associated with youth.

Alex jumps in with his own example. "We have a choice. We can vote rationally with our head," he says while pointing to his own, "or we can vote with emotion—irrationally, with this." He points to his stomach area to indicate a "gut" decision. I nod in understanding. "So, rationally with my head, I voted against the Palio, because it probably is not a good idea. But here (pointing to stomach), this is telling me that I am looking forward to the event and the excitement of the festa." Alex's introspection may indicate that he and other contradaioli are actually quite torn over the idea. It may not have been their first, or wisest, choice to hold an additional Palio this late in the year, but at this point they might as well enjoy the rare occasion and hope for the best.

Before my companions and I part ways for other obligations, I can't resist asking about the controversy over the drappellone. Alex responds first, indicating his own distaste. "The artwork isn't emotional enough. There's no symbolism that links it to the city. And the woman on the banner is like . . . Cinderella." We chortle in response to this comparison. Emboldened, Alex continues. "I have a grandmother who never wore dresses like that. But yes, my main problem is that it could easily represent any city that holds a Palio."

Don agrees, while adding his own interpretation. "Well, everybody always has an opinion about the banner, but only until the race," he explains, chuckling at his own thought. "The truth is that any contrada will be happy to have it. There is always a lot of arguing and discussion about the banner up until the Palio. Then it all stops. Everyone forgets about it." Alex and I consider these remarks while nodding in agreement. This seems to support the common Senese idiom: "We will also take it white."

While we settle the bill at the counter, Don converses in Italian with the restaurant owner. After they banter a bit, Don turns to me and explains, "The owner doesn't have any information about the prova regolamentate this morning because nobody went!" We both laugh at the thought. He then gestures to a table of men that has since attracted Alex to visit. Being somewhat of a regular here, Alex likely knows some of them and is stopping to greet them. After listening in from afar, Don says, while holding his chin, "Hmm, they're talking about the jockeys. It all seems like speculation at this point."

I respond, "I guess that's because there wasn't much time for negotiations between the jockeys and the contrade, right?"

"Yes, that's true. Usually by early summer many of the contrade already have contracts lined up with the jockeys. This time they kind of have to start over," Don confirms.

After Alex returns, the three of us say our goodbyes for now, and we part ways. I head past the Goose tents once again and begin the steep ascent up Via di Fontebranda, along the street where Linda and I lived during our first two summers here. In place of the expected pangs of nostalgia, however, my head is focused on the upcoming Palio and the complexities of making it work. Now on the eve of the four traditional days of the Palio, it is becoming clear that nearly everyone is finding themselves outside of their comfort zones—and lacking information from their fellow contradaioli.

I thus take stock of the current situation. The horses are not accustomed to racing in October, and at least some of their owners are ruminating about unpredictable conditions and training needs. As for the jockeys and the contrada leaders who hire them, negotiations must begin anew. And for their part, parents of Senese youth have been challenged with how to handle school responsibilities, and teachers are apparently resigning themselves to expect conspicuous absences from the contrada youth later this week. Moreover, many employed adults are hard-pressed to find additional vacation time, and others have already planned to be out of town for some or all of the events. Then there are the contrada and società leaders who are spending money on tents and related contingencies should the weather take a turn for the worse. Meanwhile, the municipality has been forced to determine creative approaches to pay for an additional Palio that nobody expected two months earlier.

No wonder that Siena hasn't held one of these events in eighteen years—and they may not do so again for quite some time. All of this only confirms the extent to which the two summer Palii are so intricately engrained within Siena's annual rhythm and cycle of doing things. The Senesi are really out of their comfort zone with this one, almost as if they have been magically beamed into another time zone and are attempting to adjust to a new reality. Regardless, the days of the Palio are here. Tomorrow we head into the tratta, followed by the assignment of the horses to the ten contrade. I quietly utter one thought as I lumber up the hill: *Buckle up, everyone. It's going to be fun!*

❋ CHAPTER 8 ❋

Assignment of the Horses

THE TRADITIONAL FOUR DAYS OF THE PALIO KICKED OFF EARLIER TODAY UNDER our first cloudy skies of the week, accompanied by an ominous forecast. Regardless, the rain thankfully held off for the tratta, having progressed as planned at a fashionably late 10:00 a.m. Out of the thirty-four horses tested during yesterday's prove regolamentate, twenty-nine contenders advanced to this latest event in the elaborate process that will ultimately determine the final ten horses. The tratta basically involves several groups—or batteries—of horses that are tested on various skills as they cautiously run around the track in the Campo (Figure 4). Each battery usually includes six or seven horses that are ridden by a variety of jockeys assigned to the task. The jockeys are a varied lot, consisting of a mix of younger men looking for experience in the Campo, occasional veteran jockeys of the Palio, or others associated with a particular stable or owner. Despite their diverse backgrounds, together they present an impressively unified appearance; all wear the same black-and-white attire representing Siena's striking coat of arms. The unified appearance contrasts with yesterday's prove regolamentate, which are not so scripted. Jockeys in that event could wear whatever they like, including T-shirts, vests, or jackets.

I hesitate to use the word "race" in association with the tratta, as they technically are not racing. The focus of this event is less on a horse's speed and more on assessing its skills and comfort with negotiating the unique track conditions. Still, Palio protocols are replicated to a limited extent. For instance, each group of horses and their jockeys line up at the mossa, just as they would to start the race. Although speed is not the foremost concern, they still explosively bolt off the mossa in quite a dramatic and heart-stopping display. Each group then proceeds to complete three laps around the Campo, also replicating the Palio's shockingly brief duration. Occasionally, a

ASSIGNMENT OF THE HORSES

questionable horse from an earlier battery will require an additional attempt to better assess its abilities, in which case it can be added to a later group of horses. An added attempt may also occur when a horse throws off its ill-fated jockey before completing its circuit, usually at the tricky curve of San Martino. From my experience, the tratta can include as little as four and as many as seven batteries in all, depending upon the number of horses and whether some need to be retested.

Figure 4. One of several batteries in the tratta, prior to selecting the final ten horses for the Palio. (Photo: Author)

Aside from two jockeys who succumbed to the curve of San Martino, today's event proceeded without major incident. After the last of the batteries was concluded, the horses disappeared into the courtyard of Palazzo Pubblico once again while the captains ruminated on their favored ten equine competitors.

The next step in the ongoing ensemble of Palio events is the assignment of the horses. Unlike other rituals here, this one can go by a variety of terms, causing no end of confusion. Depending upon who is talking or writing, the event could be referred to as the *extraction, drawing, assignment,* or *matching* of the horses. The media tend to favor *assignment* when reporting on the event, while others still refer to it as the *second extraction*, or lottery (the first having been the extraction of the contrade). Whatever one calls it, the event's title grossly understates its emotional significance to the Senesi and the Palio. Given that the term *assignment* seems to be the most common choice, I use it herein.

Fortunately, I have learned—as usual, from hard-won experience—that one should not expect the assignment of the horses to begin immediately following the tratta. In fact, I once stood in the Campo for a couple of hours because I had been told that the dramatic event occurs "directly afterwards." Well, some people's definition of "directly afterwards" may contrast sharply from my own. A noontime start is highly optimistic and nearly impossible, given all the necessary decisions and logistics. Although my determination to witness this event is unwavering, my confidence in its later start allows me to steal a few free hours beforehand, leading to a flurry of grocery shopping and an early lunch with Linda.

Now suitably fed, I set out into the medieval streets to find that the density of residents and visitors has finally achieved a collective human energy more typical of a summer Palio. As we have seen, the local enthusiasm this week has been slow to develop. Within only a few days, however, I have witnessed the transition of Siena from quiet, backwater town to a bustling urban core. Groups of teenagers donning their respective *fazzoletti* (silk scarves worn to represent each person's contrada; singular *fazzoletto*) are once again enjoying gelato or conversations in the street—with nary a sign of guilt about missing school. Meanwhile, adults are darting around or greeting one another, all the while dodging the occasional delivery truck or taxi. At this point, it is finally clear that the days of the Palio have arrived—albeit quite begrudgingly. Now that the proverbial alarm clock has sounded, the city is slowly stretching its limbs to prepare for the day.

As for the upcoming assignment, I am discovering (somewhat humorously) that none of my sources can pin down the official start time. Following our arrival on Sunday, Mike had indicated that the tratta would begin at an eye-opening 7:30 a.m., followed by the drawing at 10:00 a.m. My immediate reaction to this was one of dismay, due to the early timeframe. Just as intriguing, however, was this latest example of how the traditional Palio schedule was being turned on its head. Upon polling two other friends later, they impressively recited the scheduled times for the upcoming six trials, contrada dinners, and related Palio events. Nonetheless, these same voices mysteriously went silent when asked to reveal the scheduled start of the horse assignments. Finally, I held out hope last night while searching for schedules on the internet. Indeed, a veritable goldmine of information existed online, not the least being a thorough schedule for the days of the Palio. Alas, there was one thing missing: the assignment. No mention of it appeared anywhere on the schedule as if it was not even going to happen. *What's up with that?* At this realization, I shook my head and resigned myself to the probable case that nobody really knows. The captains simply require some quality time to discuss the horses after the tratta. Therefore, the event will happen when it happens! To avoid the presumed crush of the crowd, I therefore decide to be in the Campo by 1:30 p.m., which would be similar to the summer schedule.

Ceramic Shop Reunion

During my various errands *a piede* (on foot), I notice that our favorite ceramic shop is open. Remarkably, a full six years have already passed since Linda and I first stumbled upon the modest storefront of the affable Viola and Riccardo. The four of us had become quick friends after they learned we were living in the Goose contrada for our first Siena sojourn. It turned out that they were Goose contradaioli themselves. Given my own packed schedule to learn about the Straordinario, I can now finally take a breath and stop in to say hello. This also means I need to mentally prepare for a conversation in predominantly Italian. I can barely understand Riccardo with his soft-spoken voice, and, although Viola is patient enough with my hesitant language skills, the number of English words she knows can be counted on one hand. No matter, in I go. It will be fun to see them again, and I am curious to learn how their shop has fared since we last saw them in June. Their ongoing business venture has apparently served as a street-side indicator of larger tourism trends here in Siena.

At the sight of me, Viola fortunately lights up and raises her eyebrows in recognition along with a palpable amount of surprise: "Thomas, hello! You are here! How are you?" At this, her husband peaks out from his newspaper in their work room and shuffles out to greet me as well.

With equal enthusiasm, I manage, "Hello Viola, how are you doing? And Riccardo, it's great to see you," I shake his hand. Beyond this, Viola's first question is predictable: "Where is Linda? Did she come with you?"

I quickly explain, "Yes, Linda is here, but she will need to stop in later." Despite Linda's own learning curve with the Italian language, these two women have enjoyed their time together and get along like Tuscan bread and olive oil.

"Did you come here for the Straordinario?" Viola guesses correctly. "Do you have students?"

"Well, we are here all week to learn about the Palio, but we don't have students this time," I respond. Viola and Riccardo are accustomed to me dragging along various student cohorts, the members of which sometimes find their way to their shop. I happily note that their walls are once again filled with colorful merchandise, which leads to my first question: "How is your shop doing this week with the Straordinario?"

I receive a pleasant, if unexpected, response: "Very well, lots of tourists! Many of them are Americans." She then gestures to the walls around us. "We have been making a lot of new plates, and we have more in the back," she announces proudly. Her response is refreshing because only two years ago they had been considering retirement after back-to-back lackluster seasons of poor sales. Not only had their business turned around this past summer, but they had hired a college-age art student to assist with some of the production process.

"That's fantastic!" I exclaim. "Are you normally open this time of year, or did you come back just for this Palio?"

"No, we are usually open through the end of October, so the Palio is increasing our sales this week," she explains. I imagine this is the case with other visitor-related businesses in town, now elated to experience Palio-like crowds once again in mid-October.

At this point, I recognize a familiar sound approaching from the western side of the city. Both the Turtle and Snail need to pass through the hectic Quattro Cantoni (Four Corners) intersection on their way to the Campo for Palio events, and this shop is just a stone's throw away. The crescendo of unified male singing indicates that one of these contrade is now on its way to the Campo for the assignment of the horses.

ASSIGNMENT OF THE HORSES

With this audible recognition, my heart rate shoots higher while explaining to Viola, "I am interested in seeing the assignment today, so I am going to the Campo now." I promise that Linda will stop by to say hello, nearly forgetting one last parting comment: "Riccardo, congratulations on the extraction of the Goose!" To this he modestly acknowledges my gesture and smiles in return. Given his reserved, down-to-earth personality, he is not one to reveal much outward emotion about his home contrada. With that, it's time to head to the Campo to see which veteran horses have been chosen for this race and which lucky contrade will receive them.

The Palio as a Strategic Game

Stepping out into the street, I immediately find the entire Turtle contrada bearing down on me only a few hundred feet away. These determined people are in full Palio mode and are making their presence known through passionate singing and solidarity. This is all in good spirit for purposes of the Palio, of course. However, had this been a political protest I would not want to be on the receiving end of such human intimidation. A literal wall of men fills the narrow street from one side to the other as they belt out various folksongs. As tradition would have it, the contrada's devout women and children are following closely behind while adding to the spirited singing. More importantly, their appearance indicates that a comfortable amount of time remains before the assignment of the horses. Of course, the Turtle and all nine of its contrada counterparts are making their way to the event as well. The mayor would certainly not risk beginning without them! As if considering an approaching freight train, I quickly calculate that I can get out ahead of them to access the Campo through my favorite shortcut, the tunneled alley of Viccolo di Tone. This otherwise obscure, narrow flume and its side streets will literally drop me down into the Wave contrada and onward to the Campo. This route will be easier than dealing with the collective mass of day trippers who will be undoubtedly clustered around the piazza's main entrance.

As I make my way into the Campo and across the dirt track, I find a moderately populated public space in advance of the assignment. Still, the stage remains empty and the collective mood here is rather relaxed. I have arrived with plenty of time to essentially choose my own location for viewing this dramatic event. There is already a cluster of people surrounding the stage in front of Palazzo Pubblico, from which the chiarine will sound the fanfare to begin the festivities. Whereas in the past I have pressed so close to the stage that TV cameras were within reach, I am content today to remain at a more comfortable distance. Of course, I still envision standing directly opposite the stage, if not so close this time. With this goal in mind, I dutifully make my way to the emptier central part of the Campo.

While walking toward my goal, I hear my name from the left. "Tom, hello!" I naturally turn and happily see my friend from the Goose, Antonio, preparing to intercept my path! This is the second time I have seen him in as many days, the first being our previously described scheduled meeting, quite unlike this chance encounter. I silently question why he isn't accompanied by any of his fellow contradaioli. Glancing down I also notice a video camera wrapped around his hand and a small flipbook of notes designed to record horse names during and after the tratta. The notebook is standard issue for anyone fortunate enough to brush up against volunteers handing them out in the Campo prior to that earlier event. I have yet to unlock the difference in purpose between the larger cards distributed during the presentation of the drappellone and these miniature notebooks that also allow us to record the names of horses. In any case, should he end up joining me here by some strange Senese luck, I will be one fortunate fellow.

Today is everyone's first experience with inclement weather this week, and local media have been dutifully providing hourly updates and forecasts. Have I mentioned that the Senesi seem to be somewhat concerned about the weather? The sky is now unleashing some drizzle, though the assignment of the horses is continuing as planned. I do have my umbrella on reserve duty should its use become necessary. The Campo is still filling in with spectators like us, and the occasional contrada arrives to our left near the curve at San Martino, singing dramatically to announce its arrival. No sooner do we stop across from the stage when Antonio takes up our conversation from where we left off yesterday.

"Were you at the tratta this morning?" He opens. Upon my affirmative response, he continues, "Well, you likely saw that there were not many people here like there would be usually."

"Yes, that's right, I noticed that, too," I concur, now recalling an unintended benefit. "It worked out well for me. I could go to almost any of the

ASSIGNMENT OF THE HORSES

barriers and get plenty of good photos," I chuckle. "But it was strange. It didn't have the expected energy to it, like you said yesterday."

He confirms, "Sure, it is difficult for people to plan for this on short notice, and they use a lot of vacation time for the summer events. I will be curious to see the attendance for the upcoming trials." This issue with vacation time provides a dose of reality. Palio or not, many employed people need to maintain their responsibilities on the job. During the summer, it is admittedly tempting to imagine that the Senesi are magically available for the Palii and have nothing better to do. Alas, this may be one of the happiest places on earth, but it is certainly not Disneyland. People still need to earn a living and, well, pick up the kids.

Speaking of attendance, I ask, "How are the ticket sales coming for the dinners?"

"Compared to the summer, sales are slow from what I'm seeing, but so far we have about 400 for tonight's dinner, probably 500 for tomorrow. The tents are set up to handle about 1,200 people, and we are probably at 900 reserved now for the *cena della prova generale*." Antonio is referring to the contrada dinner that follows the evening trial on the day before the Palio race. He continues, "So, it's going OK at this point. It helps that people don't have to work Friday evening or Saturday."

"Well, it sounds like the Goose is on track to have some well-attended dinners, considering the challenges," I offer optimistically. Somehow, he is receiving insider information about ticket sales, though Antonio does assist with contrada social functions. I then change topics to inquire about the Goose's reaction to being extracted almost a month ago here in the Campo. "Were you and the contrada here in the Campo for the extraction last month? What was everyone's reaction to being selected fourth?"

"Yes, we were here, mostly scattered up by the entrance," he gestures toward the main ramp down into the Campo, now with the wooden judges' stand directly overhead. "We tend to stay up there and not necessarily in a group."

"Did you all run down here to celebrate?"

"No, some people ran toward the group, but we mostly stayed up there." Had he continued his sentence, I bet that he would have added, *smartly staying away from the Tower contrada*. From my observations, the Goose is a force to be reckoned with during the Palio, though they are intelligently cautious when their rival may be nearby.

At this point, another contrada is making its arrival known through its unified singing. "Did you tell me once that the Goose doesn't march in for the extraction or trials like other contrade?"

"Right, we no longer march in as a group because we have had problems in the past with the Tower. As you can see down here, we have to march past their street to get to Palazzo Pubblico," he explains while pointing out the Tower's twin streets of Via del Porrione and Via Salicotto just to our left.

As if being reminded, he gestures to his video camera. "I was asked to watch the drawing from the balcony up there and record our group as they leave with our horse."

"Oh, interesting," I manage to say while showing a hint of my surprise. I then joke, "Is this for a future documentary if you win?"

"Well, no," he chuckles. "We need to record the exit in case our members encounter any problems with other contrade. This way we can provide evidence of who started what, if there is any confusion about what actually happened—especially if there is any possibility of future disqualifications. We want to make sure the information is accurate." This throws me off guard, as I had not considered that Antonio had been sent here to assist with video surveillance. Nonetheless, it does explain why he is here on his own. His people have sent him on a mission.

"OK, that makes good sense," I say, already aware of the specific contrada to which he is referring. Still, he is strangely nonchalant about the whole thing, behaving as if he and his colleagues do this every time. I think to myself, *I wonder if the Tower films the Goose as well.*

Regardless, I follow up with a question about Goose's rival: "What concerns do you have with the Tower this time, now that you are both actually running?"

"We are mainly worried about the jockeys. And actually, we may not know the final jockeys for each contrada until a day or two from now. The trial tonight is two hours earlier than usual due to the shorter day. The jockeys may not be able to sign contracts with specific contrade by this evening, so we may see some substitute jockeys for a while—likely those who are younger and are looking for their first Palio experience," he predicts.

ASSIGNMENT OF THE HORSES

While considering his logic, my first thought is how seriously cool this is. I can't recall an instance during our past six sojourns in Siena when the jockeys have been switched during the trials. The official rule is that the contrade can change their jockeys until the morning of the Palio, after which they need to be confirmed for the race. This is yet another potential consequence of running a Palio in October, especially if negotiations with the jockeys can be interrupted by the reduced amount of daylight.

Antonio continues his train of thought: "We are particularly worried about whether the jockey, Scompiglio [Jonatan Bartoletti], will race for the Tower. When a jockey chooses a rival, he likely will not run for you again. So, for instance, we have Tittia [Giovanni Atzeni], and he might run for the Wave or Shell, which is fine. But if he races for the Tower it would be viewed by the Goose as a betrayal. That's why jockeys tend to stay with one contrada and its allies. The Goose has been interested in Scompiglio, and he has won quite often recently—twice for the She-Wolf in one year. If he goes to the Tower, this would not be good news for us. It could set us back five years or longer, to lose a jockey like that to our rival."

That jockeys tend to run for an allied grouping—practically a family—of contrade certainly is news to me. This revelation tells me that when a jockey decides which contrada to represent, the decision is not simply based on an even playing field; that is, the decision is not merely about contracting with the highest bidder. Rather, there are more contextual issues of contrada relationships at stake. Of course, local media outlets are only fueling the speculation regarding the jockeys. One news article posted on October 2 provided potential thoughts about the future matches, though apparently with little evidence. Solidly informed or not, the piece likely did nothing to diminish Antonio's concerns. While mentioning that the Tower would like to renew its association with Brio—the jockey who gave them a victory in July 2015—the article raised the possibility that Scompiglio could be encouraged to run for the Tower should they extract a competitive horse.[51]

After considering Antonio's insight about Scompiglio, I respond, "Yes, that does make sense, as I am also thinking about Tittia. Generally, he has raced for the Goose, Wave, Forest, and Shell." I realize that Antonio is the last person who needs this information. Rather, I am keen to demonstrate my basic knowledge about one of the Palio's most promising young jockeys. In fact, one may recall that Tittia ran and won for the Goose in July 2013, during our first summer in Siena. Since then, I have closely watched his progress.

"Yes, that's right, you understand." He rewards me with a smile of approval. Then he hits me with a powerful insight about the Palio in general. "This is a strategic game. Sometimes jockeys can be paid more than 70,000 euro to not run for a certain contrada. This is something that might need to be considered, but I hope we won't need to do so," he adds. The main point here, however, is that Antonio views the Palio as a game rather than a sport, which makes the partiti all the more relevant as an influential factor.

"Do you think Tittia will run for the Shell or Goose this time? Or, does it depend upon the horse?" I am admittedly fishing for more insider information, though I suspect that everything remains up in the air at this point.

After thinking quickly, he responds, "Well, as for the Shell, they still seem eager to sign Trecciolino [Luigi Bruschelli], though I do not understand why. Of course, he is still a big name here, but he has not won since 2012." He shrugs in bewilderment. This possibility is supported by the same speculative article mentioned above, which could also be the source of Antonio's information. Although the article's author admits that the Shell would much prefer Tittia to help them "get the victory they have been missing for twenty years," the second choice does seem to be none other than Trecciolino, who claims to be "ready anyway" should Tittia not run for them.[52]

I decide not to press Antonio about where he learned this, but I do follow up with, "Do you think Trecciolino's time has passed—that he will not likely win again in the future?"

"Yes, I think so. In recent years he has focused much of his efforts on helping other jockeys and contrade win, so he is still influencing races in a big way. Because of this, I think he still remains one of the most strategic and successful jockeys within this game. In my opinion, what he has accomplished with strategy is excellent. He takes money from one contrada and divides it up for other jockeys to help meet his own purposes. So, he is no longer trying hard to win, but he is instead helping others. He helped the Tower win with Brio in 2015 and the She-Wolf in 2016."

This last statement shocks my sensibilities. "Oh really, did he pull back to let the She-Wolf win?"

ASSIGNMENT OF THE HORSES

"Yes. He is good at faking his own race and making it look like he is trying to win. He did this for the Tower in 2015, and then in 2016 he pulled back to allow the She-Wolf to go past."

"Wow, so even though you support his strategy to help others, you don't think he should run for the Shell?"

"OK, look," he begins, realizing that I need more background. Now his video camera is swinging around with his hands. "The Shell is desperate to win. At this point, the Shell is the contrada that most people agree is likely to win this one, and they have been trying for a long time. And they have been a favorite in many of the recent races, including when Tittia rode for them in 2015."

"Oh yes, we were here for that one, when Veleno pulled Tittia off his horse!" I recall with some laughter.

"Yes, exactly. So, if you are the Shell, why do you want to hire Trecciolino?" He quizzes me, but then simply answers the question himself. "Why would they want Trecciolino as a jockey if he is just going to give their money to someone else? It's likely because they still want a big-name jockey riding for them, and they think that a big name still matters. They think he has 'star power' and still wants to win. But the results lately say otherwise."

Glancing to the sky, it is apparently trying even harder to rain. An occasional sprinkle hits my body, and—not to be left out—additional drops are now decorating Antonio's surveillance camera. I judge that it is not yet umbrella worthy, and most Senesi here seem to agree, for the moment. With the speculation I am hearing about Trecciolino's future, it is instructive to reflect that we may be witnessing the sunset of perhaps the most effective jockey to compete in the Campo since the 1990s—whether his tactics are appreciated or not. I have personally yet to see him win here, and this is our sixth straight year in Siena. He is definitely experiencing a drought right now, although—presuming that Antonio's information is reasonably accurate—he still commands plenty of influence behind the scenes.

Leveling the Field

As I listen intently to Antonio's perspectives on various jockeys, we are only partially conscious of an event that needs to take place first. One may wonder what happens to all the horses that were not selected for the Palio. Quite simply, they are sent home. A rather somber, single-file parade of unselected horses is now passing in front of Palazzo Pubblico as they are guided back to Piazza Mercato (Market Square). This open-air, mostly paved expanse behind the Palazzo serves as the staging area for horses and equipment during the days of the Palio. Some determined individuals may closely scrutinize the horses as they shuffle past. By process of elimination the most dedicated observers can then tell which ten horses have been selected. Although some people here are certainly doing just that, Antonio and I are not among them. Like most, we are steeped in conversation as the horses make their final appearance in near silence. With people clustered around this low-key parade, we would be hard-pressed to see much of the horses anyway. Still, I believe this is good news. The assignment should proceed sometime soon after the final steed departs the Campo.

As the sky above us darkens more with thickening clouds, Antonio eyes a fellow preparing to climb an aluminum ladder behind the stage. The ladder provides access to two massive scoreboards attached to Palazzo Pubblico, designed for the sole purpose of this event. In a refreshingly nontechnical approach, the scoreboards—separated by one of the Palazzo's massive Gothic windows—will reveal the eventual matches between the ten horses and contrade. As the drawing progresses, the attendant slides the labeled cards into each of the board's slots. His presence on the ladder signals that the assignment is about to begin.

Then with nary a fanfare or announcement of any kind, the attendant slides numbered cards into the ten slots, silently indicating which of the ten horses have been chosen to run in the Palio. Though subtle, this is the very information that expectant Senesi are eager to learn. The numbers placed on the scoreboards represent the large, white digits on the hind quarters of the horses that ran earlier during the tratta, in this case numbering one through twenty-nine. The numbers of the chosen horses are therefore now displayed for all to see.

For those armed with the horse names and numbers provided earlier by local media, their diligence is now being rewarded. Antonio is one of them, now somewhat frantically attempting to keep pace with the scoreboard attendant. I offer to hold his video camera to expedite his writing. Somewhat to my surprise, he relinquishes the camera to my care, lacking any better idea

ASSIGNMENT OF THE HORSES

as we both stand in the light drizzle. Despite all our respective technology, his two hands are now fumbling with old-fashioned pen and paper.

Although the identification of horses has befuddled me for years, the Senesi move through the process like experts. Like a mathematician solving an equation, Antonio scans the decoded list of names and reacts dejectedly. "Oh, no, this is terrible," he growls while shaking his head in frustration. I hide the fact that my own mood is just the opposite. Though not yet having unlocked the identities of the final ten horses, I could not be more delighted by having an informed contradaiolo calling the play-by-play right next to me. Better yet, he is eagerly verbalizing his instant thoughts. Disappointed or not, his real-time commentary is—for me—precious and greatly appreciated.

Antonio gestures to his damp and barely legible list. "They didn't choose any strong horses," he laments.

"That must mean that Porto Alabe is out?" I ask, curious to learn the status of Siena's 2018 Horse of the Year. This unsuspecting animal has become the city's latest equine legend, having won the last two August Palii. Readers might recall that his prior experiences in the Campo allowed him to go "straight to the tratta" this morning. He was already a known quantity.

"Yes, he is gone. I think only three of them have raced before, maybe once or twice—Rombo, Schietta, and Sorighittu. This situation completely favors the jockeys." Antonio's facial and hand gestures clearly express his disappointment.

Now intrigued, I ask the quintessential outsider question, "How so?"

"If there are no strong or well-known horses, a jockey can no longer use that excuse when he declines an offer to run for your contrada. With good horses assigned to other contrade, they have an excuse—'Well, I need to follow this or that horse to another contrada, I deeply regret that I cannot run for you,'" Antonio mimics with not a little sarcasm. He continues, "But in this case, the horses are not well known, and so the jockeys are free to move around wherever they wish, to any contrada. Without the pull of a strong horse, a jockey can go to whatever contrada he wants. *Capito?* Do you understand?" He finishes.

"Um, yes, I believe so. That's interesting," I respond with a mix of fascination and uncertainty. He is essentially arguing that the playing field for jockeys has been leveled. They are not obligated to go with a specific horse. Instead, they are free to be hired by other contrade, regardless of the presumed strength of the animal. I eventually realize that something is counterintuitive here, so I follow up with, "So, if the captains don't want to give so much freedom to the jockeys, why did they choose so many novice horses?"

"The captains are probably more concerned with taking a chance on having their rival extract a strong horse," he quickly explains. *Concerns with their rivals again*, I sigh to myself. *This seems like an ongoing theme around here.* The stage party members are now taking their places in front of us, and the trumpet players—with their elegant, long-belled chiarine—are fussing with their instruments in preparation for the event. Antonio continues, "So they choose novice horses to level the playing field, allowing their own contrada to have an equal chance if they do not extract a strong horse. I mean, if they allow Preziosa [Penelope] or Porto Alabe in again, that's a sure bet for the contrade that extract them. But what about the others? It's a big risk to take. If Porto Alabe was allowed to run, he would likely win. Did you see, he won the August race from the rincorsa position. So, this is a more conservative move, and it seems for this Palio that the captains are being more cautious than normal. Still, it's better for the jockeys than for the contrade. I'm not happy about that."

For all of his disappointment in the outcome just now, Antonio seems to be confirming suspicions that have been bouncing around Siena for at least a month. One local news writer, Lello Ginanneschi, managed to predict today's outcome quite accurately back in late September. Although Ginanneschi admitted that he could not accurately predict the ten selected horses, he may have enjoyed access to some insider information. "According to the intent and declarations of the [horse] owners and the outcomes of the last two Palio races," he began, "the only big one [veteran] on the turf could be Porto Alabe, ready to run his thirteenth consecutive Palio, an unthinkable record in the modern era".[53] He further speculated, however, that "the captains' axe could fall on him, especially if there are numerous rival pairs running that are thirsty for victory."

Consequently, the captains would likely choose mostly inexperienced horses to level the playing field, thereby minimizing the risk that one contrada could run away with the race. This scenario is precisely what occurred here just moments ago—much to Antonio's dismay.

ASSIGNMENT OF THE HORSES

The Drawing Proceeds

With his mind clearly on the ten chosen horses, I amusingly feel the need to remind him about his filming task. The assignment is about to begin. "Do you need to be up there right now?" I gently nudge.

"Oh, yes! I need to go. They are about to hold the drawing. See you later. Ciao!" Just like that, he waves and darts off toward the *palco dei priore* (platform of the contrada presidents) that overlooks the curve of San Martino. Although the track is not blocked off for this event, Antonio still needs to navigate through the human congestion near that corner of the Campo. As he disappears, I congratulate myself for having been quick-witted enough to photograph his list of horses; otherwise, I would still not know which contrada is ultimately assigned to which horse. Although I snicker when I see that his handwriting is almost as poor as mine, I can at least recognize one horse from another.

As I consider the field of horses, the level of exhilaration in the Campo ratchets up. And now the familiar notes of the trumpet fanfare erupt in perfect harmony. As if by some interstellar coincidence, the sky above us responds by unleashing a steady bout of rain. It is certainly amusing to consider that Giove Pluvio is making his presence known, perhaps reminding all of us mortals that we are not going to get off without a hitch quite that easily. I take a few seconds to scan the Campo and I see that it is now blanketed with variously colored umbrellas. My sense of wonder upon seeing as magical a sight as any in Italy is slightly dampened when several of them pop up instantly in front of me, thereby blocking my previously unobstructed view. Regardless, this is my first Palio event accompanied by wall-to-wall umbrellas, and it is quite the sight to see. October skies, indeed (Figure 5).

Figure 5. A sea of umbrellas appears in the Campo as drizzle turns to rain before the assignment of the horses. (Photo: Author)

Completely undaunted by the wet stuff, the stoic stage party soldiers onward. The crowd just as magically silences itself, although I have learned that the first words of the *sindaco* (mayor) merely involve a sort of preliminary roll call. Before the drawing, the mayor holds each slip of paper—the first set numbered one through ten, the second set with the ten contrada names—out in front of us while deliberately reading them through the microphone. The intent here is to demonstrate complete transparency before the slips are placed inside the tumblers. This admittedly belabored process caused no end of confusion on my part during our first experience here. As the mayor kept reading the numbers, I had dumbly wondered why nobody was reacting. Only well after he began did I come to the realization that the actual drawing had not even started yet.

With all of the preliminaries now concluded, it's "go time." The first number is drawn from the tumbler, and a young page dutifully delivers it to the mayor. He expertly reads it to the crowd.

ASSIGNMENT OF THE HORSES

"*Nove* [Nine]." The first horse to be matched is Terribile da Clodia, a novice.

More meaningful, however, is the next slip drawn from the second tumbler, namely the contrada to be matched with Terribile. The anxious if disciplined crowd remains pin-drop silent while awaiting this news.

"Chiocciola!"

Aside from some basic chatter amidst the onlookers, the delegates for the Snail unemotionally come forward to receive their horse. The remarkable absence of any detectable excitement tells me that the Snail is utterly underwhelmed with Terribile—despite its rather intimidating name. Still, regardless of a horse's notoriety, or lack thereof, the animal is always received graciously by the contrada and is unequivocally doted upon and cherished throughout the days of the Palio. To be sure, any horse can be a winner.

As the mayor proceeds to match each horse with its contrada, I find it more challenging than usual to interpret the various reactions of the crowd (Figure 6). There are simply too many unknown horses to spark the type of emotions that normally occur with this event. Ultimately, the three more experienced horses, if their collective history in the Campo matters much at all, end up going to the Goose, Turtle, and Forest. The outward reactions of these three contenders, however, is likewise mixed. Perhaps the Forest sounded the most enthusiastic on my unscientific "cheer meter" with its selection of Rombo de Sedini. In marked contrast, the Goose uttered practically nothing despite landing Sorighittu. It is vital to remember, however, that being a veteran horse does not necessarily correlate with its strength, let alone superstar status. Indeed, the performance of these horses may have been less than memorable.

Consequently, it is to my mild surprise that a few novice horses are receiving the bulk of positive reactions, notably from the Dragon. As Antonio had predicted, there appears to be more confusion among the contrade than one typically observes. The field of horses has clearly been leveled.

It should be noted, however, that one particular contrada defies all expectations by scoring the highest on my "cheer meter." We turn our collective attention to their instant celebration while its devoted members race down to collect an unsuspecting steed named Violenta da Clodia (related somehow to Terribile, I am told). I recall having heard mutterings about that horse as its positive reputation apparently preceded it into the Campo. Now suitably matched, the Shell suddenly seems to think it has a chance . . .

Figure 6. The stage party and scoreboards during the assignment of the horses. The mayor (standing, right) is waiting to announce the next match. (Photo: Author)

CHAPTER 9

Four Days and Three Laps

ENRICO QUIPS WHILE WE LEAN AGAINST ONE OF THE CAMPO'S MASONRY pedestals, "About the Palio, everything spoken is true, and everything spoken is a rumor". Said another way, one person's reality is another person's fiction. This is a piece of wisdom I keep in mind during my visits here, as everyone with whom I speak holds a unique and personalized perspective—as one might expect. Like any complex social event, the Palio is a treasure trove for eliciting unending speculation and personal interpretations. One of my more philosophical friends, Enrico, is of the Tower contrada, and we have now situated ourselves across from the Tower's main street of Via Salicotto for a casual conversation. Fortunately for me, Enrico speaks nearly fluent English, and I am eager to receive his own interpretations of the upcoming Straordinario. With the drawing and assignment of the horses now concluded, Enrico and I agreed to meet here in the Campo before the first trial this evening.

He explains, "For the trials, I prefer to stay down here," referring to the curve of San Martino and, more to the point, comfortably near the entrance to the Tower's rione. "The Goose area is up there," he continues, pointing to the main entrance near the judges' stand—thereby confirming Antonio's own description of the "contrada geography" in the Campo.

"Are you planning to watch the actual Palio from here as well?" I ask.

"Well, no," he contemplates. "I will not be in the Campo for the Palio because I get too emotional. I will probably just watch it myself somewhere else." In this regard, Enrico is not alone. Many contrada members have indicated—both in person and through various publications—that they prefer the isolation of their own space. To watch it inside their società or in the Campo creates more personal anxiety than some contradaioli can tolerate.

Third Places

Before asking him about the Straordinario, I am curious to learn more about a local café that seems to have disappeared from the landscape of Via Salicotto this year. When I ventured into the Tower during earlier trips, I had noticed that this vibrant place was typically filled with a mix of contrada members of all ages enjoying tasty bakery treats and espresso. The place was likewise inviting because of its rather isolated location away from the touristy hubbub of the Campo. Moreover, the staff was always friendly when I approached with my less than confident use of Italian. Thus, Enrico is the best person I know who might be able to shed some light on its status.

"Are you familiar with the café that was located on Via Salicotto? I couldn't find it this time as I was walking by, so I thought I might have missed it," I open, while gesturing toward their contrada entrance. It turns out that he knows precisely the place to which I am referring.

"Oh, yes, they unfortunately had to close permanently and will not re-open," Enrico states with some visible regret.

"Wow, I always saw people around there when I happened to walk by, so I thought it was doing well in recent years," I respond curiously.

"Well, the owners were in too much debt, and they could no longer afford to stay open. This happened in the past as well, when the owners changed hands. But the most recent owners were able to buy it and keep it going. This time, nobody was interested in purchasing it, so they shut it down," he explains. Like a true contradaiolo, Enrico is clearly informed about local happenings.

"Oh, that's too bad!" I say with disappointment. "Do you think the cost of rent was a factor?" This would be my first guess, given the continuing trend of rent increases around the Campo.

"Maybe, I'm not sure. But it's kind of like what you might call gentrification, where the local places are closing, and they are being replaced with larger chain retailers from outside the city."

"Oh, really. That's interesting," I respond, my eyebrows rising at his mention of gentrification. Until now, no one had mentioned this concept to me in Siena.

He then proceeds to describe the social impact of this loss on his contrada. "It is really unfortunate for the Tower," he laments, "because that was the main place where contrada members went to meet each other and socialize. Now, it's almost as if our territory has shrunk because the contradaioli don't spend time in that space anymore. So, the social activity has actually retreated deeper into the rione. It's almost as if we have lost territory," he chuckles, though with some clear misgiving.

With this more recent business casualty, Enrico has confirmed the importance of local establishments to stimulate community vitality. Then it strikes me. My geography education kicks in again as I recall a rather popular concept for businesses like this.

"Have you ever heard of the concept of *third places*?" I ask, knowing that Enrico enjoys such intellectual conversations.

"No, I have never heard of that. What is it?" he asks, now intrigued.

"I think you are referring to a third place that unfortunately didn't survive here," I begin. "Back in the 1990s, a sociologist, Ray Oldenburg, had been noticing how local businesses and other popular hangouts can actually encourage community interaction by bringing people together socially. His book was called *The Great Good Place*, and he seems to have invented the concept of third places.[54] It's actually still quite popular, even outside of academics." Not wanting to revert into lecture mode, I try to sum it up. "So, he described one's home as being a *first place* because of its importance to our family and daily lives. A *second place* is your location of work, or employment, where we also tend to spend a lot of time."

Enrico jumps in. "Ah, so third places are where you go for enjoyment, right?"

"Yes, basically. He described third places as the anchors of community life. You know, where you and your friends hang out and talk about everything. They're places to socialize, even maybe with people you don't know well at first. He tended to focus on American coffee shops as the most common type of third place, but they can be any inexpensive place where friends get together regularly." I then add as an afterthought, "Actually, the

Campo right here could be considered a third place, with both of us chatting near this pedestal!" I chuckle at my own thought.

"So, what you're saying is that we lost one of our third places," Enrico concludes.

"Yes, it sounds like it. I hope you find another one. I don't think these things can be planned in advance, though Americans are trying to actually *design* third places into new developments," I laugh. "But some of them work, and some of them don't. One place can attract throngs of people overnight, but another one nearby will be deserted and go out of business. I think it's one of those more natural urban processes that takes time to develop," I surmise, adding, "What I do like about Siena is that there are still so many of them here, like restaurants and cafes where the locals hang out and where they plan to meet their friends. These places are very rare in American suburbs." I try to make him feel a bit better about Siena.

"Yes, well, it's good to hear an outsider's view of Siena sometimes, because we usually just focus on what is going wrong," Enrico admits. I reflect to myself that many of us tend to think in this manner, regardless of where we live. "I still think it's a trend here, though. It's not just the Tower, but there are not as many local stores and cafes as there were, say, ten years ago." I can't disagree with him because this trend has been described in various local media and more academic publications since the 1990s. "Well, speaking of third places," he perks up, "do you want to get a snack? I need to eat something before the contrada dinner later tonight."

His question reminds me humorously of my advice to students when we make plans to attend contrada dinners during the summer. Only half-jokingly, I usually say to them, "Make sure you eat some dinner before you go to dinner." Given that such events do not even begin until after 8:30 p.m., it is wise to consume some light fare a few hours earlier. At least, this has been my strategy, though a heavy meal is neither necessary nor encouraged; after all, it is still imperative to enjoy the three- or four-course meal provided by the contrada. Strategizing one's food consumption is akin to a balancing act, which also should account for one's level of activity before the contrada event. I usually attend the evening trial in the Campo, which is energy intensive, followed by walking around and socializing at the contrada before the antipasti is served. Although only a few hours removed from my previous "light" meal, this level of activity typically allows me to enjoy the contrada's own offerings later at night. In this case, Enrico seems to be thinking similarly, hoping now to keep his stomach satisfied for the next several hours.

Palio Philosophy

Following a short stroll, I follow his lead as we duck into a smallish pizzeria and bar just off the Campo. With our pizza slices in hand, we grab bottled drinks from the nearby refrigerator and settle in at the counter amidst a few other patrons. Of course, talk of the Palio begins immediately.

"How surprised were you about the plans for a Palio in October?" I ask with a smile.

"Well, I was actually not surprised at all about holding a Straordinario." With this revelation, Enrico catches me off guard; this is counter to what I have been hearing. But there is a twist to his response, as he explains, "There is a new city administration now, since the previous sindaco was voted out this past summer. So, I expected there to be a Straordinario at some point, as a political move to score points with the people. What I did not expect was that it would happen this quickly."

"Oh, I see," I nod in understanding. "You're saying it was a political move by the new administration."

"Yes, exactly. But to have a Palio now is not a wise move. It's not wise financially, as it costs several hundred thousand euro for the city to set it up—probably 60,000 euro for the dirt track itself. The city is not in good financial shape right now to pay for a third Palio." At this news, I decide not to mention Dario's "Netflix hypothesis" about how it may have been funded.

I gladly continue as Enrico's sounding board, in between bites of our square-shaped pizza slices. He continues, "But it's about *panem et circenses*—bread and games. Give the people what they want. You know about this saying, right?" I nod with enthusiasm, as I had not expected to hear this concept outside the courses I teach.

The *panem et circenses* to which Enrico refers is Latin for "bread and circuses," also interpreted more broadly as "food and games." The concept is credited all the way back to Juvenal, a Roman author whose satirical poems in the second century AD served as his critique of social decline within his beloved Roman Republic.[55] Juvenal basically argued that the empire had risen because the people had abandoned their political responsibilities. They chose instead to satisfy themselves with food handouts and cheap entertainment—such as found at the Roman racetrack or amphitheater. The concept survives to this day in reference to any perceived decline of civic involvement in favor of more trivial pursuits.

Scholar Wolfgang Drechsler explains why, in part, the Palio survived beyond the fall of the Republic of Siena in the 1550s. In a serious attempt to prevent additional Senese uprisings, the Florentine Medici rulers encouraged the Palio to continue, thereby diverting the people's attention from their new political reality as a regional backwater.[56] And today, Enrico is invoking the concept once again to suggest why the Straordinario is happening now.

He explains further, "The thought is, keep the people happy, and they will forget about their problems. Most of those who voted in favor [of the Straordinario] were young people. I think 90 percent of those who voted 'yes' were younger. I'm sure the city knew it would be approved if the younger contrada members voted for it, even though it is too expensive for the city right now. It's like when you go into debt and then buy more stuff!" At this analogy, I laugh out loud and attract the attention of the fellow behind the counter. Enrico is on a roll now. "You try to forget about your problems, but the real problem is still there. It's not a wise move for the city right now." Enrico is referring to none other than the recent financial crisis and the collapse of the Banca Monte dei Paschi, Siena's local and once-lucrative bank. Until recently it was considered the third largest in Italy. Although its rather humorous, if accurate, signage—Serving Tuscany since 1472—still decorates various branches in and around the city, it further serves as a grim reminder of the once proud, privately owned financial institution. For the first decade in its impressive history, the bank is no longer under local control.

Deciding to pick Enrico's brain about his contrada, I ask, "OK, so the Tower voted against the Straordinario, right? What were the reasons?"

To my delight, he opens with a more philosophical perspective. "There are two worlds here: the world of politics and the world of the Palio. The politics involve the negotiations, such as with the jockeys and other deals made behind the scenes. The world of the Palio involves more of the practical matters, and this is what did not make sense to us, to hold a third Palio. The Tower voted against the idea, but it was very close, probably within thirty or forty votes. And again, it was mostly young people who wanted to have it. There were a lot of arguments against it. One was the weather and the possibility of rain or cold temperatures. Another concern was how to organize everything with so little time. We had no contract with a jockey, so we would have to start negotiating very quickly. Their contracts ended in August. And the horses are another matter. They are off season, and they even have different diets when they are not training. So, there were a lot of practical reasons that turned a lot of people against it."

"OK, that all makes sense," I respond, silently pleased that he is confirming everything learned thus far. "So why did the Tower vote 'yes' the second time?"

"The issue with the contrada votes is complicated. It's kind of like *game theory*," he hits me with yet another insight. "Once you know that the Palio is going to be held, then the first vote of the contrada really doesn't count anymore. Now you have to vote 'yes,' or you get left out entirely."

Upon further thought, game theory might help explain why the seven contrade opposed to the Palio decided to reverse their votes. In a nutshell, there are three kinds of games: skill, chance, and strategy.[57] Although games of skill are primarily based on talents or training, those of chance are based on what some would call a random act of nature, such as a coin toss or dice roll. A game of strategy, however, depends upon the choices made by players. Game theory focuses primarily on this type of game. As author Mark Burkey explains, game theory is about "how to make the best choice when your best choice both affects, and is affected by the choices of others." Thus, your own decision is not happening in a vacuum, in isolation of others making their own choices. Rather, game theory "is about interrelated decision making, looking ahead and anticipating how your action will affect others' actions, and in turn how those actions will affect you."[58] To do this well, one also has to understand the motivations of the players involved.

Enrico's comment may inadvertently help explain why the contrade were compelled to vote "yes" the second time. As I interpret it, one contrada captain can predict the actions of his counterparts elsewhere. If he decides to join and others do not, then it clearly benefits his contrada because there is no chance of the others getting drawn during the extraction. But if others are thinking like him—as he suspects they are—then there is little chance that his peers will opt out of the Palio to give his own contrada a greater chance. Strategically, why would they want to do that? So, our imaginary captain here strategically votes "yes," as do all the others who are assuming the same thing.

As predicted by game theory, one's decision is based on the motivations of the other players. It makes sense, then, that their best, self-interested decision is to join the Palio if they are assuming that everyone else will do the same.

Speculations about the Straordinario

With these thoughts left on the counter, we mutually decide to pay for our snacks and head out. Enrico is still talkative, however, and his thoughts turn to the actual Palio race. Perhaps like Alex from the Wave, Enrico may be torn between practical considerations and his emotional enthusiasm for the upcoming event. This internal conflict becomes apparent as we step back into the reality of light foot traffic around us. We join in with those shuffling toward the Campo when I ask, "Which contrada do you think holds the advantage now that the jockeys and horses are in place?"

His answer is firm. "Everything is set up well for the Shell now. They have Tittia for their jockey, and most believe they have a strong horse with Violenta da Clodia. From what I hear, they are spending over three million euro to help secure their win."

"Wow," I jump in as we stroll toward the San Martino curve. "Are they that desperate, to spend that much money?"

"Well, this is a game, remember, so if you want to win, you have to spend money. And the Shell has a lot of it right now, since they haven't won in this century. Think about it, the Shell is one contrada away from becoming the nonna of Siena," he chuckles at the thought as I shake my head in disbelief. As Antonio mentioned earlier, Enrico is referring to the derogatory title—grandmother—attached to the contrada that has endured the longest time without a Palio win. He continues, "The Shell has not won since August 1998. If the current nonna, the Eagle, wins another Palio soon, the Shell will be the nonna. So, yes, they are quite desperate to prevent that from happening."

Continuing my inquiry, I ask, "So, if that much money is spent to help them win, where does the money go? For what expenses?"

"Well, some of the money is used to buy off the rincorsa, the run-in jockey that starts the race. He can effectively control when the race begins, hopefully when his ally is positioned to make a clean start. Money also goes to other contrade that are willing to do favors for them, whether they are running or not. Of course, their own jockey needs to be paid to run, and then much more is paid out if he wins."

"So, we won't be surprised to see a Shell victory on Saturday," I conclude.

"Sure, it's all set up for them. But remember, despite all of this, there is a saying in Siena: there are four days and three laps." He snickers before explaining more. "Anything can happen during the trials, the so-called days of the Palio. Horses can get sick or injured, or simply refuse to line up at the canape at the start of the race. Did you see Trecciolino's horse two years ago? It was finally disqualified for Tartuca after a full hour because the horse refused to line up."

"Oh yes, I remember that!" We both laugh. "Not even Trecciolino could control the horse."

"Right, and nobody can predict things like that. Then there is the race itself, when accidents happen, and jockeys or other contrade can betray certain agreements. And nobody knows the final lineup for the race, since that is determined by a drawing. Anything can happen—four days and three laps." We both smile as I absorb his explanation more thoroughly. From my own experience here since 2013, unpredictability seems to be the rule rather than the exception. A certain contrada or horse is heavily favored but may ultimately come up short of expectations for a variety of reasons.

I use this as an opportunity to ask about his own contrada. "Are there any expectations for the Tower in this one?"

"This time in the Tower we probably have the worst horse," he laughs. The horse they extracted, Tonina, is one of the seven novices that have yet to run a Palio.

"Oh, would you call that a *brenna*?" I ask, using a Senese term for a presumably weaker Palio horse.

"Yes, definitely a brenna," he confirms. "For the trial this morning—did you see?—the horse was refusing to line up. It was wearing one of those—what do you call it—fuzzy things around the nose. But it was still having problems."

I laugh. "Oh yes, I believe that's called a shadow roll. I didn't know what those were used for until recently," I sympathize while also adding, "They are sometimes used on racehorses to reduce their chance of getting spooked by shadows on the track."

"Well, it doesn't seem to be working on Tonina," he quips.

FOUR DAYS AND THREE LAPS

I respond, "So I guess you don't have high expectations for the Tower this time."

"Well, no, and who knows about the Forest?" This comment triggers my recollection of how the Forest can often weasel its way into such conversations as this one, as mentioned earlier. He then explains this perplexity out loud. "The Forest has a habit of winning when there is a heavily favored contrada. They don't have a rival. Sometimes the others forget about the Forest, and that can benefit them." He then shifts gears to another contrada I hear little about. "As for the Snail, they are also desperate to win; it's been a long time for them, since 1999. Their contrada is large, like the Shell. But other contrade are more likely to help the Shell rather than the Snail." I jump in to ask why. He responds, "Well, the Snail is not in the best shape politically right now." I don't quite understand this, but I let it drop.

We have since arrived back at the San Martino curve and have resumed our standing conversation. I am fortunate that Enrico has nowhere else to be at the moment. Like many others, he had to take time off from work, so I suppose he is taking every opportunity to enjoy it.

I change the topic back to the horses. "Do you know why the captains chose so many mediocre horses for the drawing?"

He reflects, "This time, I think the captains are being more defensive. They do not want to give a big chance to another contrada, such as a rival, I believe." His opinion seems to corroborate Antonio's explanation. He continues, "For example, we are very concerned about the Goose, even though we won a Palio more recently, in 2015. We really only have three or four wins in the past four decades, and the Goose has many more. We don't want to give them another chance, since they have not won in five years. This is similar with the Turtle, I think, because the Snail, its rival, has not won in a long time. The Turtle is concerned that the Snail will end its winless streak."

"Ok, so why do the contrade worry so much about their rivals?" I ask, trying to better comprehend this twisted logic of jeopardizing your own chance to win and also prevent your rival from winning. "Why not just enjoy the race and do your best?"

"Well, we did talk about this in the contrada," he explains. "It's important for us to make sure our rival stays in a poor position over time. Look at what happened to the Porcupine. The She-Wolf—their rival—won twice in 2016, a cappotto, which was a disaster for the Porcupine. Then the

She-Wolf wins again this past August. They had been the nonna, but now they have erased that status. It's important for us to not give the Goose another possibility for a win, as it would diminish the importance of our win in 2015. It's just the logic we use here," he adds.

"That's interesting. I find it amazing how important the rivalry can be," I respond without judgment, though I can't help but wonder if this intensive focus on one's rival can backfire like a self-inflicted wound. The obsession with one's rivals seems just as true during actual races. It is not uncommon to find two rival jockeys beating each other to a pulp while missing an opportunity to win—sometimes to the Forest, or to another upstart contrada that wasn't given much of a chance.

Enrico continues, "So, as another example, we were very happy when the Goose finished in second place, and with Porto Alabe, in July. That was almost like a win for us," he reflects. The rather strange truth about the Palio, as Enrico indicates, is that a second-place finish is considered a disastrous loss, especially with a favored horse. He further explains, "If your rival has a strong horse and almost wins but doesn't, that is an excellent situation for you. It's important to make sure as much as possible that your rival is in a bad position during the race, especially if they are expected to win."

Jockeys of Past, Present, and Future

At this point Enrico spies some of his fellow contrada friends, and they are coming to say hello. We make our introductions, and Enrico confirms that he will see them later for the contrada dinner. I suspect that our time together is winding down, so I quickly ask him what he thinks about the jockeys.

He reflects, "The big news, I think, is that Trecciolino is not racing this time."

"Oh yes, I saw that in the local news headlines," I confirm. "Do you think he will race again in the future, or not?"

"No, he is done," Enrico says definitively, though I do not know to what extent this is conjecture. It is wise to keep in mind his own earlier wisdom, that one person's truth is another's rumor. That said, the local media have made a significant fuss—including front-page headlines—about the possibility that Trecciolino may have already raced his last Palio. Enrico continues, "None of the contrade wanted to hire him, so he is out. They don't think he will win anymore, and he is fifty years old," he explains with a shrug and raised eyebrows. "And he has broken nearly every bone in his body." At this news I chuckle while wincing at the same time. As we have seen in recent Palio races, jockeying can be a hazardous profession. Then Enrico speculates, "Perhaps if he spends his own money at some point—he certainly has a lot of money—he can convince a contrada to let him have one more race to tie Aceto's record, but other than that I can't see him racing again."

Enrico is referring to the standing record for the most Palio wins by a single jockey, currently held by Andrea Degortes, nicknamed Aceto (Vinegar). From 1965 through 1992, he compiled fourteen Palio victories of his own. As Aceto's career was winding down, Trecciolino represented the upcoming, younger generation of jockeys. And now he has apparently come full circle. For his part, Trecciolino needs one more victory to tie the record. Should Enrico's prediction prove accurate, however, the renowned jockey may fall short of that goal. Incidentally, Aceto's last victory in 1992 was for the Eagle contrada, which is now the nonna with no victories to boast of since then. Regardless of what may happen for Trecciolino in the future, he somewhat strangely will not be a part of this Palio, at least not visibly in the Campo. Behind the scenes may be another matter, as Antonio had explained earlier.

It seems that the Turtle was Trecciolino's last holdout. Local media outlets virtually stumbled over themselves to determine whether that contrada might hire him. However, we have recently learned that the Turtle chose a lesser known jockey, Andrea Coghe, nicknamed Tempesta. This is only his third attempt to run in a Palio, his first and second having both been for the Forest as a rookie during the 2017 races. Tempesta and his contemporaries are now representing the next generation of younger jockeys as Trecciolino's generation moves toward retirement.

I bring up this very subject with Enrico. "Well, even if Trecciolino continues to race in the future, it seems there is a generational shift taking place with the jockeys. Is that what you are seeing, too?"

"Yes, things are definitely changing with the jockeys now. For one thing they are more muscular and physical than the jockeys of the past. These guys are athletes—Tittia, Scompiglio. This is very different than the past generation, such as when Aceto and his rival, Silvano Vigni [nicknamed Bastiano], were at their height." These latter two jockeys, long since retired from racing, were also featured in the 2015 British documentary film, *Palio*, which likewise focused on generational changes. Enrico continues, "Jockeys of the past generation were basically normal people. Vigni is a farmer, for instance. Trecciolino is a professional jockey for sure, but even he admits to 'letting go' after a Palio for a few weeks when he gains some weight. But the younger jockeys are physically stronger, and they actually train."

I follow up with, "Are you happy with this change taking place?"

"I think it's probably a good thing now, for Siena and the Palio. We have a larger number of good jockeys who are attracted to the Campo, and all of them have won recently and want to keep winning: Tittia, Scompiglio, Brio, and most recently Gingillo. For probably two decades, Trecciolino tried to control everything; it was him and his band of merry men," we laugh at what is likely Enrico's last creative metaphor during my time with him today. "So, it's probably better now that there is more competition between the jockeys. I think the Palio will be healthier overall because of this."

As we part ways and I head back to our lodging, I contemplate how the Straordinario may mark a turning point in Siena. The transition to the next generation of more professional jockeys may now be complete.

❉ CHAPTER 10 ❉

A Stalloreggi Lunch

BEFORE OUR TRIP, I DECIDED TO CONTACT ANGELO, A YOUNG FRIEND FROM THE Panther contrada whom I had met several years earlier. He has been working toward a college degree while continuing to improve his already excellent command of English. Not surprisingly, this unwavering proponent of contrada life planned to return home for the days of the Palio. After confirming this was the case, I asked if he was interested in meeting to share his perspectives on the Straordinario. Various social media posts had indicated that he was not taking the event lightly.

He responded, "Sure, that's great you're coming! The Panther isn't running, of course, so I won't be as busy as usual with contrada duties."

"Do you want to set up a day and time to meet?" I asked, like the hyper-planned American that I am.

"Probably not. I'll be there by Wednesday night, so you can find me in the contrada when you are ready. OK?"

After snickering at his vague if predictable response, I replied, "OK, great. I will contact you after we both arrive, and I will find you in the Panther." By now, I know this means he will be engaged with various activities or volunteer duties at their contrada community center, Società Due Porte. Given my own plans to enjoy one or more Panther events, I could likely find him at those if all else failed.

My Shifting Universe

Now two days before the Palio, I find myself with some precious free time after the morning trial. This may be the best time to contact Angelo to see if we can meet. To my delight, he responds almost immediately. "Yes, I can meet you soon. I will be up in the Panther in about fifteen minutes." *Right*, I think with a grin. From experience, this usually means I will find him somewhat serendipitously at Piazza del Conte or at the società. Without a better idea about how to find him, I decide to linger around the Panther's second social space, the compact Piazza del Conte. Here, I can hopefully intercept his path. I have learned not to concern myself so much with structured meeting plans in Siena. Eventually, the right people seem to show up in one way or another.

With only minimal surprise, this is precisely what happens. The probability was high that we would find each other on Via Stalloreggi, the main city street that cuts through the Panther rione. He is now walking my way, with a couple of companions by his side. After reacquainting ourselves once again, he gestures for me to follow him to a place where he plans to eat lunch with some others. I don't intend to keep him too long from his lunch date, but he is eager to talk about the Palio. First, we all arrive at a restaurant that Linda and I have yet to try, Antica Trattoria Stalloreggi. I peak inside and it's already buzzing with patrons. Angelo does the same and motions for us to wait here in the street. He is going to inquire about availability. At this point, I just stand back and let things unfold. More people arrive who also seem to know Angelo, and they are decidedly curious about the plans—or lack of same—for this aforementioned lunch.

I eventually recognize Alessio, one of Angelo's closest friends in the contrada. Together they led our cohort's more recent tours of the Panther museum. While reacquainting myself with Alessio, Angelo eventually re-emerges and begins to coordinate efforts with the others. Clearly, I am not the only one who is confused. Nonetheless, following a protracted conversation in Italian, they seem to have a plan. Another lesson I have learned in Siena is to take a deep breath and allow things to play out as they should. Taking my own advice, I simply stand to one side as the apparent plan is set in motion. Somehow, I manage to glean that Angelo and Alessio are now headed back to Società Due Porte for the moment. It is difficult to contain my curiosity, however, about why.

After we all linger around the restaurant for a few minutes, an amusing sight greets my eyes. Alessio and Angelo promptly return, each carrying the end of a folding contrada dinner table. *Very cool*, I think, as I quickly realize their intention. This is just one subtle characteristic of contrada life that I have come to appreciate. Community members simply feel at home by adapting spaces to their own needs. In one sense, the public spaces of their contrada rione serve as veritable outdoor living rooms. The determined duo then disappears again, and they return with arms full of the Panther's standard folding wooden chairs. Finally making myself useful, I jump in and help the others place the chairs around the table. I can't help but grin at our emerging scene here. We are now literally in the Via Stalloreggi right-of-way, one of Siena's busier medieval-era thoroughfares. Yet, we are setting up a lengthy dinner table for their impending group lunch.

Perhaps Angelo is reading my mind during the setup process, as he stops briefly and grabs my attention. He explains, "We can kind-of get away with this if there aren't too many tables, which would break city code," he smirks. "But this one should be OK, we've done it before." Then he throws me a surprise as their group of ten people settles in. "Tom, are you staying for lunch with us?"

The funny thing here is that I don't know whether to interpret this as an invitation or not. As an American interloper I had not planned on crashing their lunch party. However, his question sets the gears in my brain into overdrive. There is an opportunity here to meet more people and learn something new. "Well, I don't want to impose, but if you have enough space, I can stay," I respond in a wishy-washy manner. Eating a full lunch right now was not something Linda and I had discussed, let alone sitting down without warning to invade a group of close-knit contrada members. Still, I suspect this is one of those opportunities that should not be so easily rejected. No doubt, a wonderful experience awaits, and beyond that—further reminding myself—I still want to speak with Angelo about the Palio.

"Yes, we have enough spaces now," Angelo responds. "So, are you staying or not?"

I laugh at his rather direct approach to this unlikely invitation. Nevertheless, I bite. "OK, I will enjoy having lunch with all of you. Thanks!" We both take our chairs next to one another, with Alessio now placed on his other side. I quickly text Linda to inform her that I may not return for a couple of hours, knowing full well how these Italian meals tend to work. She has been very patient this week as she knows I am eager to speak with people here about the Palio. She is likewise well aware that sometimes opportunities arise that should not be turned down. If there is a clearer case in point than this, I do not know what it is. I contemplate that only fifteen minutes ago I was simply trying to chase down Angelo for an impromptu conversation. Since then, the universe has instantly shifted. *I am now sitting at a makeshift contrada table in Via Stalloreggi with a group of strangers, most of whom I have never met and speak only Italian. How does it get any better than this?*

Eating in Traffic

We have no sooner established our places when we hear a sharp honk not far from our position. A small car has arrived at our table, strange as it may sound. Given our exposed location, people can simply drive right up to us. Although we are off to one side near the building walls, we are still definitely projecting out into a rather a narrow street. Suitably alerted by the car horn, we turn to see what is transpiring. This little car and its occupant are blocking traffic behind him. The honk has come from about three cars back. Had this first driver wanted to move past our location, he could have easily done so. However, a particularly unlucky situation has presented itself: the car owner's makeshift garage is almost directly across from our table. *Good golly, what are the chances of that?* With our improvised patio outside his home, the poor fellow cannot complete his normal three- or five-point turn to back into his ground-floor hideaway. Now taking the lead (as he often does), Angelo bolts up, speaks with the driver, and starts directing us like a police officer. Meanwhile I am feeling a bit embarrassed that our group has inadvertently caused a traffic jam on one of Siena's main streets. It's not every year one can say they are simultaneously *blocking* traffic while *eating* in traffic.

Angelo explains the plan to us in Italian, but I catch on quickly. It's not rocket science. We need to physically move the table and chairs to allow this guy's parking ritual to progress. Along with the others, I grab a couple of chairs and virtually throw them back toward the restaurant entrance. Then a few of us jump in to carry the surprisingly heavy wooden table downslope a bit behind us. To their credit, the other drivers are waiting somewhat patiently as they can now see what is causing the delay—of all things, a lunchtime gathering. They are undoubtedly thinking similarly: *Those damned Panthers think they can eat anywhere they want around here.* And they would be right. At least two of our companions volunteer to guide our hapless motorist as he gingerly backs his little car into a very tight space. Moving our table and chairs may not qualify as rocket science, though the near-heroic process of parking one's car in the historic center comes very close.

It eventually dawns on me how this problem-solving situation provides an opportunity to assist the others. This naturally encourages me to feel more personally attached to the group. Strangely, I don't even know the rest of these people, and they have not yet been introduced to me. Still, introductions will have to wait until we are settled once again, hopefully with no more parking hassles in our future. I give myself a symbolic pat on the back right now. Had this occurred four or five years earlier, there is little chance I would have allowed myself to join an impromptu Senese luncheon with a bunch of strangers. This clearly says something about my enhanced comfort level here.

With the crisis rectified, we claim our territory again and take our places. Always the leader, Angelo runs in and out of the *trattoria* (small restaurant) to presumably order drinks and prepare orders for lunch. We are not being provided with menus, so I suppose we will enjoy a community spread. Given my appreciation for merely being here right now, I am content to enjoy whatever type of consumables happen to appear in front of us. It takes little imagination to suspect that we will soon be enjoying some version of local Tuscan food—prodotti tipici Toscani —as Dario and I enjoyed only days earlier. Upon Angelo's return, I manage to get his attention for a minute to ask about the trattoria.

"Is this the main restaurant for Panterini?" I ask, wondering if this is where contrada members prefer to socialize and meet one another.

"No, it's not an official place for the contrada. It happens to be on Via Stalloreggi, and it is close to the società," he explains. "And there are other factors, too, for why this is a popular place," he adds. "The main chef is a Panther, and he happens to be very good. So, we like their food," he laughs.

"Do contrada members purposely support him because he is a Panther?" I often wonder how much personal connections matter with respect to the success of various local places like this.

"No, not purposely because of that. It's a lot of things, I guess. If he wasn't such a good chef with excellent food, maybe we would not eat here so often," he chuckles. "But it *is* close to the contrada, and by using our contrada table outside we are actually helping his business. This is like a free table for him," he gestures around to all of us. "We are not taking up space inside, so they can have more customers."

A STALLOREGGI LUNCH

At this point I have relaxed about being a part of this genuine social experience. They show no signs of caring whether I am present or not, and the fact that I am tagging along with Angelo should be quite obvious to them.

As water and other beverages are poured, the identities of my fellow diners are finally revealed. Angelo graciously informs everyone in Italian that I am a professor from the United States who is interested in the Palio and the contrade. No longer able to blend in silently, I am now in the limelight as all eyes focus on me. In response, I provide a friendly wave around the table and say "*Piacere* [pleased to meet you]," ending confidently with, "and I speak a *little* Italian; thank you for the invitation." A few others indicate that they speak a little English but not so well. After this veritable icebreaker, we are off and running. I decide to ask Angelo to explain who we have here with us.

Starting to my left at the head of the table, he works his way around. "OK, so everybody here is a Panther," he begins appropriately. "This is Andrea and his two daughters. They are friends of the family. This is my Mom, who owns a business in town. I am still allowed to stay with her when I come home," he jokes, to which she laughs. "Then next to her is Mom's friend, Elisa, and you know Alessio. These guys are Piero and Marco, who have lived here all their lives." Now suitably introduced, it is time to dive in.

Tuscan Antipasti

It isn't long before several large plates arrive, namely the *antipasti*. The term is Latin in origin (*ante*—before, *pastus*—food or meal) and dates to a medieval-era tradition. Although I am not a true "foodie," I am still a consummate geographer. Local and regional traditions and cultures are always fascinating, so even the particulars of traditional Tuscan food catch my interest. Given the region's timeless connection to both land and sea, it is no surprise that a typical *antipasto* plate in this region includes a mix of cheeses, marinated vegetables, cold meats, salted fish (including anchovies), and olives. Various cured meats such as salamis and prosciutto are likewise common, and I immediately see that we are blessed today with the perfect choice of traditional Tuscan food. Rounding out the meal is the expected plain Tuscan bread and an incredible bean salad, of which I take more than my share. According to various online sources, such a blend of antipasto foods is no accident, but is strategically designed to prepare one's excitement for the main meal—as if I needed further encouragement for Italian pasta and meat dishes. Regardless, the diverse mix of food types and colors is meant to engage all the senses and encourage one's appetite, but hopefully without prematurely filling up one's stomach.

After some bantering with our tablemates, Angelo turns to me and asks if I am familiar with antipasti foods like this, to which I carefully respond, "Somewhat." He then thankfully takes me on a personal tour of our mixed offerings. I tend to gravitate toward using a fork for most of my food, though I decide to play the role of an exchange student and ask if I should use my hands for the meats and cheeses.

"Oh yes, just use your hands," he responds simply. "You don't need to be formal with us," he jokes. Others are likewise using their hands, so I dive in with the rest of them. Knowing that my appetite disappears quickly, however, I take my time on this course, thinking that I may need to order some pasta to follow. It turns out that a few people are indeed ordering the next course, the primi piatti, which are always my favorite. Fortunately for me, however, most of them are ultimately satisfied with the mountains of antipasti choices. My stomach will thus be spared from a full Italian meal today. There is more than plenty of food right here for a sizable lunch.

Then, Angelo's emotional attachment for Siena and Tuscany kicks in. This twentysomething young man begins to speak as if he is four decades older.

"This is what I live for. Just the smells of this food make me so happy to be back home," he begins, with his Mom and a few others who understand English listening in. I keep in mind that Angelo only arrived last night from his British university and internship. Strangely, I have been situated here in Siena longer than him.

He continues, "These smells, this food, people hanging out and talking, this is what it's all about. In the US and Britain—no offense—but it seems like there is a clear distinction between the wealth of the people and the quality of the food. The more money you have, the better the food. I could be ten times richer than now, and I would still be eating this," he gestures to our table and plates. "And this isn't even high-quality local food. This is standard. Your wealth doesn't matter here." I chuckle to myself because of Angelo's refreshing tendency to tell it like it is.

"So, has it been a challenge to get used to British food?" I ask, hoping for more commentary.

"Oh yes, it has been very difficult," he says seriously. "There is definitely a big culture shock living there. The differences between there and here are huge." Then Angelo says, as someone his age might, "And nobody smokes there, it's like the US! It's not cool to smoke. But then they take all sorts of pills and mix them with drinks at the bar. It's crazy!" We all laugh as he translates this into Italian for the others. This has truly become a multilingual gathering.

By this point in our meal, I have already lost count of the people who have walked past our table and said hello. Sometimes there are three or four such visitors at a time, which in turn encourages one or two of our lunch mates—including Angelo—to stand up for a brief chat. I even recognize some of them from the Panther, and some recognize me as well. After five years of enjoying a variety of contrada events both with and without students in tow, it is safe to say they recognize me as a "friend of the Panther." In fact, this is how I now typically introduce myself to other Panterini. I find that they don't seem to need any further explanation than that, at least for starters.

Having planted ourselves in the path of Panterini foot traffic, we have created our own miniature contrada function. My lunch mates seem perfectly comfortable with these random visitations, which are not only expected, but are unquestionably welcomed. This is one sign of a close-knit community, I contemplate. While part of me feels a sense of being interrupted amid a family dinner, nobody here thinks twice about abandoning their food or conversation to recognize a newcomer with a handshake or hug. This is a place to see and be seen.

Thoughts on the Palio

Before the intrigue of this meal distracts me beyond repair, I somehow still recall my original intent for being here. I am first curious to know if the Panterini—or the contrada, more officially—favors one contrada to win over others. Of course, its rival, the Eagle, is not an overt factor in this one. I take the plunge, finally seeing a window of opportunity between bites, conversation, and visitors.

I blurt out, "So, Angelo, does the contrada care much about who wins this Palio?"

"No, it doesn't matter," he says with less interest than the next bite he is now loading up. Not quite expecting such an ambivalent response, my inquiry thus comes to a crashing end with the proverbial thud. Perhaps this indicates, however, that contradaioli don't necessarily always reveal a passionate favorite in a particular race. There is not always something at stake for them.

I quickly pivot to the voting process which continues to fascinate me. He explains, "As you might be aware, all the contrade were given the opportunity to vote about whether to hold the Palio, and ten voted 'yes.' After that, the seven that voted 'no' were given a second chance—within a few days, I think—to reverse their original vote."

I continue to press, "Do you agree with giving the seven contrade a second chance to join in?"

"Yes. It makes good sense," he answers unwaveringly between final bites of cold cuts. "Think about what might happen if the second vote was not allowed. If they were not given the chance to reverse the initial vote, then they all would have voted 'yes' the first time. They would not want to risk being left out of the extraction."

Given earlier conversations about game theory and contrada strategies, Angelo's perspective makes more sense to me now. "OK, I think I finally understand this," I say to Angelo with a smile. "If the second vote to overturn a 'no' decision was not allowed, then probably every proposed idea for holding a Straordinario would be approved every time—in theory, anyway."

"Yes, exactly!" He rewards my logic. He shakes his left arm toward the table for emphasis. "Every idea that is proposed, no matter how bad, would be approved by the contrade if the second vote was not allowed, to play it safe."

"Right, so this two-vote process serves as an effective filter to help sift out the less popular ideas that might occasionally be proposed," I conclude.

By this time, those who had ordered primi piatti are digging into the meal's second course. I feel silently grateful for not having been obligated to consume a large pasta dish. My stomach and taste buds are already quite satisfied with the antipasti alone.

At which point, Angelo directs a food-related question to me, "Tom, have you had truffle before? It's fantastic." His pasta dish includes truffle in the sauce. Although he is always happy to discuss the Palio, Angelo's primary interest is clearly surfacing here for the moment.

A STALLOREGGI LUNCH

I have to think a bit. "Well, I don't believe that I have purposely eaten truffle," I hedge. Then I cave. "I know it's popular, and people rave about it, but what exactly is it?" I laugh.

"Here, try some," he throws some pasta with flaky gray stuff on my plate. "It's actually quite rare, because you can't grow truffle, like on a farm. You need to find it naturally. There is actually a lot of it in Tuscany, but you have to know what you're looking for. Since it grows underground, people use dogs to find it." He takes a break to chew and swallow. I take a bite myself, not letting on that I can't distinguish the truffle from the rest of the pasta sauce. He then laughs, "So, dogs have to hunt for the special smell, but you have to stop the dogs before they dig it up and eat it themselves. There are actually people who specialize in hunting truffle, called *tartufaio*. The Italian word for truffle is *tartufo*," he adds, making me pronounce it correctly. I have seen the word often enough in menus here, but until today's culinary education, I have not consciously considered it.

I would learn later that there are more than twenty varieties of truffle found in Italy, though only a few are considered desirable by humans and are actually edible—or, one might say, marketable. More amazing, the four or five varieties found around Siena have their own distinctive growing seasons. The popular white truffle, for instance, is found predominantly in central Tuscany and around Siena. This happens to be the variety currently in season, during autumn. Angelo continues and points to the sauce, "See how the truffle here is flat? It's best if it is eaten raw, warmed up to release the flavors, and shaved onto your food." *Well, that explains the suspicious brown flakes in his pasta*, I conclude to myself. Whether the flavors have been suitably released into my own mouth, I cannot tell. But I am feeling grateful for another cultural lesson as I nod with genuine approval of the tasty dish.

Not long after Angelo's food tour, the table conversation is turning back to the Palio. "What do you think about the decision to hold the Straordinario?" I begin with purposeful vagueness. "Did you support the idea?"

"Some people say that the mayor and council started the idea for political reasons, but I think that's [expletive]," he begins with his characteristic directness. "I think the anniversary of the Great War is an excellent reason to hold a Palio. Every contrada has a monument dedicated to their soldiers. Young people my age were sent to the front line and never came back," he states seriously. "This actually got me thinking about the war, and I finally paid attention to our own memorial."

"That's really great," I respond, impressed that at least the idea of the centennial is stimulating some local education. I had wondered if this would be a consequence—intended or otherwise—of holding the Palio. I add, "I noticed that the Panther held an educational event last weekend. I would have liked to see it!"

"Yes, I was not here, of course, but the contrada hosted a showing of a film about the war and held a walking tour of local monuments beforehand," he proudly states. "You'll hear others say, 'oh, the people just wanted an excuse to hold a Palio,' but it's really not about that. And if it is, then it doesn't matter anyway. This is a good way to bring attention to or own history."

"Sure, that make sense," I say in general agreement. "Was the contrada fairly unified in its approval of the idea?"

"Yes, for us the vote was highly in favor, with maybe only forty voting against."

This gives me an opening to ask a question that Antonio had surfaced earlier this week. "Was there any concern about the Eagle?"

"Well, this was discussed, and some argued that it would give the Eagle a chance to win—you know they are the nonna now. So, this was considered," he admits.

"So, why did this argument not convince people to vote against it?" I continue to prod.

"Well, personally I think this is a selfish perspective, and I know others thought that, too." He surprises me with this response, as I am still not quite sure I understand. He explains, "Most people in the Panther were willing to take the risk that the Eagle would be extracted and maybe even win. Worrying too much about the Eagle is selfish, because it means we are only thinking narrowly about our own contrada and our rival. If it's a good idea for Siena as a whole city, then we should support it."

Wow, this is a fresh perspective, I think, having not foreseen this explanation.

Angelo continues after choosing to swallow some quick bites of lukewarm pasta. "Still, the Palio was a good chance for us as well, so why worry so much about our rival? We have a chance to run the Palio, so there are few downsides to that. We might not have another Straordinario for twenty years or more. They don't happen very often now."

I react thoughtfully, "So maybe the biggest risk was if the Eagle had been extracted, without the Panther."

"Sure," he admits. "But say we are extracted, and the Eagle isn't. Well, then there is no problem at all, of course. Or, if both the Eagle and Panther are extracted, then it's really just like a normal Palio. This case would not be very different from others. Sure, if the Eagle runs on its own without us in the Campo, then OK, we [get nervous] for four days, but that's the way it is. Being worried about your rival is not a good reason in our opinion to turn down a rare extra Palio."

I turn to the topic of attendance. "How many of the contrada members are able to be here this week? Are a lot of people working?"

To this he jokes with the others and asks them something about being away from work. "Well, Marco is here with his children. Nobody expected the children to be in school during the days of the Palio," he laughs. "But this is true; not as many people are taking vacation time. Although, since we are not running this time, there is less interest in the contrada. This is typical as well."

"Would it have been a problem for more people if the Panther was running? More people would have to take vacation," I suggest.

"I think people would have found ways to do it, to be here," he muses. "For me, this Palio was important. Like I said, this is a historic event for Siena. I wanted to come back to *live it*—to live the experience of the Palio again." Upon hearing him speak these words (and I am not making them up!), I can't help but inwardly smile as he invokes the title of my first book about Siena.

He continues to explain his own story about being here. "So, you are aware that I've been going to college, but right now I am working for an internship position. I only had two more vacation days for this year, and I used them for this," he laughs and raises his voice. "I even gave up Christmas for this! I can't take any vacation time for Christmas now." He repeats this in Italian for the benefit of the others, and everyone laughs heartily. Now Angelo is on a roll, so to speak, and continues. "I mean, they could have held a Straordinario any other year, but it had to be this one! The one time they do this, I am actually working and need to take vacation time. If this were any other year, I could just leave the university and skip class! And we're not even [expletive] running!" All of us are absolutely howling as he translates this into Italian for the benefit of the others.

From where I sit—literally and figuratively—Angelo's testimony about this Palio's significance is genuine and heartfelt. He can "walk the walk" by being here and participating. Whether or not the Straordinario is viewed as some sort of political move, contradaioli throughout Siena are now rallying to savor this historically rare event. What began as a rather lethargic lead-up to the days of the Palio has transitioned into a degree of zeal and passion more typical of the summer events. And somewhat remarkably, the weather continues to hold out; in fact, conditions should be perfect for the main event. One can almost hear the collective exhaling of city leaders and others who had placed all their cards on the table. While keeping in mind Enrico's prior words of wisdom about "four days and three laps," Siena is about to pull off the long shot in more ways than one.

PART III:
PARTICIPATION

CHAPTER 11

The Third Trial

A POLICE OFFICER ASKS ME IN BROKEN ENGLISH, "CAN I HELP YOU WITH something?" In other words, *What are you doing here?* I guess there's no point in trying to convince him that I'm a local. "No, I am waiting for a friend, to watch the trial," I respond, with the added hope that I am not already in trouble for my mere presence. "OK," he says comfortingly, "but you can wait outside." *Fine.* In this way I am politely evicted from the service entrance on the far-right side of Palazzo Pubblico. Mike had instructed me to wait for him inside this entrance at 4:45 p.m., and that time has now come . . . and gone. Although I never once used this entrance during my first six summers in Siena, I have entered the Palazzo here twice in less than a week. Of course, the first time was with Mike and Gabriele to view General Diaz's victory speech from the conclusion of World War I. Without an escort this time, however, I am summarily being "booted off the island." *Where is Mike, anyway?* We both have much in common, not the least being our typical American obsession about promptness.

Yesterday he had sent me a startling email, the likes of which I rarely see back home. Mike had somehow acquired two tickets to see the *terza prova* (third trial) from one of the windows in Palazzo Pubblico. Upon inquiring how he had pulled off this feat, he humbly explained that one of his good friends had been elected recently to the city council, so he offered Mike a couple of tickets free of charge. In turn, Mike knew I was here to learn about the Palio this week, so he naturally thought that I might like to join him. I could make up some story here about how my stature in the Senese community has grown to include prominent connections with local officials, but alas this has not yet (and likely will not) come to pass. Regardless, I was genuinely grateful that Mike had thought of me and that I was—as people joked in the 1990s—"number one on speed dial."

THE THIRD TRIAL

Stall Tactics

I had been instructed to wait for him in the service entrance, though my self-proclaimed, darn-near heroic effort to do so has now resulted in a somewhat diminished status as a loiterer outside the Palazzo. Of course, my current predicament is rooted in the very reason for being here in the first place. The city is preparing diligently for the third trial, and I am simply getting in the way. Just to get here, I had discovered through trial and error that certain back streets were necessary to arrive at the Campo, as main entrances were either blocked by security guards or were simply crowded with onlookers in the streets. Upon reaching the Campo from Via Giovanni Duprè, I was lightly searched by a line of soldiers similar to those now guarding every entrance. Backpacks and water bottles were allowed, but only after being visually screened. Having passed through the checkpoint, I literally leaped out onto the dirt track in front of Palazzo Pubblico to find throngs of people milling around, waiting for the police to clear the track in advance of the trial.

Typically, I arrive earlier for such events. The six trials in advance of the Palio serve as significant community events, and they attract many thousands of contrada members and visitors alike. While shading my eyes from the sun, I now scan around the track while trying to avoid being hit by fast-moving humans on their way somewhere else. To my right, the bleachers for the children in front of the Palazzo are filling up. Many contradaioli have already taken their own bleachers around the Campo and are occasionally singing or chanting as loud as they can shout.

With an unending stream of people filtering through the police line, I am almost like a small rock interrupting the flow of water in a stream channel. But I can't venture too far from the service entrance. What if Mike arrives to find me absent? The kicker is that the police line at Via Giovanni Duprè is actually closer to my position here than the service entrance, providing me with precious little room to maneuver while waiting for Mike. I finally decide to remove myself from the racetrack once and for all, sneaking into the empty space behind the towering children's bleachers. To the left of the bleachers is a narrow cubbyhole where a few people can access the barrier to view the track. I decide to plant myself here for the time being, in the company of a man who appears to be a city worker in a yellow vest. From here, I can spy the track and much of the entrance area for Mike (Figure 7).

Figure 7. View of the Childrens' Bleachers filling in prior to the third trial. (Photo: Author)

After a few minutes, a well-dressed gentleman joins me in the cubby and quickly sizes me up. *Drat, this isn't good*, I quickly think. As predicted, he says, "Is there a reason you are here? You need to be out there on the track." I successfully comprehend his message in full Italian as he directs me elsewhere. But this time I decide to defend myself, indicating that I truly belong here. In half-decent Italian, I respond, "I am waiting for a friend, Michael (I pronounce his name in its Italian form, *MEEK-e-ley*), for Palazzo Pubblico." Somewhat to my astonishment, he responds, "Oh, OK, that's fine," after which he simply leaves me alone. Now feeling less self-conscious, I venture out of the cubbyhole again to scan the narrow space between the bleachers and the Palazzo. I recognize the occasional familiar face, including various city officials who have served in Siena's local government for multiple years. This space appears to be doubling as the staging area from where they will begin their standard foot parade up to the judges' stand before the trial.

THE THIRD TRIAL

In some respects, I am now backstage for the first time, unintentionally witnessing the setup routine before the show.

Finally, my stall tactics are rewarded with the sight of a familiar face. Mike is arriving, clearly exasperated with his own tiresome commute. He is not one to misjudge the time, so he has my sympathies. After waving off his frustrations, he motions in a business-like manner for me to follow him through the service entrance. I am finally legitimate, albeit with an escort. Mike finds someone in the darker recesses of the entry to ask about his own friend's whereabouts. Eventually, they find each other, and Mike introduces me to Luca, who is the one who had indirectly provided the tickets. A member of the Dragon contrada, Luca is sporting his green and gold fazzoletto as one might expect. With my companions now beside me, I can now relax and enjoy the festive evening.

An Impromptu Palazzo Tour

We next make our way to the base of a wide, expansive stone staircase, suitably scaled for a government building of this stature. We immediately launch up the stairs, and I fall in behind the others. Along the way, I am treated to a veritable museum of former building columns, statuary, and centuries-old entry doors that most certainly date back to the Republic of Siena. Gnarled and worn, the massive double doors are now out of place here, displayed on one of the landings. After ascending more than a few flights, I start to wonder how far up we will go. *Are they putting us on the roof?* I have to remind myself that the height of one floor here is likely equivalent to three or four such floors at home. Finally, my companions issue us into a spacious room befitting a former palace. Mike indicates to me that we are now inside the wing of the Palazzo where the business of the city is conducted. It still blows my mind that city government has been housed somewhere within this structure consistently for more than 600 years!

Passing through one oversized doorway after another, I recall that medieval palaces like this—whether built for civic purposes or for royal families—did not include hallways. Rather, the rooms were built adjacent to one another with simple connecting doorways. As we move hurriedly from one room to the next, my eyes swing back and forth between two competing views begging for my attention. One is the continuous row of triple Gothic windows to our left. Under the windows are platforms designed specifically for viewing the Palio. Small copper plaques with numbers are installed below each opening to allow for assigned seats. My curiosity eventually kicks in with respect to just how far through the building we will go. The Torre del Mangia can't be far away now. With each window we pass, I catch my first glimpses of the populated Campo below.

Competing for my attention to our right side are the exquisite interiors of former palace rooms with their copious square footage and towering ceiling heights that far surpass the needs of the occupants. Mike then turns back to me and provides an impromptu tour of the city's business offices. "It always amazes me," he says as we pause for a moment, "how these old rooms have been retrofitted with modern office equipment." We both chuckle at the somewhat amusing sight laid out in front of us. Unsightly filing cabinets and office tables covered with computers and printers are dwarfed in comparison to the lavish, frescoed ceiling that towers over them. Let's face it; no matter how hard one tries, there is no way for electronic office equipment to seamlessly blend into the jaw-dropping grandeur of a medieval palace. Aesthetic considerations aside, however, today's office work still requires the use of modern-day equipment—whether tucked into an elegant palace or not.

The City Council Chambers

The next room causes Luca to pause with us. His smile indicates a mixture of pride and awe as he prepares to reveal something. I imagine that his impending revelation is located behind this interior wall that is essentially penning us up against the massive Gothic windows. This reminds me of walking down the side corridor of a railroad sleeping car. In any case, we have reached the end of the wall, and it finally dawns on me that we are located just outside a "room within a room." Luca opens an uninspiring corner door, and we all peer inside like school kids. My mouth hangs open at the intricate woodwork and stylish chairs, clearly matching the relative political importance of those who sit in them.

Luca explains a bit to Mike in Italian, after which Mike translates for me. "This is where the city council meets". Known more officially as the Sala del Capitano del Popolo (the Hall of the Captain of the People), this luxurious, towering palace room could not be more appropriate for the home of Siena's democratic leadership. Somewhat more complex than a typical mayor-council system in the United States, Italian local governments such as that of Siena are organized like small-scale parliamentary systems. One governing arm of the council consists of the mayor and various *assessori* (appointed aldermen and alderwomen) who oversee specific city offices. This group makes up the Giunta. Its larger counterpart is the Consiglio Comunale, or town council (often shortened to "the Consiglio"), which includes some thirty or so individuals elected by the people with various political party affiliations. The Consiglio is headed by its own president. The room we are gawking at now is designed to hold the entire council, with the mayor and assessori sitting at the head table. Flanking both sides of the head table are the wooden, high-backed seats of the Consiglio members who—perhaps appropriately for civic discussions—face each other across the room. In all, the seating arrangement forms the shape of an elongated horseshoe.

After visually absorbing the floor layout, our eyes naturally move upwards to something more astonishing. Every inch of the vaulted ceiling is covered in artwork representing a variety of different eras. No doubt an entire Consiglio member's term would be necessary just to absorb and comprehend it all (while neglecting one's civic duties, to be sure). Mike adds, "Do you see those paintings under the ceiling, between the vaults? Those are *lunettes*, and all of them tell a story about the history of Siena." I am further told that there are sixteen of them and that they were painstakingly painted by a cadre of prominent Senese artists between 1592 and 1600.

As with typical lunettes, they are painted in the upper semicircular spaces in the walls where they transition into the vaulted ceiling. These locations provide the added practical benefit of not having to strain one's neck to the extent necessary for viewing images on the ceiling. For all their artistic splendor, part of me has never quite understood the earlier fascination with using the ceiling as a canvas. One must struggle against natural human posture for five or ten seconds at a time in a rather uncomfortable attempt to view them. It's not unlike placing all the most highly desired food products on the very top shelf of a grocery store. Nonetheless, the sixteen renderings here form a veritable timeline of events during the Renaissance that are considered significant to the Senesi—with descriptions available on the internet for those curious to read more.[59]

For me, the lunettes serve as a quite humbling reminder of my own deficiency of knowledge regarding Siena's extensive history. Although I recognize some of the events depicted, many of them remain unfamiliar. The subjects on the lunettes include Pope Pius II presenting the arm of John the Baptist to the city and—most numerous, of course—various military victories, including those over Arrigo VII at Radi, Henry VI at Rosario, and the Florentines at the better known Battle of Montaperti in 1260 CE. The beloved Saint Catherine (Santa Caterina)—who hailed from the Goose contrada's rione—is also wisely included (more about her later).

With all of us suitably awed, Luca closes the chamber door and we make our final approach to our assigned window perches. Before alighting for the evening to watch the trial, however, our impromptu tour continues in the very room we will enjoy for the evening. Hung at regular intervals on the side and back walls is a series of oval-shaped, framed portraits of whom I would initially interpret as rather grumpy old men. I quickly learn why. Mike explains with a grin, "All of those men in the paintings were former popes that had some connection to Siena." At this news I focus less on their collective frowns while considering Siena's impressive role in the history of the Catholic Church.

If that weren't enough, four of these famed Catholic leaders claimed Siena as their hometown. Briefly for purposes here, Alexander III was of the Bandinelli Paparoni family and is credited with excommunicating and defeating the Holy Roman Emperor, Frederick Barbarossa (known as Red Beard). Pope Pius II, belonging to the Piccolomini family, was considered one of the most educated men of his time; he redesigned the urban center of nearby Pienza through innovative Renaissance-inspired urban design. Today the Piccolomini Library inside the Duomo is dedicated to his life and accomplishments. Then there was the presumably unfortunate Pius III, a nephew of Pius II, who served as pope for a total of only twenty-six days. The fourth pope from Siena was Alexander VII of the Chigi family; his role in carrying out the architectural renewal of Rome during the Baroque period cannot be understated and is certainly worthy of a separate book.

Beyond representing the conventional artistic approaches of that era, I cannot help but imagine that their sullen dispositions are likewise a reaction to what lies beneath them—that is, a quite unsightly collection of electronic office equipment, the likes of which we saw earlier. All but defacing their

THE THIRD TRIAL

otherwise sacred space is an anachronistic collection of plastic and metal office tables, brightly colored rolling chairs, metal desk lamps, computer towers, and monitors scattered about. Connecting all of it to some far-off receptacle is a spaghetti-like matrix of black cables and wires clinging to the floor and tables. Ugh. It is as if someone humorously transplanted the entire studio set of the American TV show, *The Office*, into the Sistine Chapel.

Despite admitted advances in time-saving technologies, no one has apparently invented a way to visually blend all this stuff into the grandeur of an Italian palace. No matter, the work still needs to get done. More horrible still would be if the entire municipal government up and left their historic city hall in favor of more spacious and modern facilities in the suburbs—a common practice that has sometimes gutted the traditional downtowns of American cities. To its highly deserving credit, Siena's municipal government has steadfastly remained here in Palazzo Pubblico for centuries, honoring the very purpose for which it was designed. And, should one ever wish to restore this room to its original splendor, I see nothing here that can't simply be picked up and carried away within an hour—thereby leaving the room's historical integrity intact.

Preparations for the Trial

Amidst the mechanisms of city government, our attention turns to the windows allocated for our enjoyment of the trial. Other fortunate viewers have already occupied the nearby windows. I am quite relieved to find none of the royal or VIP visitors one might have expected in the past. Rather, we are accompanied here by a more comfortably diverse mix of local residents. In one set of windows is a cadre of young women from the She-Wolf contrada, all of whom are wearing black and white sweatshirts designed for the Straordinario. One intriguing practice of contrada *couture* for this week's festivities is the distribution of contrada-specific sweatshirts for their respective members. I have now seen such attire adorning various groups of contradaioli representing the She-Wolf, Turtle, and Goose. The distribution of sweatshirts for this rare October event was quite the creative and rational choice!

As for our own cohort, we are now located on the eastern third of the building (bell tower side) on what Italians would call the second floor. I keep reminding myself that Italians don't count the ground level as the first floor, as we do in America. Regardless of its proper term, we are in fact perched rather high above the Campo, and the Gothic window openings are expansive enough for all of us to comfortably soak in the evolving scene below. This is the first time I have been elevated to this extent since enjoying the viewing platform of the Torre del Mangia several years earlier.

From our overhead perch, we enjoy a commanding view of the entire track and center of the Campo—with the exception of the notorious curve of San Martino below us to the right. The ever-imposing Cappella di Piazza roofline is blocking our view, but there are no complaints among us. The construction of this massive structure—whose purpose was to demonstrate gratitude for the city's mere survival following the Black Death episode of 1348—was troublesome from the outset. Portions of it were rebuilt numerous times until its final completion in 1376. The Renaissance-style roof now blocking our view was also replaced a century later, in 1461.

Now gaining courage to lean out over the thick windowsill, I first notice that the crowd is lighter than one might expect for this evening trial. The bleachers are certainly filling with contradaioli, though copious expanses of empty space still remain in the center. Normally the Campo would be packed more densely at this point as the police clear people from the track before the trial. Although still harboring untold thousands, the lighter attendance this evening appears to reflect the trend of all pre-Palio events thus far. Still, from up here we can hear the stable murmur of the crowd's collective conversations.

And then, boom! The *mortaretto* (small mortar) located near the starting line sounds off for the first time, signaling the clearing of the track. What I notice most is the reaction of the crowd. Like thousands of bees suddenly jostled awake, the always-shocking mortar explosion sets everyone instantly abuzz, and people are now nervously in motion. I can appreciate what it's like to be on the ground just now. It was this same mortaretto that caused my adrenaline to skyrocket during my first tratta in 2013. With that precise moment, I became unabashedly hooked on the Palio.

Although only just after 5:00 p.m., it is still late October. The sun has already set behind the buildings on the Campo's western side, blanketing the entire public space in early dusk. For us, the situation is different because the low-angled sun is still pouring into our windows. During the summer, the sun would be much farther north in the sky, so we are actually fortunate not to have to face it more directly. While Mike shades his eyes to scan the track, I state, "It just feels strange to hold a Palio at this time of year," I chuckle. "The sun angles, the dry air, the early start times. It's just not right!" I laugh. And this is coming from an outsider with only six years of experience here. And yet, I am already set in my ways. It can't be any easier for a true Senese.

Speaking of whom, the outer *palchi* (bleachers) have been filling in with contrada members as expected. Especially for the evening trials, separate groups of contrada men and women reserve their own blocks of seats around the Campo, usually in the same locations from one year to the next. As the track is gradually cleared by the police at a snail's pace, we are treated to a musical sound like nothing I have ever experienced. Entire blocks of contradaioli are starting to sing their own versions of Il Canto della Verbena.

To hear this song and its many variations from the center of the Campo is always a special treat. But from where we are standing tonight, the song is absolutely stunning. Members of the Shell contrada belt out the song to our right, followed by either the Turtle or Snail down to our left. Not to be outdone, the Goose ramps up directly across from us, singing over the others. Our ears are thus enjoying a veritable symphony of Il Canto della Verbena, with portions of the "orchestra" alternately erupting with their own boisterous voices. Moreover, from our elevation the music softens and blends together, reminding me of an echo chamber. This is certainly not something we would experience below; only our central, elevated location provides the line-of-site geometry required for this impromptu concert. For quite some time, I rest my arms on the deep windowsill to soak in the experience.

Eventually, we find ourselves staring down at an empty dirt track as we wait for the race to begin. From this distance, the turf loses its texture and undulations to appear more like a smooth, light-brown carpet. The center of the Campo has now been closed off and, as is customary, nobody can move across the track in either direction. Below us to the left is the elongated set of bleachers devoted entirely to the children of all ten contrade, who in their collective bundles of energy are in constant motion with their own chants or related activities. Eventually the city officials and contrada captains emerge from the Cortile di Podestà directly below us. As they begin their hike around the track to reach the judges' stand, they must first pass in front of Siena's youngest generation. While doing so, the officials are greeted with genuine glee and animation from wildly cheering children, vigorously waving their fazzoletti. Whether or not the children can identify any of these well-dressed people is not the point; tonight, the generations have come together once again to showcase both the current and future leaders of their timeless city.

With the judges' stand now suitably populated with Siena's delegation, the mayor appropriately stands in the precise center of the second balcony, as he always has. With the entire Campo stage now set, the mortaretto blasts once more, signaling the long-awaited emergence of the ten competitors. We watch them appear one by one onto the track, after which they soon devolve into an unorganized cluster (Figure 8). The children are screaming as their newest heroes trot past, and the expansive crowd roars with delight.

Figure 8. Horses and jockeys emerge onto the track from Palazzo Pubblico to begin the third trial. (Photo: Author)

THE THIRD TRIAL

The Lineup Ritual

As expected, none of the jockeys is in a particular hurry. For the trials, the order in which the horses line up at the mossa is known well in advance. The lineup consists of positions one through ten, starting from the interior of the track and moving outward. For the trials, the lineup was determined long ago, based on the order in which the contrade were extracted (or drawn) back in September.

The approach for determining the lineup for the trials during the Straordinario generally follows that of the standard summer events. In the summer, the lineup for the first trial is determined by the order in which the ten contrade were selected during the extraction. The seven already guaranteed to run had been selected the previous year. The lineup order for the second trial is the opposite of the first. Thus, if you were in the first position on the inside of the track during the first trial, you become the rincorsa for the second trial. Number two becomes number nine, and so forth.

Just when you have mastered this approach, however, Siena throws you another curve ball. The lineup for the third trial—tonight's event—is determined instead by the order in which the contrade were assigned their horses after the tratta. Recall that during yesterday's drawing, the mayor first called the number of a horse, followed by the name of the contrada that would receive it. Thus, the tenth and last contrada to be called for the final horse becomes the rincorsa for the third trial. That lineup will be simply reversed for the fourth trial tomorrow morning. For the fifth and sixth trials, the lineup is based instead on the order in which the final ten horses were selected by the captains to run in the Palio, immediately following the tratta. The Senesi have clearly enjoyed quite some time over the centuries to figure this out.

As they will do for the Palio, now two days away, the horses and jockeys begin their ritualistic circling routine, known as the *giro* (tour), on the track behind the mossa. They essentially parade slowly around in a circle until they are summoned one by one to take their places at the canape. During the actual Palio, this process can require an hour or more, depending upon how the horses behave in close quarters with one another. For the trials, the drama is ratcheted down a bit because everyone knows the lineup in advance, and nobody is desperately trying to "win" the trial. Still, the jockeys intend to practice their launch in as many positions as possible. Unlike the more predictable trials, the lineup order for the actual race will be determined by a third and final lottery as the horses circle behind the mossa.

Aside from testing the horses during these trials, the jockeys can benefit in various ways. In one sense, the six practice runs provide a bit of free time away from the otherwise stifling scrutiny of their contrada hosts and handlers. During the four days of the Palio, the jockeys are never left alone, primarily to prevent different contrade from approaching them with inducements to throw the race one way or another. However, this close supervision lightens up during the trials. While amid their peers on the track, a slim window of time exists to communicate among themselves. As noted by Dundes and Falassi, at this point "the *fantini* may be exchanging pleasantries, but more than likely they are communicating offers and counteroffers from their employers or would-be employers."[60] In this way, the officials of one contrada can also send messages to their counterparts covertly through their respective jockeys. As noted earlier, the lineup order for the horses at the mossa is known well in advance, so plans might be hatched for one jockey to speak with another during a particular trial when they are slated to be closer together.[61]

As we focus our eyes intently on the circling horses from our far-away position, each contrada is called by the *mossiere* (starter) to line up at the canape (Figure 9). Not surprisingly, they are doing so in the order expected for the third trial. Starting from the first position on the inside of the track and moving outward, the order is thus: Snail, Tower, Giraffe, Forest, Turtle, Goose, Owl, Shell, Dragon—and She-Wolf as rincorsa. I have to say, however, that from our vantage point here it does not appear they are all complying with the lineup order as directed. I wonder if certain jockeys are negotiating the lineup with their counterparts.

THE THIRD TRIAL

Figure 9. The lineup process for the third trial. Horses and jockeys are summoned one by one to line up at the canape. (Photo: Author)

Following the assignment of the horses yesterday, the news media has predicted a rather lengthy lineup process for the trials, let alone the actual race. Because so many novice horses were chosen for this Palio, the process will likely require additional efforts to calm the jittery steeds enough to launch them successfully. I am already recalling Enrico's comment about the Tower's horse, Tonina, who threw a fit while lining up last night for the first time. We may be in for a lengthy wait, therefore, despite this being only the third trial. As we soak in the essence of the Campo and the miraculously perfect weather, this prediction appears to be playing out. I turn to Mike to initiate some conversation about the jockeys. "I noticed that Trecciolino is not riding for the Turtle at this point, though it seems that the media had expected him to be racing. Did you see anything about that?"

Still hanging his head out the window, he responds, "Yes, that's very curious, as I assume he still wants to break the current record for Palio wins. But I don't think he's out there right now on the track."

I respond, "No, I didn't see him in the list for this trial, so I guess he still hasn't been hired by anyone." I am gleaning this information from a screenshot on my phone of a recent article with tonight's roster of jockeys. I continue, "And for the first trial last night, the Turtle's jockey was someone named Alessio Giannetti. He doesn't seem to have a nickname, so maybe he is a rookie. Then this morning for the second trial they switched to Andrea Coghe, nicknamed Tempesta. I think he is also running for the Turtle tonight. I wonder if he is going to be their permanent jockey; it's getting late in the trial process."

Mike reflects, "Yes, that's interesting. It's true, we don't see the jockeys change very often after the first trial, even though they're allowed to change. Usually they have settled on their jockeys immediately after the assignment of the horses."

I respond, "Yes, this is the first time I have ever seen it happen—at least knowingly," I chuckle, fully aware that I generally possess a proclivity to miss something important.

Mike adds, "Yeah, I am definitely surprised that Trecciolino has not been hired yet. There have been articles in the media this week that speculate about his future as a jockey here. He may be retiring, but no one really knows."

Mike's observation about the media is accurate. Just today an update in *Siena News* reviewing the progress of the Palio suggested that a lot of unknowns continue to surround the Straordinario. In part, the author wrote, "The question marks are many, but it can only be that way for an Extraordinary Palio that is being run with only three experienced horses (Sorighittu, Rombo de Sedini, and Schietta), along with the absence of Luigi Bruschelli, nicknamed Trecciolino, who has thirteen victories in the Piazza."[62] This author also predicted that more time would be necessary to calm the novice horses in advance of the trials and perhaps for the actual Palio. Additional speculation abounds as to why certain jockeys are running for various contrade at this point. The author of this article was admittedly as perplexed as everyone else, asking with not a little frustration, "Why is Tittia running for the Shell, Brio for the Owl, Scompiglio for the Giraffe, and Gingillo for the Goose, given that all of their horses are not experienced, but beginners?" Any normal Palio would elicit countless questions such as this, let alone those of a rare October race with little time to prepare.

THE THIRD TRIAL

A Symbolic Finish

This unpredictability is now playing out behind the mossa as the horses and jockeys valiantly attempt to assume their positions. As expected, the jockey for the She-Wolf rincorsa is holding back his horse to start the trial. It then dawns on me that the most recent Palio in August was won by that very contrada. More remarkable was that the She-Wolf managed its win from the very rincorsa position it finds itself in tonight. With our heads straining outward to see the start of the trial, I exclaim to Mike, "Look at that, the She-Wolf is the rincorsa tonight, just like in August!" He responds politely to recognize this rather obvious fact. But then I make a fun prediction: "I wonder if the jockey is going to win the trial tonight as well, just as a fun way to remind everyone what they accomplished in August," I laugh. Why not? I think that would be very cool indeed, though others may not see the humor or symbolism in it. Again, Mike graciously accepts my harebrained idea with a nod before returning his attention to the crowd below. *But still—what an opportunity!*

As predicted, the lineup is requiring some time and patience. We can discern only basic movements at the mossa due to our distant location and the darkening shadow. But then a new sound greets our ears which, in effect, gives us a heads-up that something is about to happen. As the horses appear to line up successfully for the first time, what hits our ears is a tremendous, collective roar from the crowd below, sensing that the lineup is decent enough to launch the horses. The crescendo is daunting, reminding me of turning up the volume of static on an older television or radio. Then just as suddenly, the sound dies down as the mossiere instructs the jockeys to return to their circling routine due to yet another unsuccessful lineup. This occurs two more times, no doubt because the jockeys are struggling to control a set of fidgety steeds.

At last, the crowd's roar rises to fever pitch for a fourth time, and the rincorsa jockey makes his move. The other jockeys are looking to their left in anticipation of his launch. Within a split second after the She-Wolf's horse lunges forward, the mossiere drops the canape, enabling the other nine horses to take off. I have since abandoned my quest to understand why the Goose and Forest jockeys lined up closer to the center than expected, or why the Giraffe jockey placed himself out near the Shell and She-Wolf horses. The

Turtle jockey's behavior has been puzzling as well, choosing to hang back behind everyone else until the She-Wolf jockey made his move. No matter, as the horses lunge off the starting line, a sorting-out process takes place within seconds. The Snail horse simply remains closest to the barrier in his number-one position but is quickly outpaced by the Goose and Forest. They are clearly racing at this point and assuming the lead. At the other end of the lineup is the She-Wolf jockey, who has come armed with his own strategy. Upon starting his gallop, he immediately cuts to the right and assumes an inside position of his own. With the Owl and Giraffe jockeys apparently content to remain in the rear, the front six are now barreling toward the San Martino curve, with the Goose, Forest, and now the She-Wolf in positions one through three, respectively. For whatever reason, Gingillo for the Goose has decided to practice a quick start and has now assumed the lead. At this point, the pack moves into our blind spot as the Cappella di Piazza effectively hides the action transpiring there.

Perhaps surprisingly given their speed, all ten jockeys emerge below us without incident, still atop their horses. Their order has not changed much, with the Goose, Forest, She-Wolf, Turtle, and Tower horses being the first to reach the turn of the Casato. By this time, the intensity of the trial is lessening as more of the jockeys begin to throttle back their speed. Even the fast-paced Goose horse is cooling its heels for the upcoming second and third laps.

The exception to this is found in one particular jockey who refuses to relent—one Valter Pusceddu, nicknamed Bighino. I am familiar with his name from previous summers, though I have not seen him win. In fact, he has raced in the Palio twenty-six times, including his first attempt in 1999, but unfortunately has no victories to show for it. Still, to be fair he has won other races outside of Siena. Given his less than impressive track record here, consequently, I suspect that the contrada that hired him has only modest expectations. I can humorously imagine the contrada's optimistic captain trying to explain his choice of jockey: "Well, he has raced the Palio twenty-six times, so he just might succeed with the twenty-seventh. I'm feeling it!" In turn, his colleagues would respond with a slap on the back and, "You're right, Duccio, this could be the one! Sign him up."

Regardless of his immediate future in Saturday's Palio, Bighino is clearly in racing mode. He and his free-spirited horse are careening past more conservative jockeys, who are now merely trotting around the track to await

THE THIRD TRIAL

the end of the trial. In marked contrast, we watch unsurprisingly as Bighino crosses the mossa in first place for the contrada that hired him—the She-Wolf.

❈ CHAPTER 12 ❈

Blessing at San Domenico

IT SEEMS AS THOUGH TIME IS FLYING BY THIS WEEK FASTER THAN THE racehorses competing in the Campo. Of the traditional four days of the Palio, this is the third. The actual race will be held tomorrow evening, preceded by a day's worth of rituals and activities that generally mimic the summer events. Now, following a night of much-needed slumber (it is, after all, quite the physical challenge to "live the Palio") I am eager to witness a ritual that I have not yet experienced. Despite six consecutive summers here, certain events have managed to escape my attention. One of them is the official blessing of the drappellone by the archbishop, which will occur today at precisely high noon. For many Americans like me, the arrival of 12 o'clock would normally signify a pending lunch. However, to live the days of the Palio more or less faithfully, it is wise to remain flexible with one's eating habits. If an important event or personal meeting is occurring during a preferred mealtime, one must keep in mind that the food can wait. Having cobbled together some version of brunch with Linda, I now find myself racewalking to attend an intriguing Palio ritual that is not found at its usual location.

Procession of the Drappellone

During the two summer Palii, a sacred procession little known to visitors takes place, which proceeds on foot from Palazzo Pubblico to either the Church of Santa Maria of Provenzano (July Palio) or to the Duomo (August Palio). The event's main purpose is to transport the drappellone for its official blessing by Siena's archbishop—once again signaling the cultural intersection between organized religion and the traditions of the Palio. Typically, the procession occurs in the mid-afternoon two days before the race. In this special case, however, the procession and blessing are occurring the day before the race, and at noontime rather than several hours later. Regardless of its timing, the procession's dramatic flair is not to be underestimated. Delegations from all seventeen contrade—each consisting of two flag bearers and a drummer—march in advance of numerous city officials who carry the vertically raised drappellone for all to see along the route. A variety of youth wearing historically themed costumes rounds out the procession.

Not only has the procession's timing been adjusted, but its destination has changed as well. In this specific case, the event will conclude not at the Duomo or Provenzano, but rather at the more distant Church of San Domenico located on the hill of Camporegio. Deep within the Dragon contrada, both the hill and its imposing church enjoy a commanding view overlooking the Goose's rione in the valley below. It is at this unlikely location where the archbishop will presumably bless the drappellone before it is placed on display there until the day of the Palio. I say "presumably" because the banner representing the most recent Palio in August 2018 was summarily rejected by the archbishop, as one might recall from my earlier conversation with Dario. As long as the Catholic Church can comfortably disregard the ongoing drama surrounding this particular banner, I imagine the artwork should be safe this time around.

Following the conclusion of the blessing ceremony, the banner will then be moved once again on the day of the Palio (tomorrow) and placed on the *palco dei giudici* (judges' stand), from which the city leaders and contrada captains will watch the race. The silk banner really does get around town quite impressively!

It turns out that the Senesi were surprised to see San Domenico chosen for the Straordinario. The spacious church is impressive and it is often hard to imagine that its construction by the Dominicans began many centuries ago, in the 1220s. Much of the existing nave and interior roof system still date back to that early era. About a century later, a new transept (wing) and crypt were added, and a similar Gothic-styled façade was built to face out over the valley. Parts of the church were damaged or destroyed by no less than three fires during the fifteenth and sixteenth centuries. Beyond that, its rather stubby bell tower was intentionally reduced in height following an earthquake in 1798.

UNBRIDLED SPIRIT

In 1925, the Catholic Church awarded San Domenico the status of "basilica," a title bestowed upon churches that meet certain criteria as judged by the Vatican. According to an educational website devoted to the topic, it must be demonstrated that a church has "unusual historical significance, or is especially sacred because of its architectural beauty, liturgical renown, or significance as a place of worship."[63] This was an interesting finding for me, as I had presumed that the distinction between a basilica and a church was based primarily on its physical size and scale.

Further, a church's leaders seeking the status of basilica must first petition the local diocese for initial approval by the bishop. If accepted at that level, an application can be submitted to the Office of the Holy See at the Vatican, which oversees the review process. As for San Domenico, its direct relationship to the life and accomplishments of Saint Catherine of Siena provided the appropriate significance necessary for basilica status. There are now more than 1,700 basilicas worldwide. Perhaps not surprisingly, Italy is home to most of them with more than 570 such designated places.

To this observer, San Domenico's orientation over the valley, along with its various renovations over the centuries, produced a rather bizarre architectural mish-mash. It is most certainly one of Siena's earliest Gothic-style churches, with its characteristic pointed-arch (lancet) windows. Despite the relatively light and airy Gothic design that structurally allows for its spacious interior, this timeless structure still provides an almost foreboding, fortresslike presence. Perhaps most strange, its primary entrance is through an unassuming doorway on the back side of the nave. This location is likely a matter of convenience, providing the easiest access to a busy street corner for arrivals by bus, car, or foot.

As indicated earlier, the expansive church is best known for its close association with one of Siena's most famous residents. Santa Caterina, or Saint Catherine of Siena (1347–1380) spent most of her daily life inside its very walls. Born in what is now the Goose contrada's rione, she accepted the Dominican habit in 1363 and thereby became a member of the Third Order Dominicans who met in the church every day.[64] Perhaps the most famous highlight of her productive life was successfully convincing Pope Gregory XI to return the papacy to Rome from Avignon, France, in 1376. She was eventually canonized by Pope Pius II in 1461. Both Catherine of Siena and Francis of Assisi were declared patron saints of Italy in 1939. In 1970, Pope

BLESSING AT SAN DOMENICO

Paul VI named her the Doctor of the Church. For these reasons, San Domenico and Catherine's nearby family home serve as popular international visitor attractions to this day and it is a rare time indeed when they are not packed with day trippers and tour groups.

Communing with Saint Catherine

For all the church's history and significance, none of it explains why San Domenico is being featured for the Straordinario this week. What few people knew until recently—including an untold number of Senesi—is that the storied church houses one of the city's more prominent memorials to the World War I. I confess that my first reaction to learning this from Gabriele (during our Monday "field trip" with Mike) was, "You mean they put a memorial in a church?" quite to his amusement. Correctly sensing my intrigue, Mike then offered to accompany me to see it if I had time during the coming week. Though I am fairly confident about my wayfinding skills, Mike still suggested I join him while navigating the cavernous basilica, and I graciously took him up on his offer, realizing that one could almost get lost within its expansive interior, and a typical memorial of modest size may not be the easiest thing to track down.

So, yesterday morning, Mike and I entered through the standard back-corner entryway to find the place nearly deserted, which at least provided for an appropriate ecclesiastical ambiance of solitude. Strolling slowly to gawk at our surroundings—Mike was not immune, either—he asked, "Are you aware that Santa Caterina's relics are located here?"

"Yes, I recall that some of her remains are here. Is that what you mean?" I responded.

"Right. So, over here is the chapel, with her head on display," he explained nonchalantly as if leading a tour, and then added, "And I believe her thumb is visible as well." It certainly was, with a well-manicured nail.

We both stared intently at the sacred relics of Saint Catherine, the same vestiges which visitors from around the world seek to honor. In one respect, my mind was nearly overwhelmed with trying to contemplate my proximity to an actual human being—or parts of her—who had somehow been preserved since the fourteenth century.

Although one can certainly view Saint Catherine up close as we did, stepping back a bit from the altar area allows for a more complete enjoyment of her elaborate chapel and its artistry. Surrounding the reliquary case that contains her head is what I would describe as a full-color, celebratory explosion of architectural and artistic works. Most notable are two jaw-dropping frescoes by the Renaissance artist Giovanni Bazzi (nicknamed Il Sodoma), dating to 1526. One is titled *Fainting and Ecstasy of Saint Catherine*, depicting her after receiving the Eucharist (Holy Communion) from an angel.[65] On the right side of her chapel is the fresco *Saint Catherine's Exorcism* painted by Francesco Vanni during the 1590s. These and related works of art, combined with the imposing Greek temple façade surrounding the altar, provide for an appropriately magnificent setting designed to honor her life and accomplishments.

A Memorial at San Domenico

After communing a bit with Saint Catherine, it was time to return to our original mission. I changed the subject and asked, "So, do you know where the war memorial is located in here?" Thus far, I could detect nothing obvious on the surrounding walls of the nave.

In his characteristically tranquil voice, Mike motioned for us to move further along, respectfully taking leave of Santa Caterina. "We need to turn into the transept, and we will see it in one of the side chapels, if I recall correctly," he mused. While scanning side-to-side for an object resembling a memorial, we ultimately moved through the length of the transept and ended up at the very last chapel on the left. Just as we were running out of options and floor space, suddenly there it was, seemingly tucked in a corner of the massive church. I gaped speechless at the sight of a substantial masonry plaque affixed to the main wall, adorned with probably hundreds of names honoring those who lost their lives during World War I (Figure 10). Surrounding the plaque on the floor was a tasteful wrought-iron fence extending out six inches away from the memorial as a symbol of protection and significance. Above the honored names was a second, vertical element resembling a simple Greek temple capped with a classical triangular pediment. Now that we have finally located the memorial, the decision for San Domenico to host the blessing of the drappellone makes perfect sense.

Figure 10. The World War I memorial within the Basilica of San Domenico. (Photo: Author)

Apparently, much of Siena's local population had not been aware of the memorial's existence either. For some, it was quite the surprise. Upon the decision to feature the basilica during the Straordinario, *La Nazione* featured an interview with the pastor of San Domenico, Father Alfredo.[66] As one might imagine, the announcement that their beloved church would become the symbolic site for the Straordinario was greeted with enthusiasm among its clergy. Father Alfredo described the decision as a "sign of hope," continuing with his own perspective: "I don't deny it. There is a profound meaning [to this decision]. There is a monument here to the fallen of the Great War, of which many did not know. The news that San Domenico was, for this reason, a candidate to welcome the Palio Straordinario has created curiosity. A lot of people have been coming to the church." The article led off with an image of Father Alfredo happily leaning in front of the memorial. I imagine the clergy's collective (if appropriately reserved) excitement over the Straordinario can be compared to the staff of a hotel learning that a famous person would be staying there. In this case the veritable "rock star" is none other than Montesano's drappellone, a surprise visitor to San Domenico that probably no one here would have thought possible only weeks earlier.

The Procession Arrives

Back to today, I am arriving at a safe, early time so as not to miss any of the action at San Domenico. There is no way for me to predict the size of crowd that might descend on the place for the blessing. I do know that the procession is scheduled to arrive around 11:45 a.m. in advance of this special Palio ritual. After cautiously approaching the entrance stairs to the church around 11:15 a.m., I eventually duck inside to find surprisingly few people milling around. It is therefore safe to relax a bit, not having to worry about finding a place in a densely packed throng. For now, that sort of attendance is not yet materializing. I thus spend some time scoping out the interior, trying to imagine the route of the procession through the church and where the archbishop will perform his duty. Not just incidentally, I smile at the sight of the main walls, which have been decorated with the flags of the seventeen contrade, just as they would normally appear at the Church of Provenzano or the Duomo. The sacred space of San Domenico has thus merged in this rare instance with the traditions of the Palio and contrade. Somehow seeing those flags puts me in a good mood, anticipating yet another celebratory, uplifting Palio event. Feeling a bit like a child awaiting a carnival ride, I am clearly sensing some positive energy at this moment, in quiet anticipation of the procession that will be coming through that back door.

As time passes, some people continue to trickle in and take scattered seats in the pews facing the altar. Much of the nave behind the pews is simply empty, however, providing copious room for standing. Without any better idea, I decide to hang out behind the pews but still close to the center aisle. From here I enjoy a commanding view of the interior. It is easy to recognize an upbeat Father Alfredo in his nearly angelic white clergy robe mingling with visitors on the opposite side of the nave. Within minutes there will undoubtedly be thousands of photos featuring every painting and plaster crack of San Domenico being posted on social media. Just as with other Palio traditions held inside houses of worship, it seems that the standard modicums of reverent behavior have been lifted for this special occasion.

As I soak in the evolving scene, it dawns on me that a high percentage of new arrivals are school children, clustered in class-sized cohorts with their presumed teachers and chaperones. Given the ongoing issue of whether schools should remain open this week, it appears that some teachers and school leaders have creatively discovered a good excuse for a field trip. They take their seats in a row on the floor in front of me, so I happily retreat back a few steps while the classes form a veritable receiving line to welcome the eventual procession. Though packed with the characteristic enthusiasm of youth, the children are remarkably well behaved. Less surprising is that many are already unpacking their digital devices to photograph whatever they find amusing, not the least each other. One student comes armed with her own Apple iPad, promptly shoving the wide screen in the faces of her classmates to obtain some close-up photos.

Eventually, everyone's attention turns to the back of the nave, with many of us now standing in a heightened sense of alertness. Recognizing contrada drums when I hear them, I presume that the lead units of the procession have arrived outside the church. Father Alfredo joins his colleagues—including, I believe, the archbishop—opposite the rear entrance, and everyone at that end of the nave focuses their attention on the doorway. The children rise in unison and are on their feet in seconds. The modest collection of adult onlookers with me is now falling back to enjoy some downright luxurious open space in which to stand and observe the happenings. I must say, this lack of competition for viewing space is highly unusual for anything related to the Palio. The throngs of people I had imagined would attend this event have not materialized, perhaps another casualty of a busy workweek for the Senesi.

The first drummer, from the She-Wolf contrada, leads the procession into San Domenico, followed by two of the contrada's flag bearers directly behind him. Upon stepping foot inside, the flag bearers pause to respectfully hold their flags in tandem above their heads in what amounts to a silent tribute to the basilica they have just entered. After posing for a few seconds, they lower their flags and march in behind their contrada's drummer. As they make their way toward my location, a similarly sized delegation for the Dragon enters and performs the same tribute with raised flags. Counter to what one might imagine in such a sacred place, the drummers are not going silent after entering. Rather, they are still banging away inside with near-deafening intensity. It is a remarkable sound to experience, and I am cherishing it with a wide grin.

We all watch in awe as a parade of the remaining fifteen contrade continue to perform the same tribute as they file toward us. Upon reaching our area near the pews, the delegations are directed to split to either the right or left side and line up on the outside aisles. After clustering together to form lines on both sides, they turn ninety degrees to face one another across the church. Despite their proximity to one another, the flags continue to swoop majestically through the air while all the drummers continue their wondrous racket (Figure 11). I do hope Santa Caterina is enjoying this rare festivity inside her former daily stomping grounds. It is not likely to happen again for quite some time.

As the contrade take their places, the next delegation of musicians arrives, consisting of two costumed drummers followed by several rows of Siena's blue-costumed trombettiere with their long-belled horns. This second contingent moves halfway through the nave before preparing to play. To everyone's delight, they unleash a heavenly fanfare, the likes of which I have never heard in Siena. The harmonious sound of brass horns is echoing through the building as the third contingent of the procession now arrives. *This is quite the production!* I am thinking to myself. The elegantly simple city banner with Siena's black-and-white balzana and the symbols for each of the contrade appears next, followed by the bulk of the city's municipal officials. They all make their way proudly down the center. Siena's mayor marches appropriately at the center of the well-dressed delegation, draped with his own distinct sash of colors representing the Italian flag. The city officials are followed by a small army of local police officers, providing a rather imposing, if regal scene. As if staged for a grand finale, the drappellone is carried in at last.

BLESSING AT SAN DOMENICO

Figure 11. Contrada delegations take their places for the blessing of the drappellone. (Photo: Author)

The entire procession is now within the walls of San Domenico. The resulting atmosphere exudes nothing but overwhelming joy as the traditions, sounds, and colors of the Palio happily invade the basilica (Figure 12). This may be the first such event here in generations—if not the first time in recorded history.

Eventually the drums quiet down and the church returns to a reasonable measure of peace and solitude. The vastness of the interior presents a challenge for me to see much detail of who is doing what. At this point, the drappellone has been advanced to the high altar, and the ceremony begins. The priest then recites the traditional *Te Deum* as the congregation follows suit, now suddenly sounding like a traditional mass. In what is essentially an honorable tribute to God, its name derives from its opening phrase in Latin, *Te Deum Laudamus*, meaning, "Oh God, we praise you."[67] Although often recited as a prayer, the narrative can also be sung as a hymn. Eventually, I see the archbishop perform his much-anticipated blessing of the drappellone.

UNBRIDLED SPIRIT

Figure 12. The procession of the drappellone makes its way through the Basilica of San Domenico. (Photo: Author)

Beyond these ceremonial rituals, there is one more surprise in store for all of us today. The entire municipal delegation uproots itself and shuffles the drappellone to the end of the transept. An enthralled, devoted crowd of onlookers is joining them, so I quickly decide to forego any effort to push my way in. Given their distance now, all I can make out is the vertical drappellone dangling somewhat precariously over the crowd. As for the delegation's motive, there is no doubt. They are paying appropriate tribute to the war's dead, memorialized by the wall of names that Mike and I had studied earlier.

For all its outward festivity, the procession into San Domenico may have been tempered a bit from past events. As described by Dundes and Falassi in the 1970s, even more excitement would normally pervade this ritual. The mere sight of the drappellone (palio banner, in their description) inside the church apparently once invoked near-rapturous behaviors among the devout contradaioli. They would begin with outright cheering upon entry of the procession and the drappellone into the church. These authors provided a further description of the typical experience up through that time, as follows:

BLESSING AT SAN DOMENICO

> As [the palio banner] enters through the church's portals, there is a general shout hailing the entrance. Contrada scarves are waved excitedly to greet the incoming palio. As the palio is brought down the aisle to the chapel altar, where it will receive a blessing by the archbishop or his representative, people try to touch it for good luck. The principal flag bearers of each contrada will make a special effort to be the very first to touch the palio with their contrada flags. Presumably the first contrada to touch the palio in the church may be the first to finish the race and win the palio.[68]

During the procession's final journey to the altar a few minutes ago, I witnessed no such behaviors from contradaioli or contrada delegation members. In contrast, all attendees and contrada delegates alike were the epitome of professionalism. Perhaps the event is more regulated with better protection for the prized banner this time. More practically, the contrada flag bearers alighted on the extreme side aisles where they could not easily access the silk cloth. Today's relatively light attendance is likely atypical as well, as mentioned previously. Regardless of how this festive event may have changed over time, I cannot help but feel an overwhelming sense of satisfaction at being present for this special occasion. And given recent press accounts, it is not difficult to imagine that Father Alfredo is likewise overjoyed with what has transpired here today.

One More Quest

Now back outside, I finish watching the contrada delegations emerge from the church to scatter elsewhere for the afternoon. Suddenly I make a spontaneous decision to take advantage of my location in the northern district of the city, the Terzo di Camollia (Camollia District). Mike, Gabriele, and Dario each had mentioned another memorial to the war, located somewhere near the Garibaldi statue in what is known locally as the Giardini La Lizza (La Lizza Gardens). Having presumed unwisely that it would take little effort to find it, I did not ask them for follow-up details. Regardless, my curiosity is kicking in now to see if this third, mysterious memorial does in fact jump out at me with little effort. With no pressing appointments or Palio events on my radar, I now find a rare moment of personal freedom. My first goal is to double back to Piazza Gramsci, which serves as the city's intercity bus depot. From there I can find La Lizza just to the northwest of Gramsci. La Lizza also happens to be the location of an absolutely massive outdoor market held every Wednesday morning. The market—a veritable sea of reasonably priced household goods, clothing, and knickknacks—was always a must-see event for our students during recent study-abroad programs, to the point where we would purposely schedule a Wednesday morning to allow students some browsing and shopping time. Our students and faculty alike could easily supplement their sparsely furnished apartments with pretty much any type of kitchen utensil or household good known to humans.

When not occupied by one wing of the market, however, this triangle-shaped public space provides a peaceful, tree-canopied area in which to stroll or sit. Never one to turn down a quest, I now set off for the Giardini La Lizza and its immediate environs.

After wandering through part of the park, it is an easy task to pick out the equestrian statue dedicated to Italy's founding General, Giuseppe Garibaldi. Perched probably twenty feet high on a massive, formal block of carved stone, Garibaldi sits atop his steed while craning his neck to his right side, bracing his right arm on the back of his horse to do so (Figure 13). He is likely posed as if overseeing his troops or other activities on the ground during a military engagement in the field. Of course, Garibaldi statues are a common sight across Italy given his prominent role in unifying the Italian peninsula, which ultimately resulted in the formation of the new Kingdom of Italy in 1861. Hugely popular during his military years, Garibaldi is still considered one of the most effective generals of modern history. He is perhaps comparable in status to the American general and founding father, George Washington. After enjoying some quality time inspecting the statue of Italy's famed general, I continue to stroll through this peaceful place with the hope that another monument to World War I will somehow appear in front of me. Alas, it never does.

Scanning side to side like a sleuth, I am admittedly becoming much better acquainted with the layout of the Giardini La Lizza. Still, some personal patience is required to simply relax and cover my steps at least twice. *If I were a war memorial, where would I be?* I am essentially keeping an eye out for an elevated plaque, statuary, or wall that might somehow be dedicated to World

War I. It is important, I remind myself, to expect the unexpected; such was the case with the memorial perched in the back corner of San Domenico. Regardless, Garibaldi is apparently all alone here; there is absolutely nothing out of the ordinary that would suggest the presence of a war memorial. The intelligent minds of Mike, Gabriele, and Dario can't be all wrong, so the logical conclusion is that I am missing something. *You presumptuous dummy; you should have asked for more detail,* I mutter. Anyway, it's all good. I enjoy the occasional mystery.

With the afternoon leaping quickly toward evening, I decide to cool my heels for this mission. It would be wise to touch base with Linda and perhaps enjoy a late lunch and some rest before tonight's pre-Palio events. With these immediate thoughts in mind and the grandest of the trials only hours away, I take my leave of General Garibaldi and wind my way back to our lodgings.

Figure 13. Statue of General Garibaldi in the Giardini La Lizza. (Photo: Author)

❊ CHAPTER 13 ❊

Homecoming at Due Porte

C OMMONLY DESCRIBED AS THE DRESS REHEARSAL FOR THE ACTUAL PALIO, THE prova generale is always the most festive and well attended of the six trials. Following that event are the massive and jubilant outdoor contrada dinners held on various streets and public spaces around Siena. At this point I have returned to our lodging once again after being released from the center of the Campo and the last of the evening trials. This evening's weather could not be more perfect. The Goose's tent city may not be necessary after all, though it will likely keep their attendees somewhat warmer as the night progresses. Giove Pluvio has apparently decided to grant this fine city its rare Straordinario after all.

Cena della Prova Generale

For the ten contrade running in tomorrow's race, tonight's outdoor cena della prova generale will approach the festiveness of New Year's Eve. During the summer, entire streets are closed off to both foot and vehicular traffic to accommodate hundreds and often thousands of contrada members and guests for this grandiose community affair. The cena, which always follows of the final evening trial, is when the contrade enjoy their most substantial Palio celebration, which embodies the best of community cohesiveness and social life.

Attendees during the two summer events may arrive at an usually late sit-down time of 9:30 p.m. with empty stomachs in anticipation of a three-hour, four-course meal. But they also come filled with an expectancy of seeing their jockey and contrada leadership one last time before summarily launching their horse in the final race in less than twenty-four hours. At some point during the night, those at the head table (usually the contrada president

HOMECOMING AT DUE PORTE

and captain) deliver various speeches of encouragement and appreciation. Sometimes the jockey is encouraged to share a few words as well. This is the time when the contrada leadership attempts to guide and manage their members' expectations surrounding the upcoming race. No matter the collective mood or general wisdom regarding the presumed quality of their horse, the captain generally promises at the very least that the jockey and steed will do their best as they strive for victory. As noted earlier, in this unpredictable game, every contrada enjoys some chance to realize glory.

For tonight's planned cena in the Goose contrada, Antonio has already determined that the number of visitors for their event dropped significantly from its normal summer levels. This cena is typically the one dinner of the year when guests from outside the contrada are welcome to attend—that is, if they can unlock the mystery of how to obtain tickets. Still, the Goose usually hosts upwards of several hundred guests in addition to nearly two thousand contradaioli. Tonight, however, Antonio estimated that the number of guests will be less than fifty. The low attendance likely mirrors the general trend this week, that of a greatly reduced population of foreign visitors who do not normally travel this time of year. The silver lining? For those Senesi who have dreamed of enjoying a Palio dinner without mobs of summer visitors mingling about, this will be the one to cherish.

Although I considered the Goose or Tower for tonight's cena, I chose the Panther because that is the contrada where I have had the pleasure of making the most friends in recent years. Probably a lesser known fact is that the seven contrade not running in the race still host their own dinners. Granted, their own celebratory events are not as heavily attended and do not feature a full stage with head table and speeches. Still, tonight's dinners in these seven contrade will still provide an opportunity for their memberships to rejoice around the Palio. Since well before our arrival in Siena, I had planned to join the Panther for this festive (if relatively low-key) event.

As such, tonight's pending dinner celebration is viewed as a personal homecoming of sorts, as I am looking forward to seeing acquaintances I have known for several years. To earn the trust and general acceptance of a contrada can require years of persistence and patience for an outsider like me, especially considering the ever-present and pesky differences of language, culture, and geography. Not only do such visits test the limits of one's household budget, but hitting the unforgiving wall of the language divide provides no end of frustration. Sometimes what I dream of most of all is to hold a normal, day-to-day conversation with these people.

Given these various cultural challenges, I have found that it is wise for non-Senese enthusiasts like me to take their time, earning gradual trust along the way. Also, more positively, I have fortunately discovered that if one digs deep enough, there are English-speaking contradaioli to be found who can assist with bridging the cultural divide. I confess to having relied quite heavily on such individuals. Granted, only a small portion of Senesi can speak English with some degree of confidence, but they have tended to come out of the woodwork—or stonework—as I have continued to meet more people. My recent, quite extraordinary lunch with Angelo, Alessio, and their counterparts provides one excellent example of such a bilingual affair. Though it is unwise to expect such encounters, I would certainly welcome the opportunity to meet yet another English-speaking person at tonight's cena—especially since I will be "flying solo" for this one.

Second Thoughts

Regardless of whatever friends I might claim to have in the Panther, I have been hard-pressed to identify anyone who can specifically join me for tonight's cena. This deceptively simple goal has proven more of a challenge than I had anticipated. Two factors are conspiring against me already, both discussed previously. First, the Panther is sitting out this Palio despite its earlier hope of being extracted. Consequently, their attendance at dinners like this one is reduced because they are not running. Then there is the ongoing matter of our late October timeframe, when an untold percentage of residents had simply not planned to be in town.

Undaunted as always, however, my confidence in finding a companion remained high. Linda was, of course, at the top of my list. At least we can fumble through such events together. She has since acquired a head cold, however, and is wisely taking a pass tonight to enjoy an early bedtime. Though certainly not one to turn down such occasions, she is in no physical or mental shape for the expected marathon of socializing, translating, and generally festive merrymaking. These marathon dinners are not for the faint of heart. Moreover, a multihour event in the cooler October air is probably not the smartest move for her right now.

HOMECOMING AT DUE PORTE

With Linda out of the picture, I turned next to my good friend, Carlo, and his family. I have happily counted on them quite often to guide me through various contrada functions. Unfortunately, Carlo's presence was not in the cards, either. Like other Senesi this week, Carlo was not able to escape his daily workload through the use of precious vacation time. He is therefore foregoing such late-night dinners that would usurp at least half of his good sleeping hours. He and his family will consequently watch the Palio on television from afar without coming to the contrada. Part of me can't help but find this ironic; a stalwart contradaiolo is compelled to miss his own event, while this American interloper will dine with his fellow Panterini in his place.

Fortunately, Carlo and I already had a successful reunion dinner of our own earlier this week. In fact, Linda and I joined Carlo and his parents, along with his girlfriend and another longstanding couple of the Panther for a wonderful outdoor dinner at one of their favorite Campo restaurants. Despite being under the weather, Linda soldiered through it quite well, having disguised her symptoms with various over-the-counter remedies. As tradition would have it, we followed up the two-hour affair with a short stroll around the Campo. We ended the evening at Carlo's favorite gelateria before parting ways sometime well after 9:00 p.m.

Returning to my ongoing dinner companion issue, another option would have been a grandfatherly friend of Carlo and his family, who has likewise kindly befriended Linda and me. Unfortunately, I learned last week that he and his wife were already traveling elsewhere to visit family. As for my younger friends, Angelo and Alessio, they are already spending much of their waking hours in valued service to the contrada. They also tend to eat with their own, younger contrada peers, as expected. The truth is that major contrada dinners are typically stratified by age and gender. There could not possibly be a more awkward scene than barging into a hyped-up teen and twentysomething crowd of young men. Beyond my younger friends, I will also likely see various other acquaintances I have met over the years, though I am less inclined to insinuate myself into their own social circles for this event.

Consequently, my list of possible companions for tonight has become devastatingly meagre. I must admit to harboring some second thoughts about the wisdom of joining the Panther on my own, without a support team of any kind. If that were not enough to keep me on edge, it is highly likely that

I will be one of the very few outsiders in attendance tonight, and I may actually be the only American. Finally, tonight's dinner is not one that other outsiders will easily stumble into. Quite frankly, the Panther's cloistered courtyard, hidden well from all public streets, is likely one of the best-kept secrets of Siena. Should the pesky Florentines choose tonight for a surprise invasion, the Panther will be well protected.

There is a strong likelihood, however, that I will identify someone familiar upon arrival, and I find that thought to be of some comfort. If not, so be it. I can make new friends and practice my Italian. Further, it is indeed true that they consider me as a "friend of the Panther." Thus, I might as well show up and act like one.

The Bàrberi

With all of this in mind, I arrive with a thin sweater and light coat on the contrada's narrow street of Via San Quirico. Outside the società are the expected groupings of Panterini lingering around for pre-dinner conversations. I do not immediately see any of my previous acquaintances, so I duck into the entrance of Società Due Porte. After numerous visits and events here, I am comfortable with navigating the otherwise confusing interior. Moving past the familiar contrada bar and TV room, I wind my way through one more hallway and adjoining anteroom to reach the Panther's prized possession—to my mind, anyway: their attractive courtyard, which is surrounded on all sides by two-story buildings. I am told that they were once part of a high school facility and, before that, a storied school for the deaf. When blessed with decent weather, nearly all the Panther's contrada lunches, dinners, and related events are held in this comfortable space. The capacity here is upwards of 500 people, perfectly suitable for a smaller contrada of this size.

Said another way, a full-size basketball court can fit within the space, if snuggly. This scenario is not just hypothetical, either. It is amusing to see recent images of this space retrofitted with special flooring and basketball hoops to accommodate Siena's annual contrada tournament. Only when the Panther is running the Palio is this space not large enough to host the more than 1,000 attendees for their cena della prova generale. Tonight's event, however, is a more subdued affair. The added drama and emotional intensity that accompanies a contrada preparing to go to "war" the next day in the Campo is thereby greatly reduced.

Usually the final anteroom toward the rear of the società consists of an empty space that is used to pass through to the courtyard. This time, a new surprise awaits, and my face lights up with delight. It's a bàrberi machine! I could be mistaken, though I do not recall this contraption set up here during previous visits. For lack of a better description, this "machine," as we Americans have come to call such things, is really a heavy wooden contraption that serves as a Palio game for children (or occasional adults). Its purpose is to provide a continuous string of winding inclines on which marbles can race to the bottom. Smaller though equally intricate versions of bàrberi machines can be found for sale in local toy stores and souvenir shops within the historic city center. This one is doing its job splendidly tonight. I arrive to find at least eight children screaming their lungs out and running around the device as I stand there gaping in awe.

These contraptions enjoy a historical tradition in Siena. As with their ancestors before them, these children are using a set of bàrberi, which are wooden, painted balls, each representing the horses of the Palio and decorated with the 17 contrada colors.[69] One child places them together at the mossa at the top and then releases them to gravity. The first *bàrbero* (ball) to make its way through the bottom funnel to the finish line is the Palio "winner." The scene here is akin to watching energetic bees buzzing around their hive (Figure 14). If I interpret the screaming accurately, the She-Wolf has just won the latest race here. The girl presumably assigned to that contrada is screaming "Lupa!" repeatedly, the intensity of which is only magnified by the uninsulated room. As I leave the scene for the relative serenity of the outdoors, she continues her own celebration apace.

For me, every encounter with one of these bàrberi devices is like finding a new treasure. According to Dundes and Falassi, such children's games serve as a constant reminder of the Palio throughout the year. During the 1970s when their first book was published, similar games with bàrberi were more formalized during street fairs, especially during a contrada's celebration for its patron saint.[70]

UNBRIDLED SPIRIT

Figure 14. Children playing Palio dei Bàrberi in the Panther società. (Photo: Author)

The most common of all the street games is, perhaps not surprisingly, *Palio dei Bàrberi*, which involves similar wooden balls painted with the contrada colors and the requisite series of inclined planes on which to roll them. For the purposes of a street fair, however, a designated individual sells 17 tickets for those children or adults who wish to enter the race. The event is described by Dundes and Falassi:

> After all seventeen tickets are sold, the operator releases the bàrberi and the race begins. The operator normally gives a running play-by-play of the race (usually over a blaring loudspeaker), referring to the bàrberi by their contrada names. Naturally there are cheers if the home contrada should win and jeers if by any chance the enemy contrada should win. The winning ticket is presented for the prize, which may be a live chicken, a bottle of Chianti, or the like.[71]

HOMECOMING AT DUE PORTE

Although there are no chickens or other barnyard animals to distribute tonight (and I don't quite know how children would make use of the Chianti), the bàrberi machine now entrenched in the Panther società reminds me of others we have seen around town. Recently, the Goose installed a new cement version in the elegant if simple shape of a spiral in the public park near Fontebranda. During our recent stay within the Wave contrada, one massive contraption was placed in the street during their patron saint holiday, precisely as described above. Another, more venerated, wooden setup still exists on the eastern side of town in the playground outside the Basilica of San Francesco. There are others scattered around town as well, including one near the Medici Fort.

Of course, the children can be quite creative. Such was the case recently, before an outdoor dinner in the Goose, when the bàrberi had been replaced with much "cooler" Hot Wheels cars. Visitors to Siena can find countless bags of the bàrberi of different sizes at virtually any souvenir or newspaper shop. For the Senesi, it is heartening to see that this traditional children's game is still fashionable. If my observations are any indication, the pastime may actually be enjoying a comeback if the Goose, Wave, and now the Panther have anything to say about it. Wooden balls and marble machines have fortunately not yet gone the way of other outmoded toys by the advancing digital era.

Making an Entrance

As I move into the courtyard, the emerging dinner scene brings me back to reality (and solitude). Life is buzzing out here as well, but at a more adult-centric pace. I have arrived nearly at 8:00 p.m. as had been suggested, which is only one hour earlier than the same dinners during the summer events, so I imagine we are still in for a lengthy, if memorable evening. My initial sense is that I am neither early nor late, which may be the most appropriate time to arrive—if there is such a thing. A third of the people are standing near their seats to chat with nearby neighbors, and probably another third of the seats are now directly occupied. Some chairs have been tilted upright toward the tables to signify reserved blocks.

UNBRIDLED SPIRIT

At this point my own "antennae" go up as I scan the current attendees for familiar faces. *This place seems larger than I remember*, I think nervously. The task of identifying individuals is more challenging with people spread out across the courtyard. Then as my eyes shift to the right, I see them. I don't know if my face is outwardly expressing the true glee I am now feeling. Pietro and his wife are sitting across from Massimo—all of whom Linda and I had met at previous events here this past July. I had also met Pietro and his family two years earlier when we had sat near them. Pietro's cousin, Simone, was the head of the Young People's group at the time. (Following all this?) As I now approach their long row of tables, Pietro waves in recognition and signals for me to join them. *Phew.* I believe I have just found a home for the night. I bolt excitedly toward their table on my way to personal salvation.

I turn into the narrow aisle when suddenly, bang-crash! The coat dangling from my left arm catches on the back of a standard-issue, wooden contrada chair tilted up toward the table. My momentum causes that chair to knock into its neighbor, setting off a more horrid string of events—not the least being the simultaneous crashing of said folding chairs onto the paving stones below. For those with lingering doubts, the sound of hardwood on stone can make quite a racket. The whole table may have also shifted while instinctively lunging for it to retain my balance. After a split second of assessing my error and its cause, the expected embarrassment sets in. Numerous people on this side of the courtyard now turn my way to address the commotion. Thinking my horror is now complete, I fuss with one of the chairs to pull it upright, only to find myself staring directly into the curious eyes of the contrada's priore. *This just keeps getting better.* "Hello Thomas, it's alright," he smiles and gestures not to worry. "How are you?" I quickly recover my wits and respond, "Well, I am breaking everything, so we're off to a good start!" I quip and laugh nervously. He understands basic English, so I don't even try to translate at this point. He'll get the gist of it. Eventually I make light of the whole episode, suspecting that my nearby neighbors are only sympathizing with this gangly visitor's ineptitude.

I cannot help but recall an instructive revelation—in fact one of my favorites—offered by author Robert Rodi in his book, *Seven Seasons in Siena*. Now adapting one of his own contrada dinner anecdotes, I contemplate that when wishing to convey humility as an American visitor, stumbling into dinner chairs in front of the contrada president can be downright golden.

HOMECOMING AT DUE PORTE

Guess Who's Coming to Dinner

After mentally recovering, I move more cautiously to the chairs across from Pietro and his wife. They don't seem preoccupied with their toddlers, so perhaps they are at home with someone. Across from them is Massimo, who I recognize immediately from our dinner with him and his wife three months earlier. Somehow, they have left one empty seat directly across from Pietro. After shaking hands and reacquainting ourselves, Pietro motions me to take a seat now, as more Panterini are streaming into the courtyard. The seats to my right are still empty, I notice, though Pietro mentions they are already reserved. With numerous contrada dinners under my belt (perhaps literally), I should know the drill now; empty places at tables are deceptive because keen contradaioli will visit in advance to reserve their blocks. One of them asks about Linda, and I mention that she is sick, quickly recalling various Italian words for "cough" and "sore throat" which I memorized earlier for a visit to the pharmacist. At this point I take my seat, throw my coat around the chair without further incident, and take comfort in the feeling that I have arrived.

I have also learned that it's not necessary to continuously test myself with speaking in the Italian language. Just let things settle down, watch people show up, and occasionally engage in spontaneous conversation. The last thing I wish to be is an American pest. Before settling into the obvious topic for discussion, I ask Pietro whether his cousin, Simone is here tonight. He raises his head a bit and looks around as if spying through a contrada periscope. Most attendees are now at their seats in anticipation of the antipasti.

Pietro finds his target. "There's Simone, over there," he points to two tables behind me and then yells to direct his cousin's attention our way.

I turn around to see the lanky Simone still standing, true to form. He spots me and gets excited, to my satisfaction. "Tom! Welcome! How are you?" he says in his boisterous voice with a friendly wave. I had seen him earlier in the week at Piazza del Conte, and we agreed to find each other at the dinner. Mission accomplished—though the idea of holding a conversation of any kind with him tonight is not likely in the cards. That is, if he doesn't move out of his current, hemmed-in position. The tables are too tightly packed to allow for ease of movement between them. This does speak volumes about the impressive attendance, however. As if to confirm this observation, I turn my head back once again to witness Angelo, Alessio, and a few of their peers dragging out yet more tables to set up along our side of the courtyard. More people are filing in and are hard-pressed to find seating. Many of them appear to be young people who may have been out front and are now arriving for the meal. Looking around myself to judge current attendance, I can't help but be impressed that our courtyard is nearing capacity. The Panther isn't even running tomorrow. I further suspect that few, if any, non-Panther visitors are joining us tonight, as I suspected. This is clearly a special and unique opportunity to participate in a traditional community event that is by no means oriented to outsiders.

I barely return to my tablemates and notice the individual plates of antipasti coming our way, feverishly distributed by two young women carrying a large tray. And one of them is Carmina! She quickly sees me and does a double take, voicing her own surprise: "Tom! Hi! Are you here for the Palio?" I respond in the affirmative and thank her for providing the first course. I had met Carmina along with Angelo at the Panther museum several years earlier, which was followed by several mixer events between her contrada peers and our own students. At that time, she was in college, but has since joined adulthood more thoroughly, including a recent marriage and a budding career. A lot of her friends have done the same, and learning of their successes is an expected and satisfying circumstance of paying attention to the same small community for five years now.

Turning to our plates, we take stock of the offerings. Each of us has been given a piece of thick bruschetta (toast) decorated with shaved zucchini and cheese, along with a generous helping of mixed green salad with cranberries and walnuts, and a wedge of what is probably pecorino (goat cheese) topped with marmalade. I decide to "play tourist" for once as I whip out my smartphone for a photo of the undisturbed plate of food. To my pleasant surprise, at least two others within my field of view are doing the same, including Massimo. I am consequently not completely out of line here.

Massimo opens conversation with me, first in Italian, then (if necessary) in broken English. "Did you come to Siena just for the Palio?"

"Yes, I was surprised in September to learn about the Straordinario," I begin, "and I wanted to learn about how it is different from the summer Palios." In a way, Massimo opened the door for me to ask a question without actually asking one.

HOMECOMING AT DUE PORTE

He chuckles, "It was a surprise for all of us," he says sternly. "It was much too late to plan for a Straordinario this year. The season usually ends in August. It's caused a lot of debate here in Siena," he continues. "Isn't that true, Pietro?" He asks across the table.

Turning away from another conversation, Pietro asks, "What?" while looking back and forth to Massimo and me in a theatrical way, as if to say, *What did I miss?* I do appreciate his playful humor.

After repeating his question in Italian, Pietro responds quickly, "Yes, nobody expected this. And we're not even running!"

I quickly say in a positive tone, "I am still really impressed with how many people are here tonight," gesturing around the courtyard.

Pietro can't help but agree, adding, "It's a good excuse to get together. The contrada is our extended family," he teaches me, confirming what I have heard many times.

I ask both of them, in a rare moment when I have their attention, "Do you care much what contrada wins tomorrow?" Both of them indicate right away that it does not matter. They don't seem to have a preference. I follow up with, "Are you favoring an ally, like the Owl?" Both of them agree that it just doesn't matter in this one. The Eagle is not running, which seems to have been the main concern during the extraction.

At this point, Massimo and his wife enjoy a visit from their teenage son, who was sitting at a nearby table with fellow peers. He has shuffled his way down the aisle to talk to his Dad, which makes me curious—that he is attached enough to his parents to pay them a visit. Massimo gives his son a pat on the back and introduces me before talking a bit more with him. I then watch as he heads back to his table for the night.

I ask Massimo, "Have you and your family always been members of the Panther?"

He responds with an explanation that I have heard more commonly than not. "No, I was not a member of the Panther. We moved here, and my son went to school and made friends from the contrada. It just made sense for us to join. My wife and I essentially became members because of our son," he smiles. I reflect to myself that this approach seems to be a rather recent, roundabout way of adding new contrada members. Traditionally, membership was determined largely by where one was born in Siena. Then, during the twentieth century, a family's bloodline became a more probable

• 218 •

route to membership. If one or two parents were members of a particular contrada, the children would follow suit. Beyond these venerated approaches to contrada membership, newcomers who move here are now finding themselves involved in contrada life in serendipitous ways, not the least being their children's social connections from school. This closely resembles the story of my friend, Carlo, and his parents as well. Carlo went to school with Panther kids, and his parents started to attend contrada dinners—in their case following the Panther's victory of 2006.

Massimo feels it necessary to explain why their son is not sitting here with them. "At dinners like this, people of similar ages and genders sit together. The age groups are about age seven to twelve, then thirteen to eighteen. The twenty-year-olds tend to sit together as well," he explains, a case in point being Angelo and Alessio with their counterparts now sitting two tables away. This carries over to more middle-aged men and women continuing to sit in groups of their own. Behind me tonight there is a table of women who occasionally sing various beloved melodies, just as the teenage and twentysomething groups are doing a few tables away. Then there are the persistent groups of senior citizens, usually older men who eat together and have likely known one another since childhood. If my sample of observations is any measure, these venerated contradaioli tend to eat at the same general table area for all meals here. In all, it is as though we are bearing witness tonight to the entire life cycle of the contrada (Figure 15).

Beyond these more traditional, stratified social groups, others are enjoying the company of immediate tablemates with little apparent need to mingle or network among their peers. The senior foursome to my immediate right, for instance, appears to have come here as if meeting at a restaurant. They are quietly enjoying each other's company but have made no effort to engage in conversation with anyone else.

Likewise, the seats down our table to the left have only gradually filled in with later arrivals. I notice a lone father who has remained entirely devoted to his toddler-aged son, slumped in Dad's lap and sleeping off the early evening. Before gaining more tablemates during the first course, Dad has not made one intentional effort to look around for friends or to otherwise socialize with others. Rather, he seems content for the time being to coddle his sleepy son while soaking in the festive courtyard environment. Eventually, others fill in around him and engage in occasional conversation.

HOMECOMING AT DUE PORTE

Figure 15. Panther contradaioli enjoy dinner and socializing within the contrada's courtyard. (Photo: Author)

One might presume that contrada members will more typically be found together in the larger social groups such as those discussed earlier (teens, college-aged, seniors, and so on). Granted, their vibrant group energy is often what attracts the attention of outsiders like me. However, there are other individuals and families who enter the dinner scene without a preconceived idea of where to sit or with whom they might interact. To some extent, our own small cohort is behaving similarly. While Massimo, Pietro, and various neighbors are occasionally entertained by their impromptu American friend and his curious questions, they otherwise remain content to enjoy the dinner without working the room. The takeaway lesson here is that it remains perfectly acceptable to join a contrada dinner without the expectation of being included in larger social groupings of friends. With this comforting realization in mind, I sit back and relax a bit; there seems to be little expectation that everyone will be interacting ceaselessly with others.

UNBRIDLED SPIRIT

With the antipasti plates recently collected by teenage volunteers, the primi piatti are now arriving. People are buzzing and preparing to eat, so it's difficult not to conclude that the contrada has been anticipating this moment above all others. At my first sight of the trays coming our way, it appears we are being treated with lasagna. Upon closer inspection this variety of lasagna favors the pasta and cheeses, with maybe a trace of meat sauce. It is closer in form to a *cannelloni*, which we have enjoyed previously in the Panther. Either way, we are in for a treat, and a filling one at that. Regardless of its proper title, the important thing here is that its main ingredients are pasta and cheese. Enough said.

The array of foods served from one contrada meal to another can be quite diverse. This past July, a young family member joined me for a lunch right here in this very courtyard. Mixed into the more familiar fettucine and red sauce was—of all things—tripe. I had been asked cautiously several times in advance of that meal if I was willing to eat one of the four chambers of a cow's stomach, to which I responded with a resounding "yes!" I'm always flattered to be eating as a guest in the Panther, so the food served is of little concern. Still, it was my first known encounter with this rather tough and chewy delicacy, though it was virtually tasteless within its more dominant tomato base. Slop enough red sauce across any type of food and it will taste like spaghetti. More to the point, those in the contrada eat very well, and they enjoy a variety of food items from one event to the next. There has been no cause for disappointment.

As we make progress on our primi piatti, I ask for Massimo's perspective on the contrada's vote to hold the Straordinario.

He explains, "Every contrada had to hold a separate vote to decide on the Palio," he begins. "In the Panther we voted at the assemblea generale by a simple count of hands."

"So, how many people voted 'yes' and 'no'?" I follow up.

Massimo reflects, "I guess there were about 250 people who attended, and almost everyone voted for it. Only a few voted 'no' or abstained." His recollection confirms Angelo's previous estimate.

"Were there any concerns about it, or arguments against holding the Palio?"

"Well, some were concerned about our rival, the Eagle, but most people did not think this was a good reason to vote against it," he offers. "The most important thing to consider is 'you' [your own contrada], so it was worth the risk. We have not won a Palio in twelve years, so we are interested in this extra chance. Of course, we weren't selected, and neither was the Eagle, so it really doesn't matter anyway. It's still something that does not happen very often," Massimo concludes.

"Are there fewer contrada members participating because you are not running?" I ask.

"Yes, that's true," he admits. "Many others are not here, although there are more people here than I expected. We are all waiting more for next July, when we know we will run. There are probably a lot of people here because of the decent weather," he smiles. "It could have been much worse."

On that note, I am beginning to feel my own first chill of the evening, with cool air starting to tap my neck and hands. Even with the one drizzly day, most of this week's high temperatures have been comfortable, right around room temperature. And this enclosed courtyard of stone and brick likely retained some heat a bit longer after the sun went down. Still, I note that more than a few people are already reaching for extra sweaters, jackets, or even neck scarves. I am not shivering yet in my sweater, which means I can still add my jacket, if necessary.

At this point, Pietro swings around to focus on Massimo's discussion with me. His body language suggests that he is eager to jump in at the next opportunity. He turns to me and adds to Massimo's description of the contrada vote. "The biggest problem is that there was not enough time to organize the Palio," he says in his best English, leaning intently and close to my face. "Seven of the contradas voted 'no,' so it almost didn't pass. I think it was the new mayor who wanted to hold the Palio," he volunteers. "The initial proposal and decision was to make the mayor look good after being elected. It was all political."

"That's interesting," I respond with furrowed eyebrows. "Do you agree that the second vote should have been held for those that voted 'no'?"

"I think that rule needs to be changed. If a contrada votes no, that's it," he swipes his hand across the table. "Instead, the ones that voted 'no' were given a chance to join in. Of course, they all voted 'yes.' And then what happens? The first five contrade to be extracted were those that voted 'no.' And we weren't selected," he ends with a smirk. There are clearly very different philosophies among the Senesi as to whether the second vote was a good idea.

As my tablemates turn their attention back to others, I notice that the priore is making his rounds, as he tends to do. He knows how to work a room and greet nearly everyone before the night is out. Upon making it over to this accident-prone American, and before greeting the others around me, he says hello again and asks how I am enjoying the dinner. He must be curious to find me mingling with these otherwise unassuming Panterini with whom I have previously spent little time. Although, he has by now become accustomed to seeing me in the contrada or walking the streets nearby, both with and without Linda or student groups. I have apparently established myself as some sort of a "regular," at least around during the days of the Palio.

Main Course

Tonight's main course, which is somewhat counterintuitively called the *secondo* in Italian, descends on us, and a few of us unleash our camera phones once again. Usually this course consists of what I might call a meat-and-potatoes dish, to use a euphemism for standard American fare. Linda and I rarely make it to this course when eating at local restaurants. We typically have eaten too much food already, with just some bruschetta and primi piatti. Contrada dinners such as this provide a welcome exception, however, as the serving sizes are more reasonable, and the courses are spread out over time, allowing one's body to prepare for the next onslaught.

Because I am often in the middle of various multilingual conversations during the primi piatti, the time required just to eat my pasta can be quite lengthy as well. During a similar dinner here not long ago, my Panterini tablemates were giving me a hard time because I was eating my pasta so slowly. It was all in good fun, however. When I finally finished my plate, I essentially took a bow and showed off my empty plate to those around me, causing a hearty round of applause. It still amazes me how my dining companions can scarf down their food so quickly. Perhaps this is a testament to the hearty appetites that accompany their characteristically active lifestyles, at least during the events surrounding the Palio. Regardless, this evening my stomach is now appropriately prepared to handle the next

HOMECOMING AT DUE PORTE

course—a good thing indeed, as a modest plate of beef, gravy, and potato pie has now appeared in front of me.

Just as I prepare to dig in, I am interrupted once again from behind. An "old" friend appears with a hand upon my shoulder. It's Matteo! I happily return his greeting, having now seen him every year since our first *cena della prova generale* with the Panther in 2014. For his part, Matteo is a highly devoted and involved senior member of the Panther, and his enthusiasm for seeing me in recent years has done wonders for my growing confidence. Upon turning around to face him, he says with a big smile, "Tom! How are you doing?" I have learned quickly that Italian greetings are just as generic—and thus just as manageable—as standard American ones. When someone asks, *"Come stai?"* ("How are you are doing?"), I immediately respond with *"Sto bene"* ("I am fine"). Sometimes they ask, *"Tutto bene?"* ("All is well?"), to which all I need to reply with is the exact same thing: *"Tutto bene, grazie!"* ("All is well, thanks!").

Unfortunately, such reunions with the likes of Matteo are still bittersweet, as few of them are comfortable enough with prolonged conversations in English. The same remains true with my limited mastery of Italian. That said, most people don't seem disappointed about this situation, as they are probably not that eager to make me their best friend. At least they have some idea of who keeps joining them for dinner. Not all is lost, though, as enough people are variably bilingual to at least make conversation manageable.

Further, certain modern technologies provide a welcome crutch when necessary. Various phone apps, for instance, allow for the translation of words or phrases on the spot. At one point this evening, I was bogged down with a particular word as I attempted to translate to Italian, and Massimo whipped out his phone to show me a new app I had not seen before. This one is voice activated and translates immediately in a way that Apple's Siri might. Although its use was limited tonight due to persistent background noise, such software and devices are becoming more common for multilingual events like this. I have already made occasional use of the simple Google Translate tool tonight to converse with Massimo and the others. It appears that one benefit of smartphones is their ability to help us bridge the cultural divide.

Radiational Cooling

Pietro and Massimo are now wondering about what kind of *dolce* (dessert) will show up, now that the secondi plates have been cleared. Perhaps their body language is asking more than that, however; a certain level of urgency seems to be creeping into the minds of the Panterini as they attempt to stave off the nighttime chills. Although I have not yet reached for my jacket, I am close to doing so. What surprises me more is the behavior of those around me. Many attendees have already donned a variety of thicker coats, and I even spy some scarves wrapped around women's necks. It seems that the first few casualties of the evening have now given up and are making their way toward cars and homes. Still, the dolce is coming, and most of us are hunkering down despite the oncoming chill in the air.

One senior gentleman a few chairs to my left has likewise decided to surrender as well, gesturing to me that he is dressed inappropriately for the cold and with no hat to protect his hairless head. Looking a bit frustrated with himself as much as with the weather, he bids all of us a goodnight. Despite near-perfect daytime conditions this week, the evening temperatures of autumn are providing some challenges. Having taught weather and climate, I recall that one natural process, radiational cooling, is especially potent this time of year. With the sun having set, the earth is now shedding a lot of its heat energy directly into space. The surface of the earth cools first, thereby cooling the air directly above it. Given that we humans are close to the ground, we are quite susceptible to this rapid cooling, as the poor Panterini are now discovering. Meanwhile, those over in the Goose are likely enjoying their tents, as even a thin cover will greatly reduce such cooling and contain some of the heat. The same strategy is often employed to protect plants from an early freeze or frost.

Finally, those of us who have toughed it out are rewarded. Sizeable aluminum cups filled with tiramisu have arrived, each covered with a heaping portion of chocolate powder. No complaints can be heard as we all dive in.

With more attendees calling it a night, I now contemplate that dinner events like this one seem to progress with their own unique life cycle. Throughout a roughly three-hour timeframe, everyone first moves through an arrival phase, during which early attendees mingle out in the street and in the courtyard before taking their seats. Dining locations are scouted out and

HOMECOMING AT DUE PORTE

reserved, friends are met, and initial conversations are held. The second phase involves consuming the first two dinner courses, with nearly everyone eating while seated at their places and holding various conversations with their immediate tablemates. By the third phase, the secondo course is being consumed and the younger members at their own tables begin to get antsy. They often instigate bouts of singing, which often contagiously spill over to other tables. Occasional singing can also erupt among tables of middle-aged women and the older men. It is during this time when the contrada priore and sometimes other leaders make their rounds to greet their constituents and any guests that might have joined them. Some contradaioli also make the effort to visit others elsewhere in the courtyard. Finally, the fourth phase occurs before and after dessert, marked by the first people to bid their neighbors farewell. Taking their leave is not the easiest of feats, however, as they will often be compelled to stop—or be stopped—to enjoy last-minute conversations on their way out. The dinner thereby winds down as a gradual stream of people exit for the street. We are now clearly in the midst of the fourth phase. As the scrumptious tiramisu comes and goes, we are nudging ever closer to a chilly 11:00 p.m.

A Promising Invitation

There is one last surprise awaiting me tonight, as my own veritable homecoming winds to a close. I feel yet another hand on my shoulder and a gentle, "Tom, how are you?" Normally, this would be the priore making his rounds, but he has already done so for the evening. I turn with delight to find one of my newer acquaintances: Bruno! Following a joyous handshake in return, I stand up to speak with him. Bruno is another contrada leader who I had met last year at a dinner like this one. We emailed back and forth during the year, and most recently I had sent him an email specifically about the upcoming Straordinario. He is now picking up the conversation with a heartfelt, if unnecessary, apology.

"Tom, I'm so sorry I have not responded to your email. I have been traveling and have not caught up with the contrada email lately," he says with genuine concern. Of course, this does not phase me at all.

"Bruno, there is no problem, you are all busy," I comfort him. And then the final surprise of the night arrives.

He asks, "When would you like to meet? How about we go get breakfast tomorrow, and I can tell you more about the Straordinario?" I now sense my jaw hanging open, though it probably isn't. I immediately think, *on Palio day?* I am still not beyond the ability to be starstruck, as it remains perfectly true that I am simply not worthy.

Still, I decide immediately to accept, responding, "Well, sure, if you have time! It's Palio day, so I understand if you have other obligations." Of course, I am presuming that he doesn't, because he is the one who offered.

"It's OK, the Panther isn't running, of course, though I do have to get back to change into my costume by 1:00 for the corteo storico. I will be marching with the comparsa once again," he smiles.

"Oh, that's fantastic!" At which point, I decide immediately to take advantage of his generous invitation. "Sure, I would love to join you for an early meal. When do you want to meet?" We establish a time to meet at the entrance here to the società. Somewhat shockingly, I now have a breakfast invitation with Bruno on the morning of the Palio. It doesn't get any cooler than this. And for once I am not referring to the weather.

PART IV:
PALIO STRAORDINARIO

CHAPTER 14

The Protectors

After ducking inside Società Due Porte on Palio morning, I eventually track down Bruno. He bids farewell to a friend and asks if I have any preference for a place to eat. Without any thoughts of my own, he suggests that we simply start walking to find something along the way. *Right*, I think, a bit puzzled that he doesn't seem to have a favored hangout. In truth, I could not care less where we go, or even whether the place serves food. My companion, who has made the bizarre if appreciated choice of spending time with this American, is no less than a local expert about contrada operations, and someone—I am confident—who comes armed with a variety of perspectives on the Straordinario, which is now only hours away. For my part, the wisest thing to do now is go with the flow and see where Bruno leads us. We are moving quite rapidly down the Panther's main street, where we will imminently encounter the city's western thoroughfare, Via Stalloreggi.

Uneven Population Growth

After expressing my appreciation for meeting, I open with a comment about the previous night's dinner experience.

"I was happy to see so many people at the dinner last night," I begin. "Were you surprised with the attendance?"

"Well, yes and no," he responds with a chuckle as we dodge other pedestrians. "It was great to see our courtyard filled with people, even for a [cena della] prova generale when we are not running. This is not a surprise, however. Our dinners during the Palio are much bigger now than a couple of decades ago. We now have well over a thousand people for that dinner when we are running." This confirms what others have told me about the growth in attendance numbers in recent decades.

"Does this mean that the contrada membership is growing now, too?" I follow up as we navigate some clusters of people standing in the street. As we approach the Campo, it is becoming increasingly difficult to focus on our moving conversation.

"No, the contrada membership is about the same. It's stable, about 600 baptized members," he states as we barrel down Via di Città directly toward the predicted throngs. I am a bit curious as to why Bruno is leading us into the most congested part of the city. He continues, "The problem is that during the regular year we are smaller, since not as many people come to the contrada on a regular basis. More people are coming for the Palio, but less during other times of the year. It's not as convenient for people now that many of them live outside the walls." Bruno's comment is now well documented, as approximately half the Senesi have abandoned the historic center in favor of larger, newer, and less expensive flats in the nearby suburban areas.

We have arrived above the main entrance to the Campo, at which there is a huge bottleneck. What all these persistent people think they are accomplishing is beyond me. The street is entirely blocked with humanity, and it is spilling into the side streets. No matter, we find a way to shove through as other locals are doing. At the top of the main ramp that descends into the Campo is an imposing (though friendly) line of armed military personnel screening anyone determined enough to pass the checkpoint. Bruno is curiously intent on pushing through the throng gathered here as well, so we suspend our strolling conversation to navigate ourselves to the other side of the congestion. I feel like we are driving through a thunderstorm downpour before emerging on the other side.

Now with more space to ourselves, we resume our intentional pace to find food along Via Banchi di Sotto. The entrance to this main thoroughfare forms the shape of a "Y" and is considered the premier intersection in the historic district. This spot is where the main roads of Siena's three terzi come together. Bruno can't resist making sure I know this story.

"Do you know why these two streets are called Via Banchi di Sopra and Via Banchi di Sotto?" he quizzes me. The first street he mentions veers off to the left and upwards, headed north toward Piazza Gramsci and Porta Camollia, Siena's northern gate.

"It has something to do with the early banking industry here in Siena, right?" I try.

"Yes, Siena was known for its banking operations, including the Monte dei Paschi. The Senesi were known all over Europe for their banking practices back in the Renaissance. And the Via Francigena came right through here," he says as he gestures toward the intersection and along our street. He is referring to the pilgrimage route through Europe, from England and France southeastward to the churches of Rome. Siena's businesses thrived during the late medieval and Renaissance eras because of their location along this fabled and well-traveled foot path. Bruno continues, "*Sotto* means below, and *sopra* means above. So, the banks that lined this lower street were the Banchi di Sotto, and the banks up there on the northern road were 'the banks above,' the Banchi di Sopra." Just like cities around the world, street names and other landmarks can provide strong clues as to the important historical institutions and people that shaped their past.

Although he seems strangely unphased about his continued search for food, Bruno returns to our conversation about contrada population trends. "The contrada we are in now is the Unicorn, which isn't running this time," he begins. "The contrade with the smaller populations are mostly here in the center because they don't have a city gate with access to the city outside the walls." I perk up at this lesson because writers from outside Siena also have indicated this quirk of geography. "So, the Owl, Unicorn, and Eagle are the smaller contrade. Others are growing in their membership because they have a main city gate that connects them with the neighborhoods outside the wall, like the Shell, Caterpillar, and Ram. But the Porcupine is the largest because the city has been growing mostly to the north, just outside its city gate of Porta Camollia," he explains, followed by a chuckle at another thought. "Actually we [Panther] do have a gate to the outside, but it doesn't help us. It leads out to a valley in the countryside, so there are no people to attract." I smile in a combination of understanding and sympathy.

"Are you happy with the size of the Panther right now, or is the small size a problem?" I have admittedly asked other Panterini this very question for comparison purposes.

"Yes, the size right now is good, because we know who people are when they attend events or participate in meetings," he states.

Nodding in agreement, I add, "It's been fun during the past few years to watch some of the young people growing up. I actually recognize a lot of them now," I laugh.

THE PROTECTORS

"Exactly, it's easier to get to know people in a smaller contrada. People who join the larger ones do not necessarily understand its purpose or history, so they are mostly interested in partying and wearing the outfit. They think, 'Now I am wearing the outfit, so I am a part of the contrada,' but this is not true." I laugh at his impression of newcomers. He continues along this train of thought, undeterred by the distractions around us. "As I said earlier about the Panther, more people are coming to the contrade now for the Palio, but not during other times of the year. But the contrada is more than just the Palio. It's about creating community during the year." I sense a bit of his frustration at this paradox. Although the Palio is attracting new people to sustain and sometimes build the contrada's membership, other social aspects of the contrada system may be fading.

I respond, "Yes, I have noticed that myself in the weeks before the July Palio. When I walk around the rione of the Panther or other contrade, there are very few if any people around. I guess they are mostly working and living outside the contrada now."

"Sure, the contrada just isn't as convenient for people to meet each other as it once was. We still have a lot of events during the year, but you can't just walk out your front door and be there in one minute," he states. "There are still some people who live here, but it's a smaller group now."

At this point we both eyeball a vertical sign in the street that indicates a bar or cafeteria. We have arrived at Lievito Madre, which we both agree will serve our needs perfectly. While recognizing the friendly place from past visits, I remain curious about what Bruno might order for "breakfast." It is approaching noon, a time of day that many Americans associate with lunch. At the front bar, we sneak around some standing customers and order some lunch-type offerings on display behind glass. Bruno orders a small pizza and a *panino* (sandwich) for which he feels the need to explain. "I am going to be marching all afternoon, so this is my breakfast and lunch!" he smiles. I take the safe route and ask for a turkey panino, which is perched on top of a stack of prepared sandwiches.

Contemplating Contrada Membership

We eventually shuffle with our food trays and accessories through the narrow gauntlet of standing customers to a refreshingly empty dining room in the back. We find a suitable table and immediately make good progress with our meals. Now that we are both seated and more relaxed, it feels appropriate to ask him about his background, both in Siena and with the contrada.

"How did you get involved with the Panther?" I open. "Were you a member since childhood?"

He smiles and responds, "It's a funny thing. My parents are not from Siena originally. They came here because of my father's job. One of my father's friends at work was from the Panther, and he encouraged both kids—my brother and me—to get involved with the contrada. There is no grand story to it, about me being born here or something. It was simply by word of mouth. I have enjoyed being a part of it ever since then. So, I have [my father's friend] to blame," he chuckles.

Then Bruno becomes more emotional about the meaning of the contrada system. "You know that you should be part of the contrada when you feel the emotions in your heart, here," he gestures to his chest. I am compelled to emphasize here that my companion is a muscular, in-shape, forty-something fellow who could flatten me in a split second. If he was declared to be the Italian version of a Navy Seal, nobody would blink an eye. And yet he is simply at ease with displaying his emotions in front of this American newcomer. He continues in a soft tone, "When you feel it here, this is when it's time to think about joining. I am seeing this happen with my friend now, since I've been inviting him to contrada functions in recent years. It's really interesting to see. [He] is from outside Siena, but he's now starting to show emotions about the contrada. Who knows, if you start feeling this way in the future, maybe it's something to think about," he concludes with a subtle smile.

This comment alone throws me off guard. The notion that Americans or any non-Italian speaking foreigners could possibly become close enough to these timeless communities is a challenge to fathom, to put it mildly.

"Ha, that's an interesting thought," I respond awkwardly. "I think it would be very difficult for Americans like me to become accepted if they are not living here. You all have a culture and history in common, and you all live here permanently. The language divide is also very frustrating." Looking at me intently, Bruno nods in understanding and I continue on a more positive note, "Still, I'm very grateful for everyone's friendliness as I learn more about the Panther."

THE PROTECTORS

It just seems inconceivable that any combination of events—short of becoming nearly fluent in Italian and moving here permanently—could realistically lead to being anything other than an outsider here. I even admit to scoffing at other Americans who naively think otherwise. As I ponder for a moment the challenge of becoming an involved contrada member in Siena, I then think of the various communities and organizations at home in which I continuously struggle to remain active. And I actually live there and don't have the language challenges that exist for me here. Even as a native-born American, it's still difficult enough to feel a sense of community even on my own territory, so I believe it would be an even greater challenge to integrate with the close-knit networks of a contrada. Regardless of one's enthusiasm for the communities here, it seems important for outsiders to retain some sense of what is realistically possible. I do hope I have achieved an appropriate balance by now, after several years of visiting, without shortchanging myself or others. As always, I suppose that time will tell.

Other friends and colleagues have weighed in about this topic, as recently as this week. Although some English-speaking foreigners can sometimes "catch the fever" and pull all the stops to become a contrada member, others decide to take the opposite approach and avoid contrada life altogether. For instance, two of my acquaintances here have both found a way to live permanently in Siena, at least for this chapter of their lives. Both are American, and both enjoy various teaching and administrative roles in higher education. Yet intriguingly, neither of them is consciously seeking contrada membership. Upon asking one of them recently if he had considered becoming involved with a contrada, he provided this thoughtful explanation:

> Well, I had an opportunity at one point to become more involved with the Ram. I enjoy occasional contrada activities and dinners when I am invited, but I prefer to remain more neutral here in Siena. I like to be a part of larger community organizations that are not part of a specific contrada. The Palio is always fun, and I usually watch it myself from the Campo, but I don't think I would feel attached like true contrada members.

I should add that this individual already speaks fluent Italian, so the language divide is not a concern. However, given his mild-mannered personality, it is a far stretch indeed to imagine him screaming his lungs out with fellow contradaioli as they march passionately into the Campo. I'm just not seeing it. He would likely be much more comfortable singing Broadway numbers in a choral group.

The second person I asked about contrada membership also responded thoughtfully:

> As for joining a contrada, I decided not to pursue getting baptized. However, my 8-year-old kid is baptized in the Snail. There wasn't anything about the Snail that was more special than the others here, so it was pretty much a random decision. Some of his school friends are in the Snail, so helping him keep those connections made sense. There was really no other reason than that. I don't think I would feel comfortable being a contrada member, because I just don't share the history and passion that they do. Most contrada members have been here for most or all of their lives, sometimes for generations. I mean, how do you match that? You can't. I mean, I can cheer with them and appreciate their history, but they already have their community, and I would never be able to bring that sense of passion to the contrada. I might cheer for the Snail, but really, whoever wins the Palio is fine with me (laughter).

To some extent, these comments echo my own sentiments, in part because I cannot guarantee my consistent, annual return to Siena in the future. Life can go in all sorts of unpredictable directions. I believe that pursuing the esteemed status of a baptized contrada member involves, at a minimum, a long-term commitment of some kind. Such a commitment would necessarily mean having a regular and physical presence here—around Palio time at the very least—and, even better, contributing to the community in some way.

More positively, it is immensely satisfying to consider how far I have come since Linda and I stumbled off the bus from Florence for the first time. It may be very well that I will remain content with this "friend of the contrada" status for the foreseeable future. Sometimes I wonder if I'm too focused about my standing as an outsider, and maybe I should just relax. To paraphrase, with apologies to Albert Einstein, it's all relative. Sometimes we need to look beyond our frustrations and focus on the friends and related inroads we have made. Should any of these efforts lead to future involvement in some way, that's fine. Things will likely unfold as they are meant to do.

A Protector of the Panther

While in personal reflection mode here, it is worth mentioning a modestly symbolic yet practical way to support a contrada without becoming a full-blown baptized member. Two years ago, I learned that locals and outsiders alike could enroll to become a *protettore* (protector; plural *protettori*) of a contrada one wishes to support. To be a protector of the Panther or other contrade, for instance, requires a modest annual dues payment of sixty euro, at which point you are provided with a membership card and placed on their contact and mailing lists. Higher levels of support are also possible for each contrada, with a graduated list of appropriately honorific titles to recognize these levels of generosity. The email subscription provides announcements of all contrada social and civic functions. From my personal observations, the email list for protettori and bona fide contradaioli is one and the same. The contrada will even send hard copies of the membership cards by international mail, as I have pleasantly discovered. One's place of residence in the world is therefore inconsequential, though one's ability to participate regularly in their array of tempting events may be a different story. Nonetheless, it is still enlightening to see the wealth of contrada activities, business meetings, and celebrations that regularly occur throughout the year. And I do confess to feeling a twinge of mild excitement whenever an email from *La Contrada della Pantera* pops up in my inbox. A digital presence is yet another way in which the traditions of the Senesi and contrade are being globalized beyond their medieval-era city walls.

I still believe it is important to become involved with the contrada or some of its members first before requesting such a status. Like other traditions of contrada life, they do not invite just anyone to become a protettore, much less overtly attempt to sell subscriptions on the streets. Only after several years of making friends in the Panther and attending various events did I inquire about becoming a protettore. By then, their leadership was quite accepting of the idea. I figured this gesture would represent a small token of appreciation for their ongoing hospitality and for the new friends I've made.

It turns out that the role of protettore is probably one of the more obscure but important aspects of contrada society. As I mentioned, they do not advertise such opportunities. As Dundes and Falassi describe, the basic definition of a protettore is someone who voluntarily pays nominal annual dues to the contrada.[72] This status contrasts with actual members who belong to a contrada by birth or baptism and are not required to pay such dues. During the contrada's annual *festa titolare* (patron saint celebration), their designated comparsa of medieval-themed flag bearers and drummers conducts what is known as an *onoranza* (honoring) of the more important local benefactors, even by visiting their homes while out on the march, when possible. Knowing other protettori as I do, I have learned that their contributions to a contrada can be significant in a variety of ways. One protettore for the Panther, for instance, is a permanent resident and is immensely respected and known by probably the bulk of contradaioli. He is revered to the point of being trusted to compose new music and lyrics for the next generation of Panther folk songs. Thus, contributions to the contrada can be highly diverse and variously influential to the community beyond the token payment of annual dues.

Lingering Concerns about the Race

I return from those thoughts back to Bruno, who is still devouring his lunch. The topic naturally turns to the upcoming Palio, now only hours away. I ask, "What did you think of the reason to hold the Straordinario as a commemoration for World War I?"

Somewhat surprising if refreshingly honest, Bruno replies quickly between bites, "The Great War is not a good reason to hold a Palio." My eyebrows rise at this. "It's actually offensive, because Italians don't need a positive reason to remember the event. It glorifies the war."

I react with, "Wow, so were a lot of Senesi surprised about the idea?" While already suspecting his answer will resemble that of others, I am still estimating the degree to which the city was taken aback with the original proposal.

"Well, it was a surprise to all of us. The Assoarma officially proposed the event, but it is such a small organization. It just didn't make sense that they would be involved, and they are focused on all of Italy, not just Siena." With this I immediately recall Antonio's comment about the lack of enthusiasm of contrada leaders for the proposal. Bruno seems to be another case in point. He continues, "As for the war, nobody here cares about that as a reason to hold the Palio. For the city, it costs a lot of money now to organize it, more than in the past. I think the newly elected mayor and administration are taking a big risk."

"What do you think are the most risky factors?" I ask, for clarity.

"Well, the risk with the horses is a special concern. They are not trained to race this time of year. They can also get injured. If this happens, the city government will be blamed for promoting the event. So far this week, they have been lucky. As of now, the weather has been favorable and there have been no big crises to manage. We'll see if that continues," he says grimly, but hopefully.

Then Bruno seems to remember something, and a smile returns to his face. "Did you see the Palio banner, the drappellone?" With this I gradually release a smile of my own. Upon my positive response and a brief laugh, he turns more serious. "The artwork is offensive. There is no emotion in the banner, no serious connection between Siena and the Great War. And he clearly copied it from a photo. In my opinion, he really should not have been chosen as the artist for something this important. What he does for his career is fine, but not for this." Even though all humans maintain their own standards for what constitutes "art," Bruno's comment reflects the standard perspective I have heard here all week.

I turn to my other standard inquiry about the voting process for the Straordinario. "So, what did you think about the rule that allowed for a second contrada vote?"

"I believe that was a problem," he responds directly once again. He is not sugarcoating his answers, from what I can tell, which I choose to interpret as a sign of trust. "If a contrada voted against the idea of holding the Palio to commemorate the war, then they should not be a part of it. The She-Wolf voted 'no' because they just won in August, and it is interfering with their celebration events—even this week! They are also concerned about their rival, the Porcupine, which might have been selected. And then, look at what happens. The first five contrade chosen for the Palio were those that voted against it the first time." Bruno's frustration once again mirrors that of others I have spoken with. Their message is the same, essentially asking, *Where is the justice in that?* This appears to be Bruno's primary reason for not supporting the second contrada vote. It opened the door for precisely what occurred during the extraction.

I follow up with, "I know the Panther voted in favor of it, so what were the reasons?"

"I think the vote was like 250 in favor to maybe 40 against. Almost everyone was interested in participating. Some were concerned with giving the Eagle a chance. But it seems that most people realized we have not won in twelve years, and so it was an opportunity to win another Palio if we were selected. And the chances of selection were greater than usual, of course. You know that all ten had to be extracted for this one, though during the summer only three are chosen to join the others," he explains for my benefit. "So, despite those who argued about the Eagle, this was more important for us." This explanation seems to corroborate Angelo's remarks about the Panther's rationale for not worrying so much about its rival.

I further ask, "Do you think there was a generational difference with those who voted? Were the young people mostly in favor?"

"Oh yes, it was the young people. If you think about it though, it makes sense. We have not had a Straordinario in Siena for 18 years, since the millennium. Most young people were not alive, or they were too young to remember the last one. It's an exciting thing for them." With this comment, I realize for the first time what this means for the younger Senesi, given the length of time the city has gone without such an event.

I then ask, "Why hasn't there been a Straordinario in so many years? I noticed that in the past there were several each decade." This fact has also not been lost on the local media. At least several articles have nostalgically documented the relative simplicity of organizing a Palio in decades and centuries past, including this one: "The administration's decision to run on 20 October will certainly enter history . . . At the time it was not too much to [organize]. The Palio was more a festival to be made on command, rather than the unique tradition that it has become in the last 70–100 years".[73] The author provided one case in point, when the July 1848 Palio needed to be rescheduled. The decision was made to simply coordinate the race with the scheduled visit of Grand Duke Leopold II and the opening of the Siena-Empoli railway line. The point here is that the city could throw together a Palio almost on a moment's notice to coincide with other celebrations and events as desired.

In response, Bruno explains similarly as he provides his own historical perspective. "Well, the Palio is more expensive now. It costs the city a lot of money. And now the extra security forces must be paid. After what you call '9/11,' the Italian government instituted new rules for security when gathering larger crowds. And then a year or two ago, there was an incident in Torino where people stampeded, and one person was killed. After that, there is a more heightened awareness about the need for security. So, the city created 'emergency exits,' by cutting more holes in the bleachers, but they just lead to the narrow alleys and back out here." He gestures to the main street outside. "So, if people are running and panicking, where are they going to go?"

I offer a counter argument, saying, "Even though it's not perfect, at least there is a sense of security. It may be more important to take precautions these days." For my part, I have admittedly been comforted by the military's valiant attempt to at least screen people's belongings. If nothing else, the added security and exit routes may be most useful as preventative measures. Still, I can appreciate how difficult these changes have been for the Senesi. For hundreds of years they have simply gone about their business in the Campo without worrying much about the influence of devilish outsiders.

Contrada Budgeting

I shift the topic a bit to focus on the jockeys, specifically the rumors surrounding the famous Luigi Bruschelli, or Trecciolino.

Bruno provides a fresh perspective. "There is the Palio in the Campo, and the Palio *a piede*—on foot, outside the Campo where other deals and plans are made." It dawns on me that Bruno is basically saying in another way what Enrico referred to earlier, comparing the "world of the Palio" and the "world of politics".

"Ah, are you referring to the partiti?" I try to confirm.

"Yes, this is one side of it. Trecciolino was very good at this strategy. During the winter, he makes plans and deals with different contrade and other jockeys. I guess this time was different, though. He didn't do well with his negotiations. In recent years, he has been more interested in supporting his son, who was starting to run his own Palio races. So, because of that, the contrade now believe that Trecciolino is no longer trying to win. He could have made a deal to win one more Palio to tie the record of Aceto, then negotiate a promise to have his son run for them later. But in my opinion, he did not do well this time."

I present an alternative option. "Is there a possibility that he has changed his goals, now that he is getting older? Maybe he's not interested in beating the record as much as in the past."

"Even if that's true, if he still wants to race, he needs to make people think that he's interested in winning for them. He usually races for the larger contrade, since they have more money. He is often paid much more than other jockeys."

Still trying to learn more about how these earnings are used, I respond, "So, what I don't understand is how he uses his racing commission to influence other jockeys."

Bruno explains further, "Based on the amount he is earning from a contrada to race, he can actually undercut the deals that other jockeys make with their own contrada. He can divide up his own commission to other jockeys and still pay each of them more than the contrade they are running for." He shakes his head while I express my surprise. "This is how he influences other jockeys, because he can buy them out to help him with his own interests."

I respond with, "Wow, OK. So, how does a contrada do its best to make sure their jockey is devoted to them? Is it just a matter of paying the jockey?"

"It can get pretty complicated, even for us. It can be challenging to keep track of all the deals and who promises what. As for the contrada, we have to pay the jockey just to race, and we also usually pay other contrade who can help us win. If the jockey ends up in the rincorsa position, this needs to be planned for." This comment piques my interest because I have wondered whether contingency plans exist should a jockey find himself in the tenth position. Bruno continues, "This is why it can take so long for the race to start. The rincorsa jockey is trying to remember who offered what deals for whom and then to hopefully put his allies in the best starting position."

THE PROTECTORS

"Wow, that sounds incredible. And they change the deals right there on the track!" I express my astonishment.

"And there's more to think about than that," he adds, noting my interest. "You, the contrada, can also provide alternative deals to your jockey depending upon who lines up to the left or right of you at the mossa. There's a lot to keep track of, even for us." He chuckles, shaking his head.

Unbeknownst to my companion, I am silently cheering because someone is finally beginning to explain the mysteries that surround the Palio partiti. Although we are certainly only skimming the surface of the complexity here, I greatly appreciate Bruno's willingness to open a window onto the process.

After he takes another bite, I further ask, "What are the sources of contrada income that are used to help pay for these negotiations?"

"OK, sure. First, there is income from the protettori, or protectors of the contrada. You are a protettore now, so this will probably interest you," he smiles at what is an unequivocally accurate statement. He continues, "This money is never used for the Palio. It's only used for the maintenance of contrada facilities, to maintain the uniforms, and related expenses like that. None of that is used for the Palio." Bruno seems to presume that I prefer keeping my annual donations out of the bank accounts of various jockeys. And he would generally be accurate.

"Oh, that's good to know," I react quickly, "that some of the income is used to support the contrada itself."

Beyond the annual income of the protettori, Bruno describes additional sources of income. "Then there are the dinners and related events organized by the società. People often confuse the società with the contrada, but they are two different things. There is a president of the società, or the contrada's social organization. But the leader of the contrada is the priore," he explains. Regardless of my spinning head, he continues, "So, most of the money earned from the dinners goes to support the società, but a portion of that money is given to the captain for use in the Palio. However, the big dinner, the cena della prova generale, is used almost entirely for the Palio. This is how we earn money for the race."

Thoroughly fascinated, I follow up with, "Isn't there some kind of pledge as well, from contrada members before the Palio?"

"Yes, that's true. There are pledges, or promises, but only if we happen to win. Contrada members are asked months in advance if they are willing to pledge a certain amount, but they would only pay if we win. So, this isn't really regular income," he explains. "A lot of people from outside Siena don't realize how expensive it is to win. The celebration dinners and events throughout the year cost a lot of money, along with the additional payoff to the jockey."

With that, my generous companion must get from here to the dressing room for what is likely to be a typically grueling corteo storico. Bruno will be burdened further with some fifty pounds of costume armor. His role in the Panther comparsa today will be that of the *duce* (commander), traditionally assigned to one of the contrada's more physically imposing men. There is no doubt that Bruno more than qualifies on that count. As the bona fide leader of the comparsa and as custom would have it, he and his accompanying suit of armor will be located at the center of the contingent.

As we depart the relative solitude of our hangout, we thrust ourselves back into the dense river of pedestrians now ramping up into Palio mode. While forging our own path, Bruno points out a few more things and then exclaims, "Oh, I almost forgot. We have newer cards this year for the protettori." While trying not to walk into anyone, he pulls out his wallet and hands me one. "We made them smaller, like business cards this year, hoping they would be easier to carry. This is yours for 2018–19. You can just throw out the old one from last year, if you want."

I respond, "Oh, great! The business card is a good idea. The folded one last year was fun, but it didn't fit in my wallet," I tease. Then thinking like an American unaccustomed to doing business out on the street, I follow up with, "Do you want me to send an email to remind you that I paid and have the card now, for recordkeeping?" I had given him my annual dues during one of the July dinners, which was easier than attempting to send it through international mail. Beyond that, I do not wish to presume that I will be remembered easily, given that Bruno likely works with a wide range of people on any given day.

Without missing a beat, he responds with a grin, "No, that's OK. We know who you are."

CHAPTER 15

Curve of San Martino

After absorbing a brief yet enlightening week of perspectives about the Straordinario, the illustrious event is finally upon us. The race is only hours away, and I am back in our room with Linda to contemplate packing. Not packing to return to the States, mind you, but packing for the Palio race and the historical procession that precedes it. We are now in "strategy mode," with our bed transformed into a packing table. Possible survival gear for consideration is sprawled across the bedspread. We need to determine which snacks to bring and clothes to wear (assessing the potential use of pants and jacket pockets, purses, and maybe a backpack or waist belt to store everything we need) and devise contingency plans for changing weather conditions. We are essentially planning for a short camping trip—with plenty of sunscreen. It may indeed be the low-sun season of October, but our seats in the bleachers will receive the full brunt of afternoon solar radiation. For me this is the most obnoxious part of a warm or hot sunny day. For some reason the afternoon hours between roughly 4:00 and 7:00 always seem more oppressive and less tolerable than their morning counterparts when the sun angle is still the same. Whatever the explanation might be, I don't like it.

More exciting, our location in the bleachers for several hours will be on the outside of the infamous San Martino curve, where much of the typical drama of the race tends to occur. When the Panther is running in a summer Palio, this section of bleachers is typically filled with women from that contrada. Their northwest-facing seats are the very last to receive shade, so these women come prepared with thick sunglasses to cheer and sing in unison with an unwavering zeal. Tonight, we will experience the Palio from their shoes and eyes, so to speak.

CURVE OF SAN MARTINO

Acquiring Palio Tickets

Several days earlier, we had not yet known the exact location from which we would experience the race. Dario had offered tickets, as previously mentioned. Despite the lower-than-normal ticket price, I had told him that Linda and I would discuss it later, not having planned to shell out so much cash for this event. Part of me was resigned, quite satisfactorily, to standing in the center of the Campo free of charge. I had accomplished that feat most recently this past July with a younger family member, and we congratulated ourselves for enduring the wait. The crowd was densely packed, of course, but everyone enjoyed more breathing room than in the past. This was explained by the newly imposed security regulation that allowed no more than 15,000 people inside the center. Because we had not been trying to squeeze closer to the barriers, we were able to sit down in the less-populated center of the Campo for some time before the race.

For tonight, however, Linda has wisely decided to forego standing with people taller than her for several hours straight. Her lingering chest ailment this week has only affirmed that decision. For these reasons, we decided to splurge on bleacher seats to enjoy some level of comfort for the duration of this historic event. And that's when we encountered Silvia in her office three days ago.

It turns out that Silvia had access to Palio tickets through her business. When we stopped by, she asked, "Do you have tickets yet to the Palio?"

"Well, not yet," I began. "We aren't really sure how to watch the Palio this time. Out of curiosity, what is the price?"

"They are 280 euro each," she responded, quoting the same price as Dario. *There must be a standard price*, I contemplated. This was not the case in the past, as more centralized control is now being placed on what was previously an ad-hoc process of ticket sales. There are even new posters around the Campo entrances during the summer that indicate the maximum price allowed to charge for various seats.

Linda and I gaped in silent awe as she flipped through a small book of bleacher tickets right in front of us. With a mild case of hero worship, I was admittedly stunned at the sight of them, darned-near salivating like Pavlov's dog. Quite frankly I had never seen this many Palio tickets in one place before. And here was Silvia, flipping through them like cards.

"So, where are the seats?" I asked as my interest piqued.

"Do you know where the Panther women sit for the trials? Right near San Martino. You can see the whole curve there," she added for effect.

"Oh, OK, I know where that is," I responded enthusiastically. "I've seen them sitting there from where I sometimes stood on the inside of the Campo. If we buy the tickets, when would we need to be there for the start of the corteo storico?" I was already thinking about how we would plan the afternoon, because the Palio race starting time was scheduled for an early 5:30 p.m.

"I think you should be there around 2:00, and my uncle—you know him—will be taking the tickets and guiding people to their seats." This news comforted me a great deal. She was referring to Edoardo, with whom I have enjoyed various conversations in the past.

At this point, Linda and I looked at each other and nodded, confirming that we were both on board with this plan. We would join Edoardo on the Panther's bleachers at San Martino—still for a greatly reduced price compared to the summer. After returning to Silvia with the necessary funds later, I found that I felt quite relieved. Otherwise, the question of how we should view the grand finale would continue to linger over our heads. And the final race was getting ever closer on the calendar.

Into the Bleachers

Now appropriately armed with survival gear in Linda's travel purse and our various pockets, we leave our lodging behind and plot a course to the Campo. It's just before 2:00 p.m., which admittedly still feels strange. The time is early for today's festivities, mirroring the daily schedule during the past few days. The weather could not be more perfect for a late October afternoon. The blue skies and sun are providing temperatures in the 70s Fahrenheit. For all the concern about the unpredictable autumn weather, Giove Pluvio seems to be pleased. Perhaps he negotiated with Santa Caterina today to give her hometown a break. Indeed, the weather is just short of heavenly. The city administration and entire Senese population have dodged quite the bullet here. For us, this further means that every square inch of our exposed skin is lathered with sunscreen to endure the next two hours in direct sunlight.

At my prodding and in anticipation of the same throngs that Bruno and I struggled against earlier today, we stay away from the main city streets that lead to the Campo. With the race only hours away now, the congestion around the main Campo entrances will only be worse. The most logical route to our bleacher seats will thus take us across Piazza Mercato behind the Palazzo Pubblico and up Via Salicotto, the main street of the Tower contrada. Aside from some congestion from lingering crowds where the street spills into the Campo, our brush with the security line proves rather uneventful. Our water bottles need to have the caps removed, but otherwise we pass without incident. With our approach to our bleacher area only about a hundred feet away, I already spy Edoardo overseeing his growing flock. He has also wisely protected his own head with a rather humorous if effective scarf wrapped around his scalp. Most importantly, as Silvia promised, he is here to assist us. One never knows what to expect when arriving for bleacher seats, as we have learned in the past.

Upon our arrival at the base of the bleachers, we must rely entirely on his guidance now. I greet him with, "Edoardo, ciao!" Then, I ask the obvious question "So, where do these tickets locate us?"

He responds with his characteristic smile while clearly focused on his duties. "OK, so you can sit anywhere in that section on the right. There are no assigned seats."

"Oh, that's interesting," I say with pleasant surprise. "Are you expecting the bleachers to fill up?" Only a few seats have already been taken ahead of us, so it is tempting to believe that we will have a luxurious amount of room. Of course, this fantasy is short-lived.

Edoardo explains, "It will be pretty full about mid-way through the procession. People can arrive when they want, probably up through the next two hours. Of course, earlier people like you get to choose your seats!" he adds happily. He then explains the reality that will hit us later. "After more people come, there is a special way you need to sit. There is no separate bleacher row for your feet. When people fill in below you, your legs need to spread around their waist, like this." He indicates this necessary positioning with his hands and arms, then continues to explain. "Anyone sitting above you will need to do the same. It gets pretty tight, so get comfortable first."

With furrowed eyebrows at this news of unplanned intimacy, I manage to simply agree. "OK, we'll plan on being locked in when more people arrive."

Linda looks at me with a less confident set of wide eyes. There is a good chance that we are going to learn more about our future neighbors than we might have anticipated.

In the meantime, we move into decision making mode to determine our seats while they remain in our preferred state of emptiness. Now in mutual agreement, we point naturally to the upper rows to the right, closer to the curve of San Martino. Some people are already sitting on the far edge of the bleachers, however, so we elect to climb gingerly toward their general direction. There is a significant issue to consider with most bleacher seats around the Campo, however. Numerous balconies project outwards from the buildings, slightly overhanging the top row of bleachers. There is not quite enough room for an adult to sit comfortably there. Anyone stuck under the balcony will need to assume a severely slouched position for potentially several hours. My neck is starting to hurt just thinking about it, not to mention my lower back. Normally, for me to gain an extra foot of elevation would not be worth the hassle. However, in this case, we decide to hedge our bets and claim two of the very top seats, along with the row directly below us. This is a safe bet for now, as nobody is pressing in yet. We will have some time to sniff out our new aerial environment.

Climbing up these wooden bleachers warrants further caution, even for spry, more capable bodies. But they are truly unique, a one-of-a-kind Senese specialty, designed specifically for the spatial layout of the Campo. Only adding to their character, the bleacher "aisles" consist of little more than narrow cutouts in the seats themselves. Those arriving later will typically depend upon the good will of people already seated to help them up through the maze of humanity and wooden planks.

With these challenges in mind, I elect to climb up two rows first before grabbing Linda's hand to help guide her upward. Moving gingerly, it is necessary to be patient. The process is not for the faint of heart. As we arrive at our precarious positions, the seating numbers on the benches are additionally shocking. When used for assigned seating, the numbers may be placed close enough for children to sit comfortably side-by-side, but certainly not adults. Modern-day coach-class airplane seats are luxurious by comparison. For now, we have some breathing room, however, to acclimate to our temporary home for the next few hours.

Earth-Sun Geometry

I exclaim to Linda, "Do you see these numbers? I hope they don't plan to stuff this many people in here, as there is no physical way to do it."

"Well, for now let's put our things up on the top row where nobody can sit anyway, and we'll see if we need to move it later." We proceed to do just that.

I respond, "OK, we'll stay here as long as possible and see how it fills in. Hopefully the locals are right, that attendance will be down for this one." I further recall that during the summer Palii, once the actual numbered seats are sold out, vendors proceed to sell slightly cheaper tickets for the actual aisle steps. Once those are filled in, there is no human way to get in or out of the bleachers.

Now we are satisfactorily settled in our perch about six rows up, and the time is about 2:00, so we take stock of the sun situation. It takes no more than a few minutes to conclude that the direct sun angle is going to provide its own temporary challenges.

In a state of mild disbelief, I say to Linda, "How do they deal with this in the summer? Could you imagine sitting up here in 85-degree heat with the higher sun in July or August?"

She responds, "You won't find me up here! Our seats in the shade a few years ago were just fine! Who would think we'd have this issue in October?" Linda is referring to our relatively luxurious seats complete with metal-rimmed backs near Fonte Gaia in 2015, the story of which is told in my previous book. Dario had provided us with tickets for those precious spots within sight of the mossa.

I respond with a paraphrased line from the comical *Airplane!* movies of decades past: "Well, I've been doing some research on the sun. That thing is *hot!*" Linda ignores me and grimaces, though I am laughing as always. She's undoubtedly heard this too many times. We now find ourselves squinting into the direct sun, making any decent photography down the track or across the Campo nearly impossible without an elaborate sunshade. Despite having wisely lathered up with sunscreen, the direct heat feels intense and reminds me of why the beach is not typically among my favorite of places to hang out. We do have two baseball caps to deploy, though the sun is dodging the front visors and hitting our heads on the left side. We didn't bring our standard

American wide-brimmed sun hats on this trip because, well, it's October. The unlikely possibility of sitting on the top bleachers near San Martino in the blinding sun was—quite reasonably—the last thing on our minds. I then discover the most effective if awkward position for my own hat, essentially perched precariously on the left side of my head so that the visor partially covers my neck. The downside is that Linda must essentially tap her fingers on my hat to get my attention for now.

Out of curiosity, I eventually suggest to Linda, "I'm going to try to use the balcony here to shield the sun for a while, and I'll just slouch down." I thus take the plunge onto the top row behind us. I can fit my head under the cement overhang as long as my six-foot-tall body can slouch way down, allowing my feet to dangle two rows in front of us.

Linda looks back to see me wedged into this rather uncomfortable position. "How can you fit under there? I don't see how your body will take that for too long," she predicts.

"It's OK for now." I try to find some relief for her as well. I continue, "Being short might actually help you here," I joke. "If you sit here on my left, the bracket might actually shield you from the sun." It turns out that the bench behind us is accompanied by a massive, masonry support bracket for the balcony above, and it is located just to Linda's left. It thus blocks off the top row and provides some precious shade for the fortunate occupant who can squeeze next to it. Now more desperate, Linda decides to join me on the top row. For now, we assume these awkward positions while camping out under the balcony like a pair of oversized pigeons. I take advantage of the down time to scan the Campo and test out some photography options for later, all the while sitting almost on my back like an astronaut preparing for takeoff.

If nothing else, we are experiencing yet another Senese adventure. Rather than complain about situations over which we have little control, the least stressful approach is to simply revert into problem-solving mode and find a positive way to deal with such situations. The silver lining? We both take comfort in the fact that the earth will continue to rotate on its axis, thereby lowering the sun to a manageable angle within about two hours. By the time the Palio ramps up, the issue will be the opposite. As always, the lack of daylight come race time will not only derail most decent options for photography, but it will also threaten the ability to hold the race should darkness fall. We may even need our sweatshirts if we are out here long enough this evening. Nonetheless, such a thought is particularly welcoming at this moment.

Pre-Palio Festivities

As we continue to manage the effects of the celestial object overhead, the track is now clear of humans, and the events of the day are getting underway. We know this because of the increasing din of crowd noise emanating from the opposite side of the Campo.

"Is that the procession starting?" Linda asks me while squinting toward the sun.

"Well, I think the Bersaglieri and Carabinieri are both supposed to appear, but I don't know in what order." Recalling the time schedule for today, I add, "It's just past 2:30, which is when the Palio events were expected to kick off, so I guess they're on schedule." The local media had provided the expected starting times online, including the emergence of the horses and jockeys from Palazzo Pubblico at 5:15 p.m. From where we sit at the moment, that distant time still seems a half day away.

Before we analyze much else, the crowd's roar intensifies as the mounted Carabinieri in their stunningly elegant and polished outfits emerge from the Casato, on the opposite side of the Campo. I surmise that observers sitting on that side must have seen them preparing to enter. With their entry into the Campo, the Palio Straordinario officially kicks off. As the crowd roars its appreciation, the troops and their glimmering swords slowly prance around the track with as much uniformity as possible while riding moderately nervous steeds. Their contingent soon rounds the corner of the track and is prancing directly toward our position. Typically, this renowned unit of the Italian military police remains to complete a second lap—a full-throttle gallop around the track with swords pointing valiantly into the air. Today, however, their time is split with another military group yet to perform, so the Carabinieri glide gracefully across our path and unceremoniously exit on the street to our immediate left.

Just as the dust is clearing behind the departing mounted police, we detect an upbeat military march projecting from the Casato entrance. Its source is no mystery, and I smile in recognition of the Bersaglieri unit beginning its fast-paced jog around the track. My phone camera is ready to capture the group on video when they round the corner momentarily to face us. As advertised, the unit is doing its utmost best to play a recognizable tune while maintaining a brisk jog, to the delight and cheers of the crowd. Even before they emerge into view in front of us, we keep track of their distinctive feathered helmets bobbing uniformly above the crowd. Their march music concludes as they round the corner to face us, but their fast-paced jog continues as they, too, pass us with smiles adorning their sweating faces (Figure 16). I realize as they pass within speaking distance that this is no uniform lot of twentysomething soldiers but is rather a diverse contingent of variously aged men and women thoroughly enjoying their performance. If I didn't know any better, it is almost as if they are saying goodbye to us after an eventful and educational week here. After all, it was none other than the Bersaglieri that first greeted me in the Campo within hours of our arrival last weekend. Their special performances for an equally special Palio are thus providing quite the appropriate bookends to our experience.

Figure 16. The Bersaglieri march around the Campo with their fast-paced jog. (Photo: Author)

CURVE OF SAN MARTINO

The speedy exit of this crack Italian army unit is followed quickly by the beginning of the corteo storico. No time is wasted as the first costumed contingent of this regal, slow-paced pageant emerges from the Casato onto the track. To recall, those in the procession have already been marching through part of the city for some time, requiring about one hour to make their way from the Duomo to the Campo. The participants are dressed in a colorful and artistic variety of Renaissance- and medieval-era costuming loosely representing the glory days of the Republic of Siena. About half of the procession includes uniquely costumed contingents of all seventeen contrade. Each comparsa is similarly staffed with a handful of contrada representatives donning various military outfits, accompanied by their contrada's prized alfieri. Over the next two hours, the two alfieri for each contrada will perform their own interpretation of the sbandierata no less than six or seven times before concluding the procession in front of Palazzo Pubblico.

After an eye-popping routine of physically demanding jumps, tosses, and catches, each pair of alfieri concludes the sbandierata with the same grand finale. To the sound of a continuous, stimulating drum roll, they undertake a uniform circular motion to wrap the flags tightly around the poles. Then with a snap precision that would be the envy of any American drum corps, they toss their twisted flagpoles approximately three stories into the air before they finally succumb to gravity and are miraculously caught in tandem by their masters (Figure 17). I can't think of any other routine that requires the unfathomable amount of skill and practice involved with this risky maneuver. Given our prime location here at the curve of San Martino, we are all treated to many such lively performances conducted directly in front of us.

Figure 17. The Alfieri for the Shell contrada perform the sbandierata during the corteo storico. (Photo: Author)

During the more than two hours required for the procession to move around the Campo, we gradually collect more neighbors. Off to our right near the second main entrance to the Campo is the largest gathering of police and medical personnel I have ever seen at such close range. All are awaiting deployment, if necessary, for various duties, planned or otherwise. From our lofty perch, we further see Edoardo playing host to an increasing number of new arrivals searching for their bleacher seats. Not unlike one of those marble machines in science museums—you know, with rows of pegs that scatter the marbles in various random directions—the new arrivals are scattering either up toward our direction or farther to the right. Inevitably, however, the empty spaces around us are shrinking as more humans press in toward us.

The first party to sit close to us is a family with three children of various ages. They are, quite curiously, all wearing clean and fresh-looking fazzoletti representing the Turtle contrada. They have settled just below me to our right. Soon after, a similar family (but with one less young person) has taken the plunge to occupy the seats next to me. In this case, my water and satchel must be moved to make room for them. I end up sitting immediately next to the presumed mother of the family, with the two children placed between her and her husband.

This family is also sporting bright and new fazzoletti, but in this case they represent the Giraffe. *Are these actually Senese families?* I wonder to myself, deciding finally that they are not. Their fazzoletti are too perfect and oriented all the same way around their necks as visitors might do. And, where is their emotion surrounding their home contrade? They display no more enthusiasm than anyone else waiting patiently for a sporting event to start. The parents of both families are more focused on entertaining the children than anything else.

Somewhat to my surprise, Linda bends in closer and asks, "Isn't it disrespectful for them to wear the scarves like that? They likely don't even know what it means."

"Well, presuming they are tourists, which I think is true," I begin carefully, "I think it's OK as long as they aren't doing anything embarrassing. From the years we've been here so far, it seems that the contrada members at least seem to accept that visitors will wear them around Palio time. What I find more curious," I continue, "is that everyone in each family is wearing the same scarves. Normally tourists just pick a variety of colored scarves from the vendors."

"Hmm, so these are, what—the Turtle and Giraffe?" Linda asks for confirmation, and I nod in return. She continues, "They're both in the Palio, right?" I see where Linda is going with this question, as she is pointing to an important distinction between the contrade that are running in the Palio and those that are not. The members of the contrade that are not running do not wear their fazzoletti during the days of the Palio. It is further considered bad luck for contradaioli to wear them at times other than the four days of the Palio and other approved contrada-designated events throughout the year.

"Yes, they are both running," I confirm. "So, they are not likely tourists who have pulled random contrada scarves off the shelves. Maybe there's something more to these families than we might expect."

"Well, do you think they are contrada members? If so, what are they doing up here with us?" Linda continues her analytical questioning, though she is admittedly echoing my own thoughts.

"I'm not sure. I was thinking the same thing, and I can't tell yet if they speak English. I'll plan to ask them when the time is right," I say while gauging the appropriate time to introduce ourselves.

Perhaps with a touch of irony, our whispered analyses of people sitting around us might have progressed in a completely opposite direction five years earlier. While living among the Ocaioli in the Goose contrada during our first summer, I had been quite convinced that it was virtually sacrilege to wear a fazzoletto if one was not a true contrada member. Now I am finding myself defending these families and lightening up about the whole thing.

However, Linda has reversed course as well, but in the opposite direction. To my (pleasant) surprise she is actually displaying some concern about whether it is appropriate to be wearing these important symbols of contrada identity. After all, it was Linda who bravely marched into the Goose società while wearing her new silk fazzoletto purchased not ten minutes earlier from the contrada office. Even then, we were received by members of the contrada quite graciously once they saw that we were genuinely interested in learning about their collective home.

Eventually, the moment of "first contact" with one of the families presents itself with little effort. The two younger members donning the Giraffe fazzoletti become antsy and discover the inviting cave of space behind us. With the sun low enough now for us to emerge from under the rocks, so to speak, the children are being drawn into our earlier retreat, at which point the woman next to me says in broken English, "I'm sorry, are they OK there?"

We both nod and I respond, "Oh, it's not a problem. This is a very long event!" To expect children of elementary-school age to survive in their seats without moving for three or more hours is expecting a bit much.

Then she asks in English once again, "Where are you from?" She likely took an educated guess that she should avoid speaking Italian with us.

"We are from the United States, the city of Indianapolis," I begin. "I usually teach American students here in Siena during the summer." I decide to refrain from sharing too much complicated detail for now. I thus ask in return, "Are you all from Siena?"

Mom waves this off and says, "Oh, no, no. Our town is about three hours from here."

Considering this, I decide to ask anyway. "So, are you members of the Giraffe contrada, living outside Siena?"

"No, we are not members. We have a friend in the Giraffe, so we are here to support her." And just like that, the mystery of those sitting next to us is now solved.

"Oh, that's great. I hope you see a victory tonight!" I say encouragingly.

She laughs in response and adds, "Well, our friend is not expecting to win from what she tells us. The Giraffe won the Palio last July, but I guess they could still win with luck." This statement reminds me of Enrico's comment earlier in the week: "Four days and three laps. Anything can happen . . ."

I respond with, "Yes, that makes sense. They will not likely try hard to win if they won recently." Mom seems to be aware of this, which means that neither of us hold out much hope for a Giraffe victory. Only some fifteen months earlier, the Panther hosted an impressive dinner in its courtyard for the victorious Giraffe, nearly giddy that their win had caused the Eagle to finish embarrassingly in second place. Such consolation victories may not seem all that significant on the surface, but they are often cause for serious celebration.

Eventually the Panther comparsa draws near as the procession revolves like a slow clock around the Campo. After several performances of the sbandierata, their delegation shifts around the corner to face us from a distance of around several hundred feet. Nonetheless, I smile in recognition as I pick out Bruno right away.

"Do you see the big guy in the middle with all the armor?" I point out to Linda. As she nods, I continue, "That's Bruno, he's the one I ate lunch with earlier."

"Oh, OK, so he's the one you met last night?" She asks.

I explain more than I had earlier. "Well, I met him last year at one of the dinners, and I worked with him to become a protector. So, he actually found me last night. I was pretty amazed."

"Well, I guess if things are meant to be, they just work out." Indeed.

It turns out that the Panther comparsa is the last of the seventeen contrade within the procession. I recall that Carlo had mentioned this during our dinner a few nights ago, saying "We are the very last ones," as he chuckled. He further explained that the order of contrade within the procession is also based on the extraction of the contrade last month. Although only the first ten had been selected to run in this Palio, all seventeen contrade participate in the drawing to determine, among other things, the order in which they will march in today's corteo storico. As such, we are somewhat disappointed when we realize our Panther friends will not be performing directly in front of us after all. It seems the marchers have been instructed to keep things moving in the interest of timeliness, so they are skipping their final performance. That's OK, however, as I imagine they are welcoming the respite by now.

As the corteo storico nears its conclusion, the symbolic Chariot of Triumph—known as the *Carroccio*—arrives in front of us with the drappellone perched on top (Figure 18). As Senese tradition would have it, contrada members are vigorously waving their fazzoletti in the air as the drappellone lumbers past. At this point our freedom from densely packed neighbors is coming to an end. For his part, Edoardo has been diligently identifying empty pockets of space within our section, and people are finally crowding in around us. I declare to myself that our bleachers must be filled to capacity by now as I cannot fathom where even one more individual might squeeze in. We are now assuming the positions as Edoardo instructed earlier, with our feet planted firmly on the bench in front of us—each with another human torso situated between our ankles.

CURVE OF SAN MARTINO

Figure 18. The Carroccio (Chariot of Triumph) carries the drappellone to conclude the corteo storico. (Photo: Author)

In amused disbelief, I note to Linda, "My feet are locked into the best spot possible. If I need to stand up, I should be able, but I can't move my feet!" My shoulders are further pressed inwards from Linda on my left and "Giraffe Mom" on my right. The children have since returned to their parents, so the only safety valve we have now is the narrow space behind us, taken up by our satchel and water bottles. To reach any of it, however, requires some advance planning and communication between the two of us. At some point I say to Linda, "I will never complain about the center airplane seats again!" Mercifully, as the corteo storico nears its end, the influx of humans into our area has apparently stopped for good. Theoretically, more people should be able to fit up here. I am thankful that we will not need to figure out those logistics tonight.

With literally nowhere to move her arms, Linda finally decides to resume her place under the balcony behind me. In so doing she comes to realize one advantage to her smaller size—she can fit under the overhang with only minimal adjustments. Further, she now has my torso between her

UNBRIDLED SPIRIT

ankles rather than that of a stranger. We both gain some breathing room on either side of us, and she can take photos and video over or around my head. With all these benefits, she will watch the remainder of the Palio festivities from there with no complaint from me. To our delight this revised seating strategy rewards us grandly for what is perhaps the most meaningful event of the corteo storico today—that is, the sbandierata in front of Palazzo Pubblico. Alfieri representing all seventeen contrade spread out along the racetrack's straight section and successively toss their flags into the air. This is the very tradition that was added in 1919 to honor the veterans of World War I (Figure 19).

To everyone's credit, those around us are behaving cordially and with some measure of patience. We're all here to have fun and enjoy the Palio of the century, so everyone seems willing to deal with some minimal discomfort. Of course, there is always one exception. In this case, the woman in front of me is sporting one of the largest brimmed sunhats ever manufactured. When seated, this cumbersome object presents only minimal visual disruption, as I can reach my arms above her head for my desired photos. Several times and for no apparent reason, however, she decides to stand up, remaining on her feet for quite some time.

I whisper to Linda after the third such incident, "This isn't going to work," as I point in front of me. Rather than grimace and simply accept this visual abuse, I decide to nip it in the bud before the evening's more important events. Were it not for the equatorially wide hat surrounding her head, her occasional urges to stand would be moderately acceptable. In any case, her hat is now rendered useless with the sun nearly setting behind the buildings. *Why is she even keeping the thing on her head?* I wonder with some consternation.

"Um, *mi scusi* [excuse me]," I begin with a gentle tap on her shoulder. She seems to speak Italian, so I maintain this language for now. With a combination of hand gestures and presumably poor Italian grammar, I blurt out, "Would you please sit down? I can't see well. I greatly appreciate it!"

After feigning surprise that someone is actually behind her, she politely responds with a smile and mentions something about her discomfort. I make an effort to sympathize by saying in Italian, "It is really difficult here, I understand," with a smile of my own. Though perhaps obsequiously polite, my point has been made. She cannot turn this "standing up thing" into a habit, especially when the horses and jockeys make their eventual appearance. For now, my cautious optimism kicks in that the problem has been solved once and for all. Still, if she needs to shift around and stand up occasionally for relief, I can live with that. In the meantime, I ask Linda for a match to set fire to the hat. It is a sad fact that we forgot the marshmallows.

Figure 19. At the conclusion of the corteo storico, Alfieri from all seventeen contrade perform the sbandierata in front of Palazzo Pubblico in honor of World War I veterans. (Photo: Author)

❋ CHAPTER 16 ❋

Shaken

AT PRECISELY 5:15 P.M. THE MORTARETTO EXPLODES ON ITS POST FROM ACROSS the Campo, emitting its characteristic shock wave. Only a second later, a line of ten horses and jockeys emerges onto the track from the entrance of Palazzo Pubblico to the ecstatic roar of the crowd. Undoubtedly high on their own adrenaline, each jockey grabs a nerbo from one of two police officers staged at the Palazzo's exit. At this moment, every eye and digital device of some thirty-thousand attendees in and around the Campo are focused like lasers on the ten competitors. Now, in a rather unplanned order, the jockeys guide their wary steeds slowly past the bleachers in front of the Palazzo. Some of them find their contrada's costumed delegations in their reserved sections. With arm and nerbo raised in the air, each jockey pays one final salute of recognition to those who hired him. This basic gesture of determination on the part of the jockeys effectively re-energizes the otherwise exhausted marchers, as if throwing lightning bolts into the stands. In return, everyone from that contrada's delegation is standing and cheering wildly while punching the air in vigorous support. It's *game on* now, after some two months of frantic planning, setup, dinners, trials, blessings, and the unending litany of concerns expressed about the weather, horses, track conditions, school attendance, vacation time, political rationales, and voting practices. It has all come down to this moment.

Lining Up for the Race

Nobody in our seating area is talking much. Rather, all eyes are intent on discerning every possible detail about the competitors as they gradually make their way to the mossa for the lineup process. I manage a few photos as the jockeys pass the bleachers, thinking that I can play with the software's cropping feature later to better frame the images. Meanwhile off to our right, all the contrada presidents are standing shoulder-to-shoulder and leaning over their elevated, wooden gallery, the palco dei priore. This structure is a smaller version of the palco dei giudici from which the mayor, city dignitaries, and contrada captains view the Palio, perched over the main entrance to the Campo. I can't help but imagine that there are some rather jittery, nervous individuals located in both observation stands right now. With a highly inexperienced field of horses, the implications of that earlier decision are about to be realized in likely unpredictable ways.

As all jockeys and horses now settle down into their giro, one of humanity's most remarkable achievements begins. If there is another place on earth where more than 30,000 tired and impatient onlookers can suddenly go silent, I do not know where it would be. But this is exactly what happens in the Campo at this precise moment before the race. What nearly everyone knows is that there is one more drawing, or lottery, to endure. Nobody knows the final lineup order of the horses until it is announced over a rather nasal-sounding speaker system near the mossa. In its defense, however, the system is designed primarily for the mossiere to communicate with the jockeys nearby. People here have thus wisely adapted to its auditory limits by forcing themselves and their neighbors to go stone-cold silent. Those who are new to this ritual are thus admonished with a fitting round of "shushing," including within and around our own faraway section. To be sure, the utter strangeness of this practice, that of a densely packed outdoor population going silent within a few seconds, is incomparable. Everyone really, truly wants to know the lineup!

One reason for holding this final lottery just before the race is to prevent more partiti than what have already transpired. For this purpose, a one-of-a-kind metallic device is employed, which in some respect resembles a miniature, handheld bàrberi machine. The contraption includes a central chamber in which the ten wooden bàrberi, each representing its contrada, are placed. After some shaking and mixing, the bàrberi are then allowed to drop into an attached, cylindrical tube in a randomized order from one to ten. Three officials on the judges' stand are designated to oversee the device, also in the presence of the ten captains. To see the order of bàrberi inside the pipe, it was constructed with windows by the local artisan who designed the contraption in the early 1950s. The windows are not opened, however, until the horses and their jockeys have reached the Casato on their way toward the lineup for the race. Only then is the lineup order written down and handed carefully to the mossiere located on his own platform beneath the judges' stand. After the giro has commenced, the mossiere finally approaches the microphone and reads the name of each contrada from one to ten, inviting them to approach the canape.

At this moment, the crowd knows instinctively to go silent, desperately hoping to hear the mossiere across the Campo. Soon thereafter the first lineup attempt begins. For today's race, the mossiere calls the following contrade one by one as listed below, allowing each to approach the canape before calling the next:

1. Snail
2. Giraffe
3. Forest
4. She-Wolf
5. Tower
6. Turtle
7. Owl
8. Dragon
9. Shell
10. Goose (rincorsa).

Of course, a rumble of subdued muttering moves through the crowd like a wave after each contrada is called. People can react with any number of emotions, not the least being utter surprise or disbelief, various degrees of elation, or dejected expressions of disappointment. It is not uncommon to hear scattered screams of surprise from elsewhere in the Campo. Then the crowd's collective reaction naturally dissipates once again as each horse reaches the canape.

As expected, the giro and lineup process behind the mossa is taking some time tonight. Given the relatively large number of inexperienced horses, the earlier forecasts of a lengthy wait time are proving accurate. Starting the actual Palio race can easily require an hour or longer after the lineup order is announced. During our current wait, we are all treated to two false starts, which are only adding to the delay of the race. Both times, the canape drops and the horses bolt forward, with or without the prodding of the rincorsa. Although we cannot see details of what is transpiring behind the mossa tonight, the mossiere will occasionally drop the canape to prevent injury to the horses. The false start is indicated to everyone quite clearly with an instant blast of the mortaretto. During the false starts, the crowd becomes antsy, and we all watch as the jockeys guide their horses cautiously around the track. If certain horses did not leap forward with the others for some reason, they might simply remain at the mossa until the lineup routine begins anew.

In between the false starts, the lineup process behind the canape is providing some intrigue. Much of the drama appears to be incited by the Shell's jockey, Tittia, who is pulling some antics of his own. While in position number nine, he appears to be conspiring with Gingillo, riding for the Goose contrada. This activity does not surprise me because the Goose is usually Tittia's home contrada. While most other horses are attempting to line up in the required order, Tittia occasionally enjoys a field trip to the sixth position and forces his way in between the horses for Tower and Turtle. Even between the false starts, he is moving back and forth between positions six and nine—back and forth, back and forth.

For his part, Tittia is no doubt under a ton of stress. He rides one of the more experienced horses today, and he is considered one of the favored jockeys in the Campo. He has also signed on with the contrada most desperate for a win. This race is the Shell's to lose if one is to believe all the Palio gossip and scuttlebut. Tittia also must be concerned about other jockeys who are likely making deals with one another, either in the Shell's favor or not. Regardless, whatever Tittia is up to, he is no doubt participating in some last-minute partiti of his own. Furthermore, he can't be very happy with the ninth position, which might provide one reason for his conversations with the rincorsa. It would not be too farfetched to imagine that Tittia is making an offer to Gingillo to help start the race in the Shell's favor.

Well after the two false starts, there is a point during which Tittia finds himself wedged awkwardly in the sixth position, with a yawning gap opening between the Owl and the Turtle next door. Whether planned or otherwise, this is when Gingillo makes his move to start the race. With the sudden lurch of Gingillo's horse, the canape is dropped. The Straordinario has finally started!

Three Laps of Chaos

As all ten competitors desperately launch off the mossa, the Snail assumes the early lead, benefitting handily from its first position. Tied for a close second are the Giraffe, Forest, and She-Wolf, which, along with the Snail, are revealing the expected advantage of positions one through four. As for the Shell, Tittia's efforts to position himself favorably offered little reward because he quickly assumes a position within the rear of the pack. With the leaders banking into the gentle curve behind Fonte Gaia, the Snail continues to hug the inside barrier and maintains a narrow lead ahead of the Giraffe and Forest. All bets are off now as the first four bolt at speed into the San Martino curve, deflecting just to the right of our bleachers as they face us. As they barrel through the curve, the Snail, Giraffe, and Forest wisely take a cautious, wide arc. Somehow all three survive as they whip past the Cappella di Piazza. Amazingly, the Owl manages to navigate a sharper turn to gain inside leverage, now awarding its jockey, Brio, with fourth place. Now in fifth and six places are the Dragon and Turtle, which have yet to put up a serious fight for the lead. Tittia finds himself here in a disappointing seventh place, probably hoping now for a major shakeup somewhere. Nonetheless, he and the other six in front of him make it through the San Martino curve unscathed.

As the leaders speed up in front of Palazzo Pubblico, the last three jockeys are not so fortunate. The She-Wolf is barely ahead of the Goose and Tower, and those two rivals are neck and neck. The Tower takes the inside corner with the Goose immediately to his left, and then they all reach San Martino, almost directly in front of us. The Tower's momentum prevents him from making the turn cleanly, so he literally shoves his rival toward the mattresses along with him. The She-Wolf on the outside gets caught up in their mess, and all three collide into the protective mattresses. We are all yelling personalized versions of "Oh my God" while fumbling with various digital equipment.

It turns out that Gingillo for the Goose is knocked around the hardest. He falls onto the turf near the mattresses and is trampled by at least one horse. All three jockeys have fallen, and only two are recovering without assistance. As for the horses, they all shake it off and proceed down the track for an enjoyable gallop. They are now running *scosso* as the Senesi say, which means "shaken"—without jockeys on their backs.

We now have a front-row seat to a troubling scene. Gingillo is lying motionless on his back near the mattresses where he fell. In an impressive bout of humanity, the jockey for the She-Wolf, Bighino, runs up to him to briefly offer assistance. At the same time, a small legion of medics is racing toward Gingillo. The jockey for the Tower has also recovered and, seeing there is nothing he can do, scurries up the track in front of our bleachers to reach the exit. Whatever transpires now, everyone has about ten more seconds before they all need to get out of the way of the next lap.

Eventually, Bighino is prodded by the medical staff to abandon Gingillo and run for safety. For a few brief seconds, a team of medics attempt to lift Gingillo's limp body onto a portable stretcher, but they fail to do so before danger sets in. The leading horses are seconds away from the San Martino curve. The medics thus abandon Gingillo and race back to the corner to remove themselves from harm's way.

While all of this transpires, the leading seven are moving into their second lap. Rounding the Casato first are the Snail, Giraffe, and Owl in that order but on each other's heels. Now the Snail has serious competition. Quite unexpectedly, the Owl has taken the inside and is now assuming the lead. But the Owl's jockey is Brio; he knows what he's doing. As they shoot around the gentle turn behind Fonte Gaia, not much changes, with the Owl desperately hanging onto its new lead. Though surprising, the Owl is clearly benefitting from the absence of its rival. The Giraffe is in third place, followed closely by the Turtle, Forest, and the Shell (Figure 20). Tittia is still in the running here despite being in the back of the pack, and he barely survived the pile-up at San Martino. From where we sit, things have not looked favorable for the Shell since the race started.

Just when their positions appear to be locked in place, the Owl and Snail suddenly switch positions heading into San Martino. The Snail takes to the inside of the track while the Owl does the opposite. *What is Brio doing?* Soon thereafter, my mouth hangs open in disbelief. Rather than turning to fight the Snail, the Owl proceeds nearly straight ahead toward our bleachers. A split-second later the Owl's grasp on the lead ends permanently as horse and jockey careen full speed into the mattresses with a quite audible whuummp! Fortunately, all is well. Just as unbelievably, Brio remains on his horse, and they both bounce off together. From there they now recognize their fate, however, and merely continue at a slow gallop down the track. Why Brio did not make that turn is beyond me.

Figure 20. The six leading horses enter the curve of San Martino during the second lap. (Photo: Author)

As for the Owl's counterparts nearby, the Snail, Giraffe, Turtle, Shell, and Forest remain clustered together, vying for the coveted lead. All negotiated the San Martino curve successfully for the second time, so we definitely have ourselves a race! However, a brief sense of horror crosses over our faces as the Snail hugs the outside along the mattresses and essentially leaps over Gingillo's listless body, but after that the medical staff return to gingerly carry him to safety. Meanwhile, the Turtle, Giraffe, Snail, Shell, and Forest still make up the first five, in that order, and they are now banking into the Casato turn for the second time. The Turtle has just now briefly assumed the lead along with the beneficial inside position, and Tittia for the Shell has finally overtaken the Snail, which is now on the outside of the pack. The Snail thus takes the widest arc around the Casato, doing nothing to assist its own campaign for the lead. With all of this in mind, one more lap remains.

Then disaster suddenly strikes the Giraffe. Having just assumed a very brief second place, its horse passes by the Casato turn's inside corner. As he leans into the turn, his angle is too steep. His legs instantly slide out from underneath, just like the wheels of a motorcycle that succumb to an overly sharp turn. The horse, Raol, takes a horrendous fall as his feet get tangled together. Racing in the same trajectory directly behind him is the Snail, which careens right into the fallen duo. Amazingly, the Snail survives the crash, but only briefly. Still somehow confused, its horse and jockey still fail to make the turn and plow into the outside barrier. The hapless jockey first bounces off the barrier, then topples onto the track in front of his horse, only to be trampled by his own steed. His is not one of the Palio's more elegant falls. For its part, the horse continues apace following this annoying interruption.

While the Snail is wiping out at the barrier, the Turtle runs into its own problems. Although escaping the Giraffe's spill behind him, something manages to disrupt the Turtle's footing while coming out of the turn. This takes them off course and sends them into the barrier closer to the mossa. The jockey endures his own serious beating as he falls and gets pinned between horse and barrier. His body then bounces down onto the track and is likewise overrun by his own horse, which now plods ahead unphased. It is here where the fate of the Snail and Turtle collide, quite literally. The momentum of the Snail's earlier mishap sends its jockey down to join that of the Turtle. Both jockeys are flailing on the track together as the Snail's horse awkwardly leaps over each of them. With the jockeys rolling around on the ground, their respective horses are now scosso.

All this mayhem near the Casato provides for an intriguing outcome: the scosso horse for the Turtle, Remorex, now enjoys a commanding lead as the third lap begins. Likewise, the Snail's horse has not given up either and is now in a distant second. This is rapidly becoming the "Palio of the Horses," now that six of them no longer carry a jockey. And the full third lap still awaits.

Now crossing the mossa for the second time, Remorex is now enjoying a pleasant gallop and—what is he doing? If I didn't know better, he appears to be bowing to the crowd as he passes by, nodding his head both right and left. Now untouched by any other competitor, the leading horse appears to be saying, "Yeah, that's right. I am all that. Thank you; thanks very much." Quite far behind, the Snail's horse lops along in second place. And who is that coming up behind him in third? Well, it's Tittia for the Shell! He is now one of the few jockeys remaining atop his steed, and his serious competition consists of two scosso horses well out ahead of him. Still in the lead, Remorex shoots past Fonte Gaia, and then some unexpected human activity appears on the track. Someone is wielding a flag of the Turtle with its dominant yellow background—it's their *barbaresco*—the groom for Remorex! Just like in an auto race when a flag is vigorously waved to signal the drivers, this brave individual takes his own flag and excitedly whips it through the air to encourage Remorex onward. *Is that legal?* (It turns out that it certainly is not. The overzealous fellow would eventually be heavily penalized.) Whether there is any immediate impact is uncertain. No matter, this is certainly not the craziest thing we've seen today.

We now witness one of the strangest sights in recent Palio history. As the competitors glide into the San Martino curve for the final time, five of the six first horses are scosso. In third place is the lonely Tittia, now completely surrounded by riderless animals running amok (Figure 21). For his part, Tittia has his work cut out for him if the Shell is to realize its dream. But he is not yet out of contention, as there is no other jockey nearby to disrupt his progress. In this way they all plow through the San Martino curve in front of us for the final time today.

Just when we think it's safe, the Dragon shows up. Its all-but-forgotten jockey, Federico Ares (nicknamed Ares) is one of four survivors—that is, until he pulls the same stunt as the Owl. Instead of banking early to negotiate the curve he and his horse careen right past our bleachers on a direct route toward the mattresses. And then—being the wise animal it is—the horse stops short. Momentum carries Ares onward, however, and he bounces almost harmlessly onto the turf and slides into the mattresses (Figure 22). As usual, the horse escapes and carries on, now the seventh horse to go scosso.

SHAKEN

Figure 21. The Shell's jockey, Tittia, races through the curve of San Martino surrounded by riderless horses. (Photo: Author)

Figure 22. The jockey for the Dragon, Ares, tumbles onto the track at San Martino. (Photo: Author)

Essentially the race has fallen into complete chaos in front of our eyes. We are squinting into the remaining western daylight now to see how the race finishes. With most competitors lined up on the straightaway in front of Palazzo Pubblico, I let out a laugh at the most bizarre sight of seven empty horses and a jockey bumbling their way toward the finish. Tittia remains determined as always, of course. This is a jockey with an unwavering resolve to win—every time. There is no doubt that he is doing everything in his power to bring home the drappellone for the Shell. Whatever human influence he might still wield is being fully deployed as he strains to surpass the other two horses. As the threesome leans into the Casato turn for the final time, Tittia does enjoy a chance here. He soon finds a way to fight into second place, barely passing the undeterred steed for the Snail. At this point we detect screams of shock and desperate encouragement from across the Campo.

Now on the final length of track heading for the finish, Tittia knows that only seconds remain to outgain Remorex. Will the Shell realize the victory it so desperately has tried to obtain? Should Tittia deliver this unlikely win, he would undoubtedly become the hero of the day—the new King of the Square—having pulled off the upset victory of the century. Thus, with everything on the line, Tittia makes his move. His nerbo is shaking up and down violently for all it's worth. He puts his head down and takes off for the unwitting Remorex. Pushing hard, Tittia slams across the finish line at full tilt. But alas, it is not enough, as Remorex had crossed the line slightly ahead. In this manner, the first Straordinario in eighteen years comes to an absolutely stunning close. The unlikely win goes to the Turtle contrada without its jockey—the first to win scosso in the Campo since the Giraffe managed this rare feat in July 2004.

Aftermath in the Campo

Upon confirming with our neighbors that the Turtle had indeed won, we all just turn to stare at one another to absorb what has transpired. My first reaction to Linda is, "Oh my God, the horse won on its own! That's just awesome!" I am feeling genuinely pleased for the Turtle, as we have not yet seen them win on our watch. Then the additional reality sets in. "Oh wow, the poor Shell. They just can't catch a break," I say, shaking my head. The Campo is transitioning into a massive swirl of people in motion, with excitable throngs gravitating to various clusters of activity, or generally scattering away from others. We are now witnessing an unscripted theatrical production with various actors moving through the scene. The Turtle contradaioli are currently mobbing the area near Fonte Gaia, where their expected behaviors of joyous hugging, screaming, and bouncing around with unfettered ecstasy have commenced. Various horses have been contained and are being surrounded by their *barbareschi* (grooms) and contrada members. With amazing efficiency, the flag bearers of the seventeen contrade have already started the colorful routine of the sbandierata, continuing the practice that began with the conclusion of World War I. Meanwhile, the inside barriers near our location have been opened, as is happening around the entire Campo. Untold thousands of people are now spilling onto the track around us, only adding to the ongoing sense of mayhem. Still content to watch the evolving scene, Linda and I remain standing near our seats as do most others around us. There is no rush for us to scale down the bleachers into the sea of humanity.

Within a few minutes we notice two centralized activities unfolding. To our left near the Cappella di Piazza, the level of excitement is only intensifying. I ask Linda, "What is going on over there? They seem to be unified and are starting to chant something."

She responds with a shoulder shrug, "I don't know, are they part of the Turtle? It's like they're celebrating something," she surmises. Soon we see the full manifestation of their solidarity, as fists rise into the air simultaneously. Along with their unified chant, it is almost as if their energy is being directed across the Campo, rather than in celebration with one another.

I think aloud, "I don't think they're the Turtle, as they seem to be on the other side. The Turtle is focused on bringing the banner down from the judges' stand." I am referring to the tradition of victorious contrada members to form a veritable human pyramid—conveniently aided by the steep bleachers nearby—to retrieve the drappellone from its perch on the judges' stand above. We can now barely pick out that activity transpiring across the Campo from us. Then it dawns on me, so I tell Linda, "You know, I bet that's the Tower. They are probably taunting the Goose because it did so poorly with a strong jockey—and maybe because of its wipeout, too. That's my guess, anyway. They're probably rather pleased that they disrupted their rival."

Linda asks, "So, do you think it was intentional? I thought it was an accident when the three collided here."

I respond by thinking aloud, "That was my thought as well, but I suppose it could have been intentional. We'll have to watch some video to see what actually happened—it was all so fast. I couldn't quite tell how it started." Then I counter myself with, "But they were all so far back in the pack, and none of them really had a chance. Why would they cause a pileup?" At this point, I was not considering that sometimes a contrada will pay a jockey to disrupt a rival in various ways regardless of their position in the race. Taunting a rival can be a primary goal. Logically, the Tower had not extracted a strong horse, so they likely focused on giving the Goose a hard time.

Whether intentional or not, the Goose and its jockey, Gingillo, certainly experienced a hard time, to say the least. I am admittedly still concerned about the fate of Gingillo, who had to be carried off the track. We will hopefully find some news later as to his condition. Jockeys may be accustomed to occasional bruises and broken bones, but serious head injuries are a rare thing here, even for the Palio. Even with tonight's uncharacteristic level of chaos, we watched other fallen jockeys skedaddle away under their own power, more or less.

With the Tower continuing its joyous chanting to our left, a smile appears on my face. The victorious Turtle is coming our way, and we are about to enjoy front-row seats to the budding celebration right here in the Campo. By this time, the contrada has attracted many more revelers—easily into the thousands. As if reacting to a cosmic, gravitational pull, a continuous influx of people is now taking over this side of the Campo.

I begin to excitedly state the obvious to Linda—a practice to which she has grown accustomed. "Oh, wow—here comes the drappellone; they're holding it up above the crowd, and it looks like the jockey is being carried above their heads!" With the scene developing as we watch, I now realize that we are witnessing the very first—albeit impromptu—contrada victory parade materializing in front of our eyes. This is normally where a winning contrada begins its rapturous march to the Church of Provenzano. This evening, however, they will be headed a bit further north to celebrate within the Basilica of San Domenico in honor of that church's role in Siena's commemoration of the end of World War I. After that event, the Turtle contradaioli will return together on foot to their own territory to celebrate well into the night.

The jockey is soon staged directly in front of us, atop the shoulders of a highly dedicated contradaiolo. The joyous men around him are enjoying a bit of hero worship, reaching out and shouting their collective voices of support for the surprise victory he is now being credited for. Hundreds of others are clapping wildly for him as he and his ecstatic entourage make their way across our path to exit the Campo. Thousands of other onlookers like us have filled in this corner of the Campo, their arms and hands raised not in celebration, but to reach their digital devices over the heads of the crowd to capture the building procession.

As we stand watching the scene unfold, Linda asks, "So, is he a well-known jockey? Or is it a surprise that he won?"

"Um . . . Actually, this is his first Palio victory—and he's only raced here two other times, so the guy is pretty new," I review his history for Linda's benefit, after sneaking a peak at a phone snapshot of information. "So, his name is Andrea Coghe, nicknamed Tempesta." Then I chuckle and shake my head, adding, "It's kind of interesting that they are all treating him like a hero, even though the whole thing was an accident. I don't know if the Turtle would have won if he hadn't been thrown from the horse. Nobody will ever know."

Linda asks, "But does the win still count for him?"

I respond, "Yeah, it sure does. I admit that it's strange. Palio victories are counted for a jockey whether he stays on the horse or not—like Trecciolino, who is credited with thirteen victories, though he fell off during one of them." Without much thought, I add with a chuckle, "It's Siena—it's their thing. I can't explain it."

Whether he finished the race atop Remorex or not, Tempesta must be enjoying the positive attention that now approaches idol worship. He has still managed to keep his racing jacket on, though it will probably be confiscated by overzealous contradaioli well before he makes it to San Domenico. What is now an unorganized if jubilant procession is now making its way out of the Campo in front of us, with Tempesta and eventually Montesano's drappellone disappearing into the streets (Figure 23). What a perfect time in life to be affiliated with the Turtle. For their contradaioli, it does not get any better than this particular hour, right now.

UNBRIDLED SPIRIT

Figure 23. The victorious jockey for the Turtle, Tempesta (center right) celebrates among joyous contradaioli and photographers. (Photo: Author)

Exit Strategy

As the masses of humanity pour into the streets, Linda and I contemplate how to accomplish the same thing. Our bleacher friends are gradually parting ways, and only now is our own adrenaline dropping to pull us back into reality.

"So, how do you think we should get out of here?" Linda asks pragmatically.

"Well, it's going to be a big mess on the other side over there, so maybe heading out here through the Tower?" I gesture to the entrance of Via del Porrione to the left of us.

"Is that how we get back to the Mercato?" She asks.

"Yes, it will probably take a while, but it's the most direct route," I say, hopefully. Because our lodging is over in the Panther contrada on the west side of town, we'll need to cross Piazza Mercato behind the Palazzo and head up through the Wave contrada. From there, we will take our uphill shortcut to Via di Città. That's the current strategy, anyway.

"Well, maybe we can get something to eat on the way. How about Trattoria Papei?" Linda is referring to our old standby restaurant on the side of Piazza Mercato. She is not only tired like me, but she is still recovering from that annoying chest ailment from earlier this week. It would be good to find sustenance and relaxation sooner rather than later.

"Makes sense to me! Let's head out and see how it goes."

After scaling down the bleachers, we spend another five minutes just to make the turn onto Via Porrione. With upwards of 20,000 people still lingering around or shuffling into the narrow streets, clearing a space the size of Piazza del Campo does not happen on command.

What would normally require maybe five minutes at my normal clip to cut over to Piazza Mercato takes probably four times as long tonight. When navigating dense throngs of people this way, either Linda or I take the lead while the other tails right behind with a hand attached to the other's shoulder. We wind our way through an unending tunnel of people lingering to talk and reconnect after quite an extraordinary Palio. We have no choice but to take our time and maneuver around one group after another as many others await café and restaurant tables, which only adds to the festive street scene.

Finally, just as Linda begins to wonder about my wayfinding skills, we duck into one of the tunneled alleys that leads to the heart of the Tower contrada. Despite their loss in the Palio, a lot of people, still adorned in their contrada fazzoletti, are outside chatting with one another. I yell to Linda next to me while scanning the crowd, "These people don't seem very upset; they actually seem like they're having a good time and are energized for some reason."

"Yeah, they're definitely in a good mood, so maybe they were happy about the Goose," she surmises. "Is that a reason to celebrate?"

"I think it is, from their perspective," I say while navigating around circles of men and women holding various drinks. "This is really interesting to see; these people are certainly not disappointed." We then coincidentally find ourselves at the back of a moderate crowd that has gathered around a rectangular piazza, just across from the historic synagogue of Siena. What we witness next confirms everything we have already suspected. The barbaresco is walking Tonina in circles outside the stable while members of the Tower press up against the protective barriers to see their four-legged rock star. We arrive just in time to further watch various contrada leaders—we presume—hugging one another in their two-piece suits not far from the horse. I say to Linda, "Yeah, they're pretty happy. Must be because they disrupted the Goose."

I now realize how lucky we are to haphazardly find ourselves in the center of the Tower contrada at this very point in time. We are unwittingly playing witness to a contrada celebration that does not involve winning the Palio race. Losing is almost as exciting as winning for this contrada because the Tower's rival, the Goose, not only lost the race, but better yet, crashed and burned at the San Martino curve. I can all but hear the cash register now (or should I say, "crash register"?) as the Tower jockey is paid for his efforts. We briefly hang out in the back of the pack to obtain some photos of our own. I manage to capture the men hugging, contrada members honoring the horse, and giddy people drinking and conversing in the streets. Still, I can't help but consider Gingillo's limp body in the back of my mind. I wonder if there is any lingering concern among the Torraioli.

I suddenly recall Linda's empty stomach and tired eyes, so I completely understand when she retorts, "OK, how do we get to Mercato? Let's go." For her part, Linda has understandably communed enough with the Tower for one day. Minestrone soup and fettuccini await. Although we are not regular patrons of Trattoria Papei, we have alighted there often enough for me to have the menu all but memorized. And Fanta goes quite well with all of it.

Dario's Revelation

While finally winding down in our room, I check my email one more time—something one should never do before bed, of course. But I do just that. With cell service once again restored after the race (it never works with so many people clustered in one place), I have also managed to post a few favorite photos for enthusiasts back home. Next, I open my inbox to find a pleasant surprise. It is a characteristically brief note from Dario, whose style on digital media is to use as few words as possible. This is in stark, if amusing contrast to his otherwise prolific authorship. "Let's keep this simple," he begins. "If the Turtle jockey doesn't fall off of his horse, the Shell wins." For a brief second my tired mind labors to absorb his meaning here. Now intrigued, I continue reading to see his explanation. "Had Tempesta remained on his horse, he would have pulled back to let Tittia go by and win the Palio."

Wow, I'm thinking with my mouth now open. Dario is implying that Remorex—in his temporary state of freedom—inadvertently won the race, even though it was supposed to have been won by the Shell. His was an accidental victory because, well, Remorex had simply not gotten the memo. While considering the implications of this possibility, my questioning skills are naturally kicking in. Why does Dario think this is the case? He can't leave me hanging without an explanation! I thereby respond to his email with an equally short yet friendly question urging him to elaborate. Despite my suspicion that someone like Dario probably has hundreds of emails to answer nightly, I cannot resist barging back into his inbox.

Not long afterwards, I am delighted to see an email in response, just as we are turning in for the night. *Does Dario ever sleep?* He writes, "It was expected that the Turtle would help the Shell—they are allies. And it also explains why Gingillo with the Goose was waiting for Tittia to line up properly at the mossa. Tittia has won three Palii for the Goose, so it makes good sense that Gingillo was also helping Tittia get a fast start." In a nutshell, tonight was apparently supposed to unfold much differently, and the contrada that had been most expecting to enjoy a celebration right now is instead rather quietly absorbing yet another difficult loss. Indeed, for the dispirited Shell tonight, winter has suddenly and unsympathetically descended upon them once again.

❄ CHAPTER 17 ❄

A Walk in the Park

MIKE SAYS WITH A SMILE AND A FAKE RUB OF HIS CHIN, "SO, YOU COULDN'T find the other war memorial? Very interesting". He is clearly enjoying my continued sense of geographic confusion. I can almost imagine Gabriele snickering behind my back, only adding to my light-hearted embarrassment. *They could have just told me where it was to begin with!* In any case, today Mike and I are meeting briefly on the morning after the Palio at one of his standard café hangouts deep inside the Porcupine contrada. We are just a stone's throw from Porta Camollia. We have met here before; some might even call it a *third place* for people like Mike and his friends to meet for a break from their daily schedules. Mike has certainly adapted well to Italian culture.

I laugh in response, while also revealing some latent frustration. "Well, I walked through the Giardini at least twice, and I guarantee the only thing sitting in that park other than pigeons is Garibaldi!" Mike laughs, now amused. I add, "Did they put a plaque on the ground or something? Is it a living tree? I didn't see anything stapled to a tree there."

Mike smirks and responds, "OK, did you happen to see any children when you were there?" He must be continuing our apparent game with a new clue.

"Um, no, maybe with some families walking around, but that's it. Why would you ask that?"

Rather than answering directly, he instead asks about our departure plans to gauge how much time we might have. "When are you leaving town—this afternoon?"

"Yes, we're taking the 3:00 bus down to the airport. We're pretty well packed, and Linda is relaxing after a tiring day yesterday."

A WALK IN THE PARK

"Well, if you have some time now, let's walk down to the Giardini, as it should be on your way back to your room, right? I can help you solve this final mystery," he chuckles.

"Sure, that sounds great! I would appreciate your company one more time before we leave." Then I take a stab at one final guess. "So, you're not going to tell me that the park is the actual memorial itself, are you?" I just now think of this possibility on a whim.

"Well, let's go pay for our snacks, and we'll take a walk." He deflects my question and prepares to head out. Our stroll down Via Camollia is precisely the opposite experience from my frenzied walk with Bruno not twenty-four hours ago. Somehow the streets have magically emptied of locals and visitors alike, and the city is instantly returning to normal. A person dropped into Siena right now might have a hard time believing a Palio had just occurred—save for the cleanup and dismantling of infrastructure frantically underway in the Campo. It's Sunday morning, though, which reduces the street traffic even further.

Mixed News from the Palio

As we walk, I remember to ask about some Palio aftermath. "Have you seen any updates on the jockeys after the race yesterday? Gingillo took a hard hit and was lying unconscious near our bleachers."

"Um, oh yes, I think he'll be fine," Mike reflects nonchalantly. Maybe I'm the one taking these jockey injuries too seriously; no one else I've seen has expressed much concern. He continues, "I saw a news article this morning that showed him waving to the cameras inside his hospital room," he chuckles as I give a sigh of genuine relief.

"Oh, that's good. We were pretty worried, as we don't see many head injuries during the Palio," I say, adding, "I'm still amazed how the human body can recover from serious incidents like that."

"I guess another jockey was in similar shape, but he is recovering, too. It was kind of funny in the news article—Gingillo was more concerned with his fellow jockey than with himself, kind of brushing off the seriousness of his own injury yesterday," Mike laughs.

"Well, I know the Senesi don't care quite as much about the jockeys as the horses, but I am finding that the jockeys have their own life stories to tell;

they certainly play an important role in the whole Palio process," I say reflectively with my own train of thought, continuing with, "That's why I found that documentary about the Palio so intriguing, I guess."

"You mean *Palio*, where they followed Trecciolino and Tittia through several races?" Mike asks for clarification.

I respond affirmatively, "Yes, that's the one, directed by Cosima Spender. They focused on the same July 2013 race when we were here in Siena the first time. As an outsider I viewed it as an important window into the lives of the jockeys from their own perspectives. I don't think the overall story of the jockeys is told very often."

"Yes, that's true. I thought the generational changes with the jockeys was a valuable story to tell, and I think we are kind of continuing to see that shift to the next generation of fantini. For one thing, Trecciolino didn't race yesterday, as you saw," Mike offers. Then as we divert off Via Camollia up to Piazza Gramsci, Mike hits me with some very bad news indeed—something I had yet to learn for myself this morning.

Mike gives me a look and asks grimly, "Did you hear about the horse?"

With this my curiosity and concern spike upwards at the same time. "What horse? What happened?"

"Well, it was Raol, he was racing for the Giraffe. They had to euthanize him after the race yesterday," Mike says haltingly, as if providing some bad news about a family member. In a way, all Palio horses can be thought of as veritable members of Siena's extended family.

I respond in shock, "Oh, are you serious? Wow. I knew he took a tumble, but we couldn't see much detail while following the other horses."

"Yeah, it seems that the Senesi are taking it pretty hard. I'm seeing a lot of social media posts. A lot of people are frustrated and wondering already whether it was something that could have been prevented."

"Oh, that's terrible. Everything seemed to be going so well with the Palio this week, despite all of the concerns," I shake my head, already feeling like a hard reality is setting in. I continue with, "You know, people have been telling me their concerns all week about the condition of the horses. I guess their worst fear has played out. One person even told me that there would be 'hell to pay' by the city administration if something bad happened."

"Yes, I suppose so," Mike agrees, "It probably wasn't wise to have so many novice horses in the race. They are not used to the track yet, and the

A WALK IN THE PARK

October timing just provided more unknowns. Or, maybe it would have happened anyway? I think they will have to investigate the details of what happened, whether it was just a rare fluke, or if something could have been done differently." He then concludes, as many a career educator might do: "Maybe this will be a good learning experience for everyone here. This type of event—the Straordinario—isn't very common, so hopefully a lot of lessons can be learned. A lot of things went very well, it seems, although losing a horse might overshadow the successes. The Senesi do not take such accidents lightly. We'll see how this all plays out over the next few months, I guess."

About a week later we would learn that Raol's unfortunate fate had been declared a rare, freak accident that nobody could have prevented. The conclusion of the investigation was, according to one news report, "a question of pure fatality."[74] Absolutely no one was found to be directly responsible, not the least being the veterinarians, the jockey, the contrada or barbaresco, the municipality of Siena, or even the condition of the turf. The report continued, "The type and dynamics of the accident therefore indicates only that misfortune itself was the triggering element and direct cause, as has happened (even if very rarely) in the past." Basically, the injury that led to Raol's demise was attributed to bad luck.

The article's author further took the opportunity to remind the Senesi and outsiders alike about how far Siena had advanced with respect to the treatment of Palio horses. Apparently, one of the watershed events that led to a series of continuous, positive changes was another serious accident in July 1993. That incident unleashed a series of "very difficult days" for Siena and the tradition of the Palio, which came under increased scrutiny, especially in the national media. The city considered the incident as an "opportunity for change," and all of the major controls and regulations enacted since then have boosted Siena's status as a national leader in the caretaking of racehorses. Some two decades worth of these gradual changes have been adopted elsewhere, which is a tribute to the collective successes of Siena's treatment of the Palio racehorses.

The first change was a municipal resolution, referenced in an earlier chapter, which specified that only "half-blood" (mixed-breed) horses could be eligible for the Palio. This trendsetting legislation was deemed the "most significant piece of a very long path" in improving conditions for the Palio. Siena later saw the creation of a special training circuit at Mociano to replicate Palio conditions, along with highly detailed protocols for filing the horses with the veterinary clinic and for rigorous testing to determine a horse's health and stamina using a variety of measures. An additional protocol protecting the horses from inappropriate drugs and doping was also enacted.

The author noted another improvement, of which the city seems equally as proud: its unique *pensionario*, a free-range retirement home for Palio horses. Located west of Siena outside the village of Radicondoli, the full-service facility came about through an agreement between the city of Siena and the State Forestry Corps.

Nonetheless, the article's author suggested that room for improvement certainly still exists, stating:

> All said, is it possible to totally eliminate accidents in all horse races? Absolutely not. However, there are approaches that over time can lead to their decrease, as the Palio and Siena have taught. It is in fact evident that there is no risk-free activity of [humans], as for animals. But this is another matter, which will shift today's analysis to future discussions.[75]

Time will tell how this latest incident with Raol will help Siena move forward and continue to reduce risk for all involved. As with all such longstanding traditions, it is already quite evident that the Palio will continue to evolve with the times. I have no doubt that Siena will emerge from the other side of this current tragedy with even more resolve to continue its national leadership in the treatment of horses and will most likely set the bar for safety even higher.

A Social Memorial to the War

With this sad news admittedly hanging over our heads, Mike and I scoot across Piazza Gramsci to arrive at the Giardini La Lizza. I have been here so often that I can easily pick out the imposing statue of General Garibaldi, sitting atop his horse in all his grandness.

Mike directs us off to the right, saying, "Let's walk over here to the edge of the park." I still have no idea where we are going; I might as well be blindfolded. We eventually arrive next to a tasteful, black metal fence behind which stands a more modern, symmetrical building of probably two stories. The center of the structure was built in a Renaissance Revival architectural style. It consists of an impressive, triple-arched loggia with a set of stairs and porch underneath it, designed in the fashion of the round-arched, open-air loggias of the Renaissance. This central feature is flanked on either side by smaller wings.

Not one to simply reveal the whereabouts of the memorial, Mike begins with a story. "As we discussed last week, you know that Italy participated in the construction of many, many monuments of various shapes and sizes during the 1920s. This period of monument building was celebrated and promoted by the budding Fascist regime as a way to rally national sentiment."

I jump in with, "Right, it was Mussolini's way to hopefully make up for how Italy was so poorly compensated after the war. He wanted to harness the widespread anger about how badly things had gone."

"Yes, so Siena participated in this wave of monument creation, and in this case a local architect of some importance was chosen to design a new monument for the city in 1924. His name was Vittorio Mariani, and he's known for other big projects in Siena, such as the renovations on the Monte dei Paschi bank and the new post office. And, are you familiar with the huge memorial in Rome to honor Vittorio Emanuele II?" To which I nod. "So, he participated in that architectural competition in 1883 as well. Oh, and you are familiar with Piazza Matteotti right down here, with its grand traffic circle? He designed that, too."

I react with, "Huh, I had not known about him. I was wondering where that traffic circle had come from, as it seems like a Baroque-era addition to the city, in the tradition of grand, wide boulevards and circles. It's definitely not part of medieval Siena," I conclude.

Mike continues, "Right, so Mariani was already quite well known locally and somewhat nationally when he landed the job to design this new monument to the Great War.[76] And here it is." Mike gestures to the Renaissance-style structure, which is now in front of us, but well protected behind this fence at the edge of the Giardini.

While absorbing this news, I respond, "Oh! OK, so it's an actual building. No wonder I didn't pay attention to it. Duh!" I tap myself on the head. "I should have looked at the park's surroundings, not just what was inside," I add.

"Sure, well, this is not just any building, either. The entire structure actually doubles as the monument. You can see the memorial's inscriptions under the eaves there, over the arches."

"Oh wow, OK. Now I get it. How very cool!"

Mike continues, "This is known as the *Asilo*, which translates roughly to kindergarten or nursery. It was designed as a nursery school for local orphan children of the war, and it also served as a sort of living monument to the city's fallen soldiers from World War I. So, this is a social monument, not just a physical one," he summarizes while looking up at its central arches (Figure 24).

"Huh, that's fantastic. Is it possible to go inside?" I ask hopefully.

"Well, it's pretty well protected today, which is actually one reason why we didn't encourage you to come up here and take tons of photos," he laughs. "It still serves as a school—here's the sign," he adds, pointing to a hand-painted board below the stairs. "You can't just walk in, so in all fairness, the odds of you finding this on your own were pretty small," he says with a chuckle. "They actually have a security guard in there during the week."

Absorbing all of this, I respond, "Ah, so this isn't really accessible to the public. That makes sense. And what a great way to memorialize the soldiers, by building something to serve the younger generation!" I make the instant connection.

With this new knowledge from our final field trip this week, my personal quest has satisfactorily concluded. Memorials are not always where we expect them to be, nor are they always found in the expected shape and form. More important, my hunt for memorials has provided me with a greater sense of meaning for this Palio's official rationale. Further, I was certainly only one of countless individuals who became better educated about the war and Siena's role within it. Some portion of the local population—young and old alike—apparently also learned more about the war and the memorials that exist here. Putting aside for a moment the various opinions about holding a Palio this late in the year, its overall, understated purpose of education and awareness may have been handily fulfilled.

Figure 24. The Asilo, Siena's social monument dedicated to the fallen soldiers of World War I. (Photo: Author)

Personal Takeaways

Speaking of learning, various expectations of mine were summarily turned on their heads this week. The most significant was that the community's decision to stage an additional Palio was by no means taken lightly. Previous proposals for such Straordinarii failed to pass their high bar of standards. Although conventional wisdom may hold that any half-baked excuse to hold an extra Palio would meet with uncontested celebration, the opposite is in fact true. Even this one almost did not happen. The laundry list of practical concerns was daunting and speaks to the reality of holding a major cultural event at a highly inconvenient time of year. From the perspectives of teachers, parents, and school administrators, an extra Palio would greatly disrupt the school year. Even this Palio was not deemed a legitimate excuse to lose precious instruction time—creative ways around it notwithstanding.

Then there were the adults, who had to find extra vacation time or figure out how to enjoy an extra Palio and still manage the obligations of everyday life. An untold portion of the Siena community apparently could not afford yet another week off for the festa. Even a good number of my own friends and acquaintances had already planned to be out of town or were simply too crunched for time to participate much, if at all. In a way, this community-wide scrutiny and careful consideration were refreshing to see. For an event that some compare unfavorably with the concept of "bread and circuses," the evidence points to a rather more complicated conclusion. Not only did a sizable portion of the community vote against holding a Straordinario, but some Senesi ultimately did not participate at all—whether they had wanted to or not.

Even with these limitations, the community managed to muster enough collective enthusiasm to almost re-create the crowds and emotions of the summer, and there is no doubt that this special Palio treat was greatly enjoyed. It seems the Senesi wisely, and necessarily, participated in this Straordinario only after realistically considering such challenges as weather, vacations, and school. Given what I have heard and read as of this writing, it was the young people that did indeed "push it over the top." Without the understandable idealism of the community's youthful population, I am convinced, along with others, that this Palio would not have happened.

The issue of generational difference was one of my more fascinating findings, a topic that could certainly be explored further beyond my one-week visit. There was general agreement among those I spoke with that younger residents were predisposed and more likely to vote in favor of holding the Straordinario, whereas more mature generations were less inclined to do so. As Antonio had inadvertently observed, this seemed paradoxical because older citizens are still more emotionally attached to the war and its various family connections. In contrast, the younger people are still learning about the war and likely feel less attached to it. Yet it was the younger folks who were more likely to vote in favor of the idea. What remains unclear is whether this vague difference in generational perspective is due to young people "just not getting it" at this point in their lives, as Donald believed, or whether the younger generation is influenced by the global economic and cultural forces that encourage holding the Palio because it is a mere product for consumption and entertainment. The former Mayor Piccini appears to believe the latter scenario, claiming to see an actual cultural shift now occurring in Siena.

A WALK IN THE PARK

However, given Angelo's take on the debate, he and other young people clearly not only appreciated and learned from the Palio's connection to World War I, but they are deeply and emotionally involved in the Palio overall. In their case, they do "get it," and were nonetheless in full support of the idea. Perhaps the younger generations in our respective communities are not always given the credit they deserve. At other times, as expected within the so-called circle of life, they are still naïve and trying to find their way. In this respect, Siena's young people probably do not differ remarkably from youth in other communities around the world. If one could return in thirty or forty years and find that the Palio has indeed been reduced to a festival for outsiders, then perhaps Mayor Piccini will have been vindicated.

Given my own observations of some younger Senesi, however, my bet is that the traditions and rituals of the Palio will remain in good hands. After all, it has been the conscientious adult generations of Siena that have been diligently grooming the children for contrada and Palio life in the first place. It makes little sense, therefore, to conclude that their collective educational efforts would suddenly be for naught after all these many centuries.

That said, it would likewise be naïve to think that the Palio will not continue to change and evolve with time. In fact, this community game, festival, or ritual war—whatever one wishes to call it—has been gradually evolving with its longstanding community since medieval and Renaissance times. Perhaps change will come more rapidly than some might hope; as a global society, we are all still coming to terms with the implications of our new digital age and the accompanying trend of "overtourism"—a recent term describing the negative effects of the increasing numbers of visitors saturating their host cities. For Siena, both trends mean increased visibility and certainly more scrutiny from outside the city, something this community largely has not had to face. Only recently do we all find ourselves confronted with a society where nearly anything can be posted and found instantly on the internet—whether of reliable accuracy or not.

Even as the turf is being removed from the Campo, leaders are likely bracing for the inevitable fallout from the unfortunate death of Raol. Time will tell whether the incident leads to more accelerated changes with respect to Siena's relationship with the horses, regardless of whether Raol succumbed to a freak accident or from something more preventable. Siena is clearly not alone in this ongoing challenge. As of this writing, more than 24 mysterious horse fatalities have occurred during the first half of 2019 at one American race track alone, indicating a more global concern.[77] In our still nascent era of digital communications and surveillance, however, the Palio and the city that supports it will continue to be judged on their own merits and presumed flaws.

Two Parallel Paths for Siena

Moving forward, it is likely that Senese leaders and constituents will forge ahead along two parallel paths in response to intensifying scrutiny. The first path will—quite rightly so—involve continued and perhaps accelerated efforts to further improve the safety of horses and jockeys alike. The past two decades have, to the credit of the Senesi, seen substantial improvements in this area, though there is arguably always room for more. Of course, it is no easy feat to reconcile centuries-old traditions with modern-day sensibilities. Supporters of the Palio might be comforted that the city's primary tradition has persisted through centuries of gradual changes to regulations, processes, physical infrastructure, and technological advances. In fact, the Palio has continued to thrive and gain momentum as Siena's main source of cultural identity—for better or worse, depending upon one's perspective. It is thus reasonable to expect that conditions for the Palio's equine and human competitors will only continue to improve, while the local authenticity and meanings of the Palio will be no worse for wear.

Even I, an admittedly outside observer, can conjure a variety of ways to improve safety without overtly disrupting the most significant traditions. Perhaps readers can humor this author for a moment while considering a few ideas. The behaviors of the jockeys themselves could be more regulated. They undoubtedly contribute to—if not blatantly cause—an untold percentage of accidents on the track, and they can and do get disqualified for one or more future Palio races for various transgressions. Still, it is no secret that they are often promised a healthy compensation by fellow jockeys or contrada leaders to disrupt a rival's horse in one way or another. Through stricter regulations and unfavorable consequences, it is not unreasonable to imagine additional ways to discourage this kind of behavior. If the singular action of the Tower's jockey during this Straordinario was indeed intentional, then his behavior could be interpreted as a blatant disregard for the horses, let alone his fellow jockeys.

As for the safety of the jockeys, would it be unreasonable to require some minimally protective equipment that could be tucked under their contrada outfits? Regardless of their level of compensation, there are certainly ways to reduce, if not eliminate, serious injuries to the jockeys. Of course, this additional protection could reflect a national (that is, Italian) concern within horse-racing circuits that extends beyond Siena. In all fairness, sports organizations around the world continue to struggle with improving the safety of athletes; this struggle is perhaps most visible in the United States, where there are increased concerns that football players are not protected well enough from long-term head injuries. Thus, Siena does not find itself alone in struggling with this challenge, either.

As for the training and experience of the horses, it is also not difficult to envision potential improvements in this area. A high percentage of horse injuries occur at the two most hazardous turns, the curves of San Martino and Casato. This is well documented, including one study that was conducted over a two-decade time span.[78] Consequently, training and experience are two areas where attention could be focused more immediately. For instance, it was common knowledge throughout Siena that the number of novice horses in this Straordinario was higher than usual. Perhaps there a lengthier, more cautious approach is needed to acclimate newer horses to the racetrack, even beyond the extensive veterinary assessments, the tratta, and ensuing trials. Perhaps the training of novice steeds could begin a year earlier, whereby they become accustomed to the track and its dangerous turns more gradually with increased surveillance. They would therefore not be "thrown into the fire" so quickly.

The city could even create a new tradition, whereby future Palio horses are trained and showcased for additional days in the Campo during an expanded prove regolamentate. These horses would not run in the current Palio, however; rather, they would be considered more carefully for the following year. Would such an event not attract a sizable crowd and generate enthusiasm for future years? In this way, horses could be more carefully vetted for potential strengths and weaknesses without the pressure of performing in a dramatic Palio only several days later.

Additionally, the stronger horses which repeatedly endure the hazardous track unscathed have something to teach us. Indeed, a more immediate change would involve simply choosing a pool of more experienced horses for upcoming Palii. If captains remain concerned about seeing a particularly strong horse run away with the race, then put several of them in there. Over time, novice horses can be gradually integrated into the process—maybe one or two per race, but not seven.

These are only some initial, premature, and unvetted thoughts about what possibilities might exist for improving safety without sacrificing vital traditions. Beyond this point, I will gladly defer to the local Senesi and the regional or national experts who have dedicated their lives to the horse-racing circuit or organization of the Palio in one way or another. The fundamental point to make here is that plenty of creative and substantive changes have yet to be discovered, even those which do not diminish the Palio's vital cultural traditions and the incomparable role it plays in community viability.

The second parallel path for the city is likely one of intensified educational outreach. More local leaders are awakening to the need for an expansive educational campaign ahead of a Palio. They are recognizing the potential to help promote further awareness of Siena's positive cultural and community traits, along with its captivating history and traditions. This educational effort will require tackling the ever-emerging myths and untruths being propagated about the Palio and its host city, an issue becoming only more pressing in the age of social media. One recent, heartwarming attempt at such outreach appeared in the form of short video clips on YouTube that highlight the culture and history of the contrade.[79] Such educational videos have been oriented primarily to external audiences, but they have also been shared proudly on social media by local community members themselves. The sharing of such media may serve as one small indicator of Siena's collective approval of the material that was developed and presented.

Memories of the Straordinario are still fresh, and there are early signs that the aftermath is already influencing educational efforts. The writer of one local news article, for instance, admitted less than a month after the race that the city's unique retirement home for Palio horses remains largely unknown to people outside Siena. In part, it reads as follows:

The Pensionario of Radicondoli is still not too well known today. While the Senesi are largely aware, certainly those from outside the city are not aware of its existence, of this real corner of Paradise on Earth for many older horses which were injured or have accomplished great deeds in Piazza del Campo. "It's true, outside of Siena this place could be better known," confirms Lieutenant Colonel of the Carabinieri Forestali, Carlo Saveri.[80]

Likewise, the former mayor, Pierluigi Piccini, offered his own perspective on how Siena might take the lead on educational outreach.[81] His views appeared in a local news piece only four days following the race, as criticism over the death of Raol was already mounting from outside the city. Piccini's argument in favor of improving awareness through education is translated and paraphrased in part as follows:

> Modernity is not fought by closing the doors of the city. But using the tools of regulatory protection and international recognition is how a communication strategy must be created, including an in-depth analysis of historical, social, and anthropological information, and asking for help from the University of Siena. Education will come only through constant and continuous work. A city that is active and not passive ... can dismantle any controversy in advance, rather than merely allowing the television cameras to tell the story.

Thus, it seems as though the Straordinario provided one more necessary—if unfortunate—wake-up call for Siena to further enhance its educational outreach, thereby shaping its own narrative more poignantly. And Siena certainly has a fascinating story to tell that is singularly unique on the planet. An untold number of lessons can be learned from its vibrant community and social life that even its young people find hard to resist. Aside from the thrill of watching horses dart around the public square, it was this community vitality engendered by the seventeen contrade that encouraged the continuation of our study-abroad program here. For our part, many Americans have never seen the likes of Siena's level of community activity, active street life, and social involvement. Thus, Siena has much to teach the rest of us as we strive to strengthen our own communities from within.

What Future for the Straordinario?

With rapid economic and social change occurring on both sides of Siena's medieval walls, the question remains as to when we will see the next Palio Straordinario. I believe that Siena will move down one of three possible paths. The first would see the Straordinario—as a distinct *type* of Palio—quietly wither away to become a thing of the past. It had almost already done so since the year 2000. Given the elevated complexities and costs with organizing such an event in the twenty-first century, it is at least remotely possible that we just witnessed the last Straordinario. As recently as two decades ago, to create a third Palio in any given year proved to be a much simpler and less costly feat. It is further instructive that this particular Palio barely managed to occur in the first place, while other relatively recent proposals for such events have been rejected outright. Perhaps the world in which Siena now finds itself has become too complex to warrant another shot at a Straordinario. This may be unfortunate indeed, though it would not come as the biggest surprise.

A second possible future for the Straordinario would be the direct opposite of that described above. Having learned the consequences of waiting almost two decades between such events, we might see this type of Palio occur more often in the future—perhaps even once or twice a decade. This presumes, of course, that the city finds sustainable and creative approaches to fund them. It is almost as if the community nearly forgot how to run and organize a Straordinario following the last one in 2000. In this most recent case, many Senesi were downright nervous about the whole thing, from the city administration downward—although a lot of that anxiety was the result of a very tight schedule so late in the year. In one sense, however, perhaps Siena needed a "shakedown" Palio like this one to get the bugs out. From an educational perspective, it was probably beneficial for the Senesi to step outside their comfort zone from the normal, well-established Palii of the summer. The best learning takes place when people are forced to confront new situations and experiences. From my own observations, this is precisely what Siena accomplished, and it did so quite handily.

Consequently, one possible lesson is that the Straordinario is still considered to be an important *type* of Palio that is worthy of becoming more normalized and frequent. Will we thus see an increased regularity of proposals moving forward? This is admittedly one possible outcome. Should a more standardized, well-documented approach be fine-tuned and perfected, the city will avoid the need to relearn how to execute a Straordinario every time one comes along.

Beyond these two potentially extreme paths, however, is a third, more balanced scenario that may very well be the most likely. In such a case, we might see a Straordinario held every fifteen to twenty years, which has been the case since the 1980s. Should this be the chosen path—whereby such an event continues to be held, but only rarely—then we are likely already experiencing the "new normal." Within this potential future, the Palio Straordinario would be held only intermittently, which would also presumably elevate it to an even more valued and special event. As the saying goes, absence makes the heart grow fonder. Given the lessons learned from this most recent effort, Siena should have a strong baseline from which to improve future events.

Of course, it would not be unreasonable to expect future city leaders to plan ahead with a bit more advance notice—perhaps five or six months sooner than what transpired this time. The city clearly moved off track in this respect (no pun intended). Whether for political motives or otherwise, to surprise its own people with a proposal of questionable origin as late as September could be considered by more reasonable voices as irresponsible. A too-short timeframe is still one aspect, however, that can be easily avoided in the future. Beginning the process of decision making sometime in winter or spring would be more in line with past practices and would make a lot more sense for nearly everyone—and every animal—involved. Hopefully, most of the hassles, worries, and outright dissent that we witnessed in this case would simply evaporate with this single, logical change. Sometimes the simplest adjustments and decisions can lead to exceptionally beneficial payoffs.

Given this third, more balanced scenario, an occasional Straordinario would likely encourage its survival well into the future. In this case, the event will not merely wither away like a grape that dies neglected on the vine—becoming yet another casualty of accelerating globalization. Rather, this special breed of Palio can occasionally be savored as a truly *extraordinary*

UNBRIDLED SPIRIT

variety that enjoys its own unique identity within Siena's storied way of life. If this comes to pass, Siena's Straordinario would most certainly live up to its name for generations to come.

A WALK IN THE PARK

Postscript

Should the Palio that was held the following year in July 2019 be viewed as a de facto referendum on the chaotic Straordinario of October 2018, it was most evident with the ten chosen horses. In short, none of them were rookies as all ten competitors came in with previous Palio experience. Moreover, three of them were previous winners, namely the legendary Porto Alabe, Rocco Nice, and none other than Remorex, the surprise victor of the Straordinario that won scosso for the Turtle. With this development, it appears that the pendulum has swung the opposite way from the October race, when a full seven of ten horses were newcomers to the Palio.

During the emotional assignment of the horses, the Owl came out the big winner, landing Porto Alabe. The Tower and Snail were likewise enamored with their matches, Rocco Nice and Violenta da Clodia, respectively. Even the Caterpillar was pleased with its well experienced horse, Solu Tue Due. Dario hoped they finally had the winning combination, with Brio as their jockey. And although Remorex had won the most recent Palio on its own accord, the Senesi know this occurred more out of luck than skill. Thus, the Dragon could be forgiven for its underwhelming enthusiasm for drawing Remorex during the assignments. Nonetheless, one was hard-pressed to recall a recent Palio when the ten horses came in with this much collective experience.

As for the race itself, the only rival pair consisted of the Panther and Eagle. Those who believed that the veteran jockey, Luigi Bruschelli (Trecciolino), had retired once and for all were as surprised as I was to see him hired by the Panther. While the contrada offered him a gracious sendoff during the Cena della Prova Generale the night before the race, few probably thought that he had what it would take to win another Palio. And they were right, at least in this latest case. Though Trecciolino gave the Eagle a hard time right from the start, it was the Snail and Giraffe that took the lead during the race and retained it for all three laps. The Snail most certainly tasted victory as its experienced horse, Violenta, kept them in the lead for most of the race. But they unfortunately found themselves up against Giovanni Atzeni (Tittia), one of the Palio's most determined young jockeys. Only on the final leg of the race was Tittia able to push hard with a horse named Tale e Quale to edge out the poor Snail right at the finish line. Tittia thus gave the Giraffe its second victory in three years, making it the sixth win in the Campo for the storied jockey. There is little doubt that Tittia's generation is now largely in control of the Campo—at least out in public view. The bottom line? All ten jockeys finished the race atop their uninjured steeds. Perhaps we are witnessing the future of things to come.

And what of Remorex, the equine victor of the Straordinario? Perhaps he was not a fluke after all. As one of numerous veteran horses in the Campo once again, the underestimated steed would go on to win his second Palio in August 2019—but only after throwing Tittia off his back at the San Martino curve. Siena's newest budding legend has now won twice in two years amidst fierce equine competition, and both times on his own accord without a jockey. For his part, Tittia thus enjoyed the second summer in which he has officially won both the July and August Palii, his first having been in 2013 for the Goose and Wave, respectively.

But wait, let's review the last few details of Remorex's latest win. With Tittia on the turf, Remorex had to finish the job. Unlike the Straordinario, when he enjoyed a quite accidental advantage against a field of novice horses, this time Remorex had to fight every inch of the way for the win. Tied for the lead, the determined steed barely edged out Brio and the heartbroken Caterpillar for the contrada fortunate enough to have extracted him—a contrada frequently overlooked and forgotten until it is too late—that of the Forest.

Acknowledgments

To plan and organize a substantial research effort in Italy on short notice would have proven even more formidable without the enthusiastic assistance of numerous individuals. I am especially grateful to David Walthall, who assisted with the identification and translation of local news articles related to the Straordinario. He further endured my countless follow-up requests to elaborate on specific pieces of information or to clarify local processes with respect to the Palio. I likewise appreciate the perspectives and knowledge of two additional local experts related to various aspects of Siena history and culture, namely Tuscan author and contradaiolo of the Bruco, Dario Castagno, and scholar of Italy's role in World War I, Gabriele Maccianti. Both the narrative and information presented within the book have been measurably improved with their collective contributions.

When it came to improving earlier manuscript drafts, I welcomed the assistance of several individuals. I am indebted to Alexandra Carpino, Nancy-Rose Netchy, and David Walthall for their careful review and constructive feedback on a later draft. In addition, Dario Castagno carefully examined the narrative for accuracy while graciously responding to my occasional questions for clarification.

Of course, this book would not have been possible without the generous and trusting contributions of numerous Senese residents and contrada members who shared their personal perspectives on the Palio Straordinario, along with their intricate knowledge of their community, the Palio in general, and contrada traditions in particular.

Regarding the book's development, the quality of my writing and overall narrative have been substantially improved with the accomplished editing skills of Elizabeth Koozmin. Her enthusiasm for this project was surpassed only with her unwavering attention to detail and suggestions to improve the clarity and flow of my earlier draft. Likewise, a special round of thanks is owed to Anna Burrous for her skillful design of the book's cover, which successfully captures the essence of the story told within. I am further grateful for a Butler

Awards Committee (BAC) Faculty Research Grant which provided partial funding for the project through Butler University.

Most important through this entire project was the support of my family. As my wife, friend, and travel companion, I could not imagine undertaking such an endeavor without her consistent enthusiasm, ideas, and encouragement. And it is to my parents' credit, Ken and Dee Paradis, that they instilled in me an unwavering interest in learning, teaching, and experiencing new places and cultures. For that I am eternally grateful.

Glossary

alfiere. One of two flag wavers representing a *contrada* and its official delegation known as the *comparsa*.

balzana. The coat of arms for the city of Siena, usually displayed on a flag or shield with its upper half white and its lower half black.

barbaresco. A *contrada's* official caretaker, or groom, of the horse while it is in possession of the *contrada* for the Palio race.

bàrbero. The Senese term for racehorse, originally referring to horses from North Africa or, more specifically, the Barbary States. The term also refers to one of a set of wooden balls used in a children's game called *palio dei bàrberi*.

brenna. A racehorse perceived as relatively unpromising and not likely to win the Palio.

Campo. The main public square, or piazza, of Siena, where the Palio is raced in July and August. Its more official name is the Piazza del Campo. Locals and visitors alike learn to simply refer to this open space as the Campo.

Campanone. Known more informally as the *Sunto*, the large bell at the top of the Torre del Mangia that once summoned the Senesi to battle or to public meetings. Today it rings during the entire *corteo storico* prior to the Palio.

canape. The thick hemp rope that serves as the starting line for the Palio race.

Il Canto della Verbena. "The Song of Verbena," one of the more beloved and commonly heard folk songs sung by the Senesi during the Palio and other citywide events. *Verbena* refers to the grass or herb that has traditionally grown between the bricks of the Campo.

capitano. The captain is elected by each *contrada* to take control during the days of the Palio. The captain is entrusted with complete authority to run the contrada and its operations related to the Palio, especially with respect to making deals (*partiti*) with other *contrade*.

cappotto. The *contrada* that has won both the July and August Palio races in the same year.

Casato. One of eleven streets that leads into the Campo. The turn at Casato is one of the two most dangerous places on the Palio racetrack.

Cena della Prova Generale. The *contrada* dinner that follows the final evening trial on the day prior to the Palio race. This is typically the only *contrada* event that guests are allowed to attend, if tickets are purchased from the *contrada* office (*segretaria*) or directly from the *società*. Viewed as a good-luck dinner for *contradaioli*, the dinner usually occurs on a main street of the *contrada* with a special head table for elected officials and the jockey who has been hired to race the next day. Hundreds or even thousands of *contradaioli* and guests will typically attend this important, pre-Palio social event.

chiarine. (singular: *chiarina*). The long-belled trumpets used to play the fanfare prior to various Palio events. The players are known as the *trombettiere* or *musici*.

comparsa. A costumed contingent of *contrada* members (*contradaioli*) representing the *contrada* in the historical procession (*corteo storico*) and related events. Participants in the *comparsa* include a drummer (*tamburino*), flag wavers (*alfieri*), and various other medieval-themed positions.

contrada. One of seventeen wards or neighborhoods existing within the historical, walled city of Siena. Each *contrada* constitutes a social structure that inhabits a physical territory (*rione*) within the city walls.

contradaiolo/a. A generic term referencing a member of a *contrada* (male/female).

corteo storico. The historical procession, or parade, that marches from the cathedral (Duomo) to the Campo before the Palio race. Participants are dressed in elaborate costumes loosely representing the political, social, and military components of the Republic of Siena prior to the city-state's downfall in 1555. The parade marches around the Campo in the hours before the race, with each *comparsa* demonstrating its flag-throwing and percussion skills.

drappellone. The large silk banner awarded to the *contrada* whose horse wins the Palio race. This is the only prize for winning the Palio. *Drappellone* can be used interchangeably with the term *palio*, which also refers directly to the banner itself.

estrazione. An extraction or drawing. Two extractions occur before each Palio: (1) extraction of the *contrade* and (2) extraction of the horses. The first determines the three additional *contrade* that will compete with the other seven *contrade* that did not race the previous year. The second matches the ten horses with each of the ten *contrade*.

fantino. In this context, the jockey hired by a *contrada* to race in the Palio. Jockeys (*fantini*) in the Palio generally come from outside Siena and are the equivalent of mercenaries paid for their services to the *contrade*. Jockeys can ride for different contrade throughout the trials (*prove*) until the morning of the Palio, after which the jockey for a particular *contrada* can no longer be changed.

fazzoletto. The square-shaped, silk scarf given to each individual baptized into a *contrada*, either as a baby or later in life. The *fazzoletto* serves as the primary symbol of identity for a *contradaiolo*.

mangino. An assistant to the captain in charge of a *contrada* during the Palio. Typically, two *mangini* assist the captain with deal making and related negotiations (*partiti*) to help realize a victory for the contrada.

mortaretto. Literally a "small mortar" or cannon-type device located near the starting line (*mossa*) that detonates as a signal to clear the track, to announce the appearance of horses as they emerge from the Palazzo Pubblico, to indicate a false start, and to recognize when the winning horse crosses the finish line.

mossa. The location where the race starts, indicated by the starting rope (*canape*) strung across the track. This location doubly serves as the finish line for the race.

mossiere. The individual assigned to start the race. This person is responsible for calling the order in which each horse lines up at the start (*mossa*), assuring their successful lineup prior to starting the race.

nerbo. The whip provided to each *fantino* as he enters the track from the Palazzo Pubblico to line up for the race. The *nerbo* is created from the dried, stretched phallus of a calf.

nonna. Literally the "grandmother," a derogatory title assigned to the *contrada* that has endured the longest time without a Palio win.

Palio. A horse race run by ten of the seventeen *contrade* in Siena, Italy, on July 2 and August 16 each year, both in honor of the Virgin Mary, or Madonna. The term *palio* further derives from the Latin word *pallium*, or piece of cloth, referring to the cloth banner earned by the winning *contrada*. The Palio banner is also known as the *drappellone*.

palco dei giudici. The judges' stand, or balcony, from which city officials and *contrada* captains observe the Palio race and its trials. Siena's mayor (*sindaco*) typically stands precisely in the middle of these observers.

palco dei priore. A similar though smaller balcony than the judges' stand (see above) overlooking the curve of San Martino, from where the *contrada* presidents (*priore*) watch the Palio.

palchi. The stands or bleachers erected around the outside of the Campo racetrack. Groups of *contrada* members and paying visitors can sit in these bleachers as an alternative to standing in the center of the Campo to view the Palio and its trials.

Palazzo Pubblico. Literally, the "public palace," or city hall, of Siena. The medieval, Gothic-style structure has served as the seat of city government since its completion in the first half of the fourteenth century.

partiti. Agreements or deals made secretively between the captains and *mangini* of two *contrade*, in a strategic effort to influence the outcome of the Palio race. Agreements typically involve promises from one *contrada* to pay another in the event of a Palio victory.

prova. Trial race in which the horses assigned to the ten *contrade* are tested for various skills in advance of the actual Palio. A total of six morning and evening trials (*prove*) precede the Palio. Each trial closely simulates the Palio race, with a total of three laps around the track.

Prova Generale. The final evening trial on the day before the Palio. Translated as the "General Trial," the Prova Generale constitutes the fifth of six total trials and is treated as a dress rehearsal.

rincorsa. In this context, the *rincorsa* is the horse assigned to the tenth position for the starting lineup of the Palio. Together with the *mossiere*, the *rincorsa* jockey holds the power to start the race when he pleases, by rushing from behind the starting line at a full gallop.

rione. The physical territory or built environment occupied by a *contrada*. The current-day boundaries were finalized in 1729.

San Martino. One of three districts (*terzi*) of Siena, comprising the southeastern third of the city. The corner of the Campo closest to the district is referred to as the curve of San Martino, infamous as the most hazardous turn on the Palio racetrack.

sbandierata. The performance of the *alfieri*, or flag throwers, during the *corteo storico* prior to the Palio.

scosso. Literally, "shaken." If a jockey falls off his horse during the Palio, the horse is said to be running *scosso*. The horse can still win the Palio without its jockey, as long as its head ornament, the *spennacchiera*, remains attached.

società. The social hub, or clubhouse, of a contrada. Typically, the facility includes various gathering halls, a bar, and an attached outdoor patio or garden area open for use by contrada members. Its primary purpose through the early twentieth century was to provide mutual aid to contradaioli, while it now primarily serves as the focus of social events and activities.

tratta. An event held in the Campo before the six Palio trials (*prove*). Approximately thirty-five horses are tested on the racetrack in groups of six or seven at a time, with each group running three laps around the track as they would during the Palio. Following the *tratta*, the ten *contrada* captains decide on the final ten horses to run in the Palio. The *tratta* is then followed at midday by the extraction (*estrazione*), or drawing, of the horses, at which time they are assigned by lottery to the *contrade* in a public ritual in front of the Palazzo Pubblico.

Notes

1. Dundes and Falassi, *La Terra in Piazza*, 31.
2. Ibid., 23; Burckhardt, *Siena, City of the Virgin*.
3. Dundes and Falassi, *La Terra in Piazza*.
4. Comune di Siena, *Regolamento per il Palio*.
5. Dundes and Falassi, *La Terra in Piazza*, 75.
6. Corriere di Siena. "Una contrada correrà d'obbligo il Palio."
7. Siena News. "L'ultimo Straordinario di ottobre: era il 1745."
8. Dundes and Falassi, *La Terra in Piazza*.
9. Corriere di Siena. "Palio Straordinario: è il giorno dell'estrazione."
10. Ibid.
11. La Nazione. "Palio straordinario, estratte le contrade, 20 mila persone in piazza."
12. Toscana Media News. "Palio straordinario, estratte le dieci contrade."
13. Dundes and Falassi, *La Terra in Piazza*.
14. Il Palio di Siena. "La Storia del 'Cencio'".
15. Ibid.
16. Ibid.
17. Ibid.
18. Italian Sons and Daughters of America. "The Bersaglieri: Italy's Spectacular Military Group".
19. Edizioni Tiperti. "Montesano Gian Marco".
20. La Nazione. "Montesano firmerà il drappellone: 'Sto inviando i bozzetti al sindaco'".
21. Ibid.
22. Il Palio di Siena. "I Masgalani".
23. Dundes and Falassi, *La Terra in Piazza*.

24. Siena Free. "Palio di Siena Straordinario del 20 Ottobre 2018: Presentato il Drappellone realizzato da Gian Marco Montesano."
25. Siena News. "Il drappellone di Montesano nella bufera social: 'E' un copia e incolla'".
26. Ibid.
27. Il Palio di Siena. "La Storia del 'Cencio'".
28. Palazzo Ravizza. "The history of the Noble Contrada of Bruco."
29. Il Palio di Siena. "Tutti i palii non ordinari dal 1700 a oggi."
30. Siena News. "Lo Straordinario più straordinario: oggi l'estrazione del Palio del 20 Ottobre."
31. Siena Free. "Palio Straordinario, installata centralina meteo."
32. La Nazione. "Piazza del Mercato, test sul tufo per il Palio."
33. See McNulty, "Unraveling Italian Culture: What is Aperitivo?" and Davies, "Italian Table Talk: The Aperitivo."
34. Hemingway, *A Farewell to Arms: The Hemingway Library Edition*.
35. Ibid.
36. Mellow, *Hemingway: A Life without Consequences*.
37. Hemingway, *A Farewell to Arms: The Hemingway Library Edition*.
38. Llewellyn, "The Italian Front."
39. Ross, "World War I."
40. Ibid.
41. Wilcox, "From Heroic Defeat to Mutilated Victory: the Myth of Caporetto in Fascist Italy."
42. Llewellyn, "The Italian Front."
43. Clodfelter, Warfare and Armed Conflicts: A Statistical Encyclopedia of Casualty and Other Figures, 1492-2015.
44. Llewellyn.
45. Wilcox, 10.
46. Ibid.
47. La Nazione. "Palio straordinario, si studiano soluzioni per proteggere il tufo."

48. Ibid.
49. Siena News. "Pierluigi Piccini, il sindaco dell'ultimo Palio straordinario: 'Provai un senso di vuoto'."
50. Piccini. "Il Palio straordinario, emblema di una deriva populista."
51. La Nazione. "Scompiglio: 'Al Leocorno ho portato rispetto. Ma ha fatto scelte diverse."
52. Ibid.
53. Corriere di Siena. "Una contrada correrà d'obbligo il Palio."
54. Oldenburg, *The Great Good Place*.
55. Brantlinger, *Bread and Circuses: Theories of Mass Culture and Social Decay*.
56. Drechsler, "The Contrada, the Palio, and the Ben Comune."
57. Burkey, *Game Theory: Anticipating Reactions for Winning Actions*.
58. Ibid.
59. Siena Guida Virtuale. "The Palazzo Pubblico."
60. Dundes and Falassi, *La Terra in Piazza*, 69
61. Ibid.
62. Siena News. "Straordinario con tanti esordienti: monte assestate, Trecciolino grande assente."
63. Catholic Basilicas. "About Basilicas."
64. Basilica Cateriniana di San Domenico. "La storia della Basilica."
65. Wikipedia. "Il Sodoma."
66. La Nazione. "Palio straordinario, scelta la Chiesa: sarà San Domenico."
67. Our Catholic Prayers. "Te Deum."
68. Dundes and Falassi, *La Terra in Piazza*, 71.
69. Ibid., 134.
70. Ibid., 133.
71. Ibid., 135.
72. Ibid., 212.
73. Corriere di Siena. "Una contrada correrà d'obbligo il Palio."
74. Corriere di Siena. "Noi di Siena che facciamo scuola nei cavalli."

75. Ibid.
76. Wikipedia. "Vittorio Mariani."
77. Washington Post. "California considers the unthinkable: Canceling horse racing at Santa Anita Park."
78. Tulini, "The Race-Track."
79. Facebook. "Il Palio E' Vita."
80. Corriere di Siena. "Palio, ecco il pensionario dei cavali."
81. Corriere di Siena. "Palio bene culturale, lanciata la proposta."

Bibliography

Basilica Cateriniana di San Domenico. "La storia della Basilica." Accessed 08 September 2019. https://www.basilicacateriniana.it.

Brantlinger, Patrick. *Bread and Circuses: Theories of Mass Culture and Social Decay*. Cornell University Press, 1983.

Burckhardt, Titus. *Siena, City of the Virgin*. Bloomington, IN: World Wisdom, 2008.

Burkey, Mark. *Game Theory: Anticipating Reactions for Winning Actions*. Business Expert Press, 2013.

Catholic Basilicas. "About Basilicas." Accessed 08 September 2019. https://www.catholicbasilicas.com.

Clodfelter, M. Warfare and Armed Conflicts: A Statistical Encyclopedia of Casualty and Other Figures, 1492-2015 (4th ed.). Jefferson, NC: McFarland, 2017.

Comune di Siena, *Regolamento per il Palio*. 1949. https://www.comune.siena.it.

Corriere di Siena. "Una contrada correrà d'obbligo il Palio." 27 September 2018. Accessed 08 September 2019. https://corrieredisiena.corr.it.

Corriere di Siena. "Palio Straordinario: è il giorno dell'estrazione." 29 September 2018. https://corrieredisiena.corr.it.

Corriere di Siena. "Palio bene culturale, lanciata la proposta." 24 October 2018. Accessed 09 September 2019. https://corrieredisiena.corr.it.

Corriere di Siena. "Noi di Siena che facciamo scuola nei cavalli." 26 October 2018. Accessed 08 September 2019. https://corrieredisiena.corr.it.

Corriere di Siena. "Palio, ecco il pensionario dei cavali." 16 November 2018. Accessed 09 September 2019. https://corrieredisiena.corr.it.

Davies, Emiko. "Italian Table Talk: The Aperitivo." 30 July 2013. Accessed 07 September 2019. http://www.emikodavies.com

Drechsler, Wolfgang. "The Contrada, the Palio, and the Ben Comune: Lessons from Siena," TRAMES 10 (2006): 99-125.

Edizioni Tiperti. "Montesano Gian Marco". June 2011. *Biografia di Montesano Gian Marco*. Accessed 3 September, 2019. https://tiperti.it.

Facebook. "Il Palio E' Vita." Accessed 08 September 2019. https://www.facebook.com/sienasienasiena/videos.

Hemingway, Ernest. *A Farewell to Arms: The Hemingway Library Edition*. Scribner 2012.

Il Palio di Siena. "I Masgalani." Accessed 3 September, 2019. https://www.ilpalio.org.

Il Palio di Siena. "La Storia Del 'Cencio'". Accessed 3 September, 2019. https://www.ilpalio.org.

Il Palio di Siena. "Tutti i palii non ordinari dal 1700 a oggi." Accessed 07 September 2019. https://www.ilpalio.org.

La Nazione. "Montesano firmerà il drappellone: 'Sto inviando i bozzetti al sindaco'". 18 Sept 2018. Accessed 3 September, 2019. https://www.lanazione.it.

La Nazione. "Palio straordinario, si studiano soluzioni per proteggere il tufo." 18 September 2018. Accessed 08 September 2019. https://www.lanazione.it.

La Nazione. "Piazza del Mercato, test sul tufo per il Palio." 21 September 2018. Accessed 07 September 2019. https://www.lanazione.it.

La Nazione. "Palio straordinario, scelta la Chiesa: sarà San Domenico." 26 September 2018. Accessed 08 September 2019. https://www.lanazione.it.

La Nazione. "Palio straordinario, estratte le contrade, 20 mila persone in piazza." 30 September 2018. https://www.lanazione.it.

La Nazione. "Scompiglio: 'Al Leocorno ho portato rispetto. Ma ha fatto scelte diverse." 02 Ottobre 2018. Accessed 08 September 2019. https://www.lanazione.it.

Llewellyn, Jennifer, et al, *"The Italian Front"* at *Alpha History*, 2014. Accessed 07 September 2019. https://alphahistory.com.

McNulty, Michael. "Unraveling Italian Culture: What is Aperitivo?" 06 September 2018. Accessed 07 September 2019. https://dotravel.com.

Mellow, James. 1992. *Hemingway: A Life without Consequences*. Boston: Houghton Mifflin.

Italian Sons and Daughters of America. "The Bersaglieri: Italy's Spectacular Military Group." Accessed 3 September, 2019. https://www.orderisda.org.

Palazzo Ravizza. "The history of the Noble Contrada of Bruco." Accessed 07 September 2019. https://www.palazzoravizza.com.

Piccini, Pierluigi. "Il Palio straordinario, emblema di una deriva populista." 19 September 2018. Accessed 04 October 2018. http://pierluigipiccini.it.

Oldenburg, Ray. *The Great Good Place*. Paragon House, 1989.

Our Catholic Prayers. "Te Deum." Accessed 08 September 2019. https://www.ourcatholicprayers.com.

Rodi, Robert. *Seven Seasons in Siena: My Quixotic Quest for Acceptance among Tuscany's Proudest People*. New York: Ballentine Books, 2011.

Ross, Stuart. "World War I." Encyclopedia Britannica, Inc. 2015.

Siena Free. "Palio Straordinario, installata centralina meteo." 04 October 2018. Accessed 07 September 2019. http://www.sienafree.it.

Siena Free. "Palio di Siena Straordinario del 20 Ottobre 2018: Presentato il Drappellone realizzato da Gian Marco Montesano." 14 October 2018. Accessed 07 September 2019. http://www.sienafree.it.

Siena Guide Virtuale. "The Palazzo Pubblico." Accessed 08 September 2019. http://www.sienaguidavirtuale.it.

Siena News. "Lo Straordinario più straordinario: oggi l'estrazione del Palio del 20 Ottobre." 30 September 2018. Accessed 07 September 2019. http://www.sienanews.it.

Siena News. "L'ultimo Straordinario di ottobre: era il 1745." 30 September, 2018. http://www.sienanews.it.

Siena News. "Il drappellone di Montesano nella bufera social: 'E' un copia e incolla'". 15 October 2018. Accessed 07 September 2019. http://www.sienanews.it.

Siena News. "Pierluigi Piccini, il sindaco dell'ultimo Palio straordinario: 'Provai un senso di vuoto'." 18 October 2018. Accessed 08 September 2019. http://www.sienanews.it.

Siena News. "Straordinario con tanti esordienti: monte assestate, Trecciolino grande assente." 18 October 2018. Accessed 08 September 2019. http://www.sienanews.it.

Toscana Media News. "Palio straordinario, estratte le dieci contrade." 30 September, 2018. https://toscanamedianews.it.

Tulini, Rudi. "The Race-Track." Translated by Helen Elizabeth Sadler. Accessed 08 September 2019. https://www.ilpalio.org.

Washington Post. "California considers the unthinkable: Canceling horse racing at Santa Anita Park." 12 April 2019. Accessed 08 September 2019. https://www.washingtonpost.com.

Wikipedia. "Il Sodoma." Accessed 08 September 2019. https://en.m.wikipedia.org.

Wikipedia. "Vittorio Mariani." Accessed 08 September 2019. https://it.wikipedia.org.

Wilcox, Vanda. "From Heroic Defeat to Mutilated Victory: the Myth of Caporetto in Fascist Italy." In *Defeat and Memory: Cultural Histories of Military Defeat in the Modern Era*, ed. Jenny Macleod. (London: Palgrave, 2008), pp. 46-61.

ABOUT THE AUTHOR

Thomas (Tom) Paradis is a professor of geography and community planning at Butler University in Indianapolis, Indiana, USA. He was previously a professor at Northern Arizona University where he was recognized as a President's Distinguished Teaching Fellow. In addition to his broad teaching experiences in human and physical geography, he taught and led study-abroad programs in Siena for five consecutive years. He has also authored and edited various books and articles related to architectural history, downtown redevelopment, tourism geography, history of the American home, and—also about his adventures in Siena—*Living the Palio*.